28 June 1984
Love   Mom + Dad

DRUSILLA BEYFUS

The BRIDE'S BOOK

Allen Lane

RICCIARDI 1980

With love to Alexandra,
who helped

ALLEN LANE

Penguin Books Ltd

536 King's Road

London SW10

First published in 1981

Copyright © Drusilla Beyfus, 1981

Illustrations copyright © The Condé Nast

Publications Ltd, 1916–1980

ISBN 0 7139 1310 X

Designed by Yvonne Dedman
Set in Monophoto Photina by
Filmtype Services Ltd, Scarborough, Yorkshire
Colour separations by
Culvergraphics, Lane End, Buckinghamshire
Printed in Great Britain by
Butler & Tanner Ltd, Frome and London

CONTENTS

ACKNOWLEDGEMENTS

The information in *The Bride's Book* has come from a number of different sources, and I wish to thank everyone who has helped, either knowingly or unknowingly, in the compilation of the book. I must first of all thank many members of the editorial staff of *Brides and Setting Up Home* magazine and the publication's photographers, illustrators and contributors on whose published work I have freely drawn. Special thanks are due to Christine Knox for her advice on fashion; Paul Bowden for his art direction of many of the photographs published originally in the magazine; Miranda Alexander for her contributions to the text; Dr F. E. Kenyon for his chapters on health and medical advice; Weight Watchers for their guidance on dieting; Debrett Peerage for their guidance on forms of address; and to the photographers whose published work in British *Vogue* is reprinted here.

I must also express my gratitude to the various denominational authorities for their guidance on the admittedly complex subject of denominational marriage service procedures; in this connection I am indebted to Clifford Longley for his recommendations.

Three of the people without whom this book would not have come about and whom I would like to thank are Esther Sidwell, for her help in preparing the manuscript, Eleo Gordon for her encouragement of the author, and Alex Kroll who suggested the idea of a Bride's Book in the first instance.

Finally I should like to express my thanks to the many readers of *Brides* magazine and others who have sought information from me on the event of marriage today. The knowledge of what people need to know provided the guidelines for this book.

INTRODUCTION

*Marriage remains one of the three major experiences in human existence –
birth, marriage and death. Of these, only the act of marriage allows you to
make all the arrangements. So make the most of it.*

The Bride's Book *is for the individual who is getting married and her future
husband. My hope and intention is that some idea or approach mentioned will
help the day to go with some special distinction and success.*

*It must be said that the event of marriage is by reputation successful and
happy, which is perhaps one reason why the ceremonial has been with us for so
long. Part of the reason for the survival of the time-honoured wedding
procedures is their very elasticity. They absorb shocks and alarms, and have a
built-in acceptance of the occasional mishap and error. Every wedding day has
them – they are almost as much part of custom as the proprieties and may add
to the pleasures of recollection.*

*So wide and varied and specialized are the possible demands on a practical
guide to the wedding that I cannot claim to have all the answers. I have set out,
not only the usual way of doing things, but also some options and alternatives
which are in themselves becoming part of convention.*

*Anyone who is getting married will want their marriage ceremony and
celebration to contain a generous measure of their own tastes, interests and
personal judgement. To some extent, the wedding will be what you wish to
make it. The arrangements can follow tradition or break fresh ground and still
receive everyone's blessing. Without anticipating problems, I must readily
acknowledge that organizing a wedding is rarely accomplished without family
friction. My own loyalty on principle is to the bride – it is her wedding and her
views should be listened to.*

*Finally, a word of instruction about making use of this book. The same
subject is likely to be covered in several different sections. When seeking
information always check the entries in the index.*

There is no legal or social reason, however, for any engagement at all. A licence to marry only takes one clear day to obtain, as long as at least one of the couple has been resident in the area for fifteen days before the licence is requested.

Attitudes towards the length of an engagement vary from person to person. Much depends, of course, on the individual circumstances of the couple. For those living with their parents, for example, even a few months may seem an eternity to wait, while couples who are already living together often feel less urgency about the length of their engagement.

There are often many unavoidable external reasons for delaying the wedding. One of the most common reasons is financial. Many young people would prefer to start their married lives together in their own home, rather than live with either set of parents; with the ever-rising cost of accommodation, this can sometimes mean a wait of several years. Others may wish to delay the wedding until they are sure that their income is sufficient for starting a family.

Religion, too, often plays a part in determining the length of an engagement. In the case of a marriage between different denominations, it may be necessary for one of the couple to convert to the other's beliefs. This can sometimes take many months, even years.

Almost all the reasons for delaying a wedding are practical ones – and when you are in love and impatient to be married, these may be the least persuasive ones. It is, however, always better to wait now than be sorry later. Often, the reason for a long engagement is to allow one or both to finish their studies. Sometimes, parents bring pressure to bear because they feel the couple are too young, or that they should wait a year or so to make sure they really want to marry. Sometimes the couple are separated for reasons of work, or because they are studying at different schools, colleges or universities.

Another reason for a long engagement might be family considerations. If, for example, a sister or close relative is marrying too, most couples would feel it only fair to give the family a breather before launching into another full-scale wedding. Apart from all these considerations, a couple might want the kind of wedding that takes many months of planning, or want to be married at a certain time of year.

Whatever the reasons, however, it is as well to remember that a long engagement has both advantages and disadvantages. On the down side, there is the frustration of waiting, the problems of separation, the tensions between yourselves and your families that inevitably arise when emotions are running high. On the plus side, there is the fun of being together without the responsibilities of marriage, the enjoyment of being the focal point of friends' and families' attention, and the opportunity to get to know each other and make plans for the future.

But what about the short engagement? There are as many reasons for haste as there are for delay when it comes to marriage. The reasons may be legion; a hurried move abroad to take up a particular job, perhaps; or a family illness; or the bride may be pregnant. Whatever the reason, there is no need for delay nor is there any need to declare the reason for the short notice.

An Engagement Party

Formal engagement parties are no longer widely held, although most couples would like to celebrate the announcement of their intention to marry with a few of their close friends. This kind of party can take any form whatsoever. You might prefer several small gatherings, or dinner parties, or a drinks party or a big party with food and music, or to combine a party with some other family celebration such as a twenty-first or other birthday party. The celebration could consist of the two of you and a bottle of champagne. You might like to invite a few members of your family and your fiancé's to a small, informal party to meet you both, or your parents might like to entertain you both with the rest of your family. A toast to the couple can be proposed, if wished.

In-laws

The two sides meet

It should be said that it is important for the two sets of parents to meet each other at least once before the wedding. The usual arrangement is for the groom's parents to invite the bride's parents to their house. It is generally better if the engaged couple is present, too, since they are, at least for the first time the parents meet, likely to be their chief common interest.

In-laws or outlaws?

Getting on with the in-laws is proverbially the worst part of getting married, and the problem is at its most thorny at the beginning of marriage and during your engagement. The view that you are marrying him, not his family, is questionable. When you marry a man, you marry into his family – and the same goes for him and your family – and although it is not precisely a case of 'love me, love my dog' (though it could be that, too), it may well be one of 'love me, tolerate my family'.

In-laws are the victims of a thousand music-hall jokes, funny postcards and cartoons. This may be simply because these are part of the paraphernalia that we employ as devices to come to terms with the situation. Couples choose each other, but mothers-, fathers-, daughters-, and sons-in-laws are thrust upon each other and are often expected to behave as if they had known each other all their lives. The word 'in-law', a cheerless, hostile word, does not help.

Your own family life is what you make it, but the family's lifestyle is going to be there whatever you do. And although no one is going to expect you to be as fond of your husband's family as of your own, or even to like them at all, you might as well get accustomed to the fact that they are going to play a part, and an important one, in your life from now on. First impressions are important, and it is sound advice to make sure that yours at least are acceptable.

One of the biggest hurdles for many young people is the first time they spend an evening/day/weekend with their prospective in-laws. There will inevitably be a certain amount of 'sizing-up' going on on both sides, but it is important not to let nervousness get the upper hand. Be as natural and normal as you can and most families will do their best to reciprocate. All families do, of course, have their own rituals, some of which are more pagan than others! You will undoubtedly notice all kinds of things which are done differently from the way they are in your own family. But it is better not to fight the system. If you ride roughshod over their way of life, you're in for trouble – at least until you know them better.

Another important point about in-law relationships centres on the question of loyalty. Being a good daughter-in-law or son-in-law is not simply a question of you versus them. However you feel about your in-laws, your partner will have loyalties that are to a certain extent divided. It is better not to discuss his/your parents too much, since the less you criticize, the less your partner will feel the need to defend his/your parents. Apart from that, if he/she is foolish enough to repeat your feelings to them it will set up an atmosphere of resentment which will do little to smooth your path.

It is also important to try occasionally to see things from the in-laws' point of view. Many parents find it difficult to adjust to the fact that there is a new, and in many respects more important, person in their offspring's life – particularly if he or she is the first to marry, or is an only child. What may be considered possessiveness, jealousy or interference could be only parental concern on their part.

At home with the in-laws

Entertaining prospective in-laws at your home can be even more nerve racking than going to stay with them. There is, of course, the reassurance of being 'on home ground', but it is an unnaturally confident person who will not feel a few twinges of nervousness. Obviously you will want to make the best impression possible and to impress them with your suitability as a future wife for their son. Try, however, not to overdo things in an excessive desire to please and don't be over-ambitious. If, for instance, you have invited your prospective in-laws to a meal, it is far better to cook something simple that you feel confident about than to try a new and complicated dish.

Dear mother-in-law

What to call your mother-in-law is a longstanding subject of jokes, indecision and suppressed embarrassment. From a daughter-in-law's standpoint, her mother-in-law may be a relative stranger, yet as her future husband's mother, she is one of the family. Matters are not improved by the fact that it is in the nature of the dilemma that neither side is prepared to come out into the open and admit to a need for a lead.

To refer to and address a mother-in-law as 'Mrs Somebody' appears a shade formal in the circumstances. To go right ahead and use her first name could seem over-presumptuous if you have met only a few times and is particularly inappropriate if she is unaccustomed to the instant intimacy of the moment.

A pet name in general use, or an affectionate nickname, if such exists, could be a get-out. Otherwise, you will be in good company if you take refuge in the honorable expedient of not calling her anything at all. Anyway, this is a problem that time may ease. If grandchildren arrive, the whole matter is resolved at once, as the nameless mother in limbo can become 'granny' to one and all.

Planning for the Future

One of the great advantages of the engagement is that it gives you both time to plan for the future and to decide between you what you both want out of your lives. Do you both want children? How soon do you want children? Will you continue to hold a job if children are born? How will your finances be organized? Is he prepared to help in the house, or does he expect you to cope singlehanded? All these questions are far better settled before the wedding, at least in outline, otherwise there may be recriminations and disappointments later on. How often it is said 'If only I'd known how selfish/mean/untidy he/she was, I'd never have married him/her.' An engagement is the ideal time for smoothing out the wrinkles of your future life together before it is too late.

Togetherness and separation

Sometimes, problems are caused by the simple fact of geographical separation. If the man lives in the north and the woman in the south, keeping in touch can be a costly and time-consuming process. It can also be extremely frustrating emotionally and sexually. If the couples are only able to be together for brief, infrequent periods, it is often difficult to maintain a natural, relaxed relationship on any level. All the anticipation and excitement invested in looking forward to the visit may result in disappointments on both sides and a depressing sense of anticlimax afterwards. There is no magic formula for ensuring that this does not happen, but in the case of enforced separation, to be forewarned is at least to know what to expect. Keeping in touch in other ways, by telephone or by that much neglected means of communication, letter-writing, goes a long way towards alleviating feelings of loneliness, neglect and even jealousy. Many people find it difficult to express themselves freely on paper, but letters exchanged during the engagement period will not only give much pleasure at the time, but will often be treasured long afterwards.

Another difficulty facing young engaged couples revolves around the problem of doubts and uncertainties. These are often compounded in cases where there is opposition to the match from family or friends. Often, of course, these doubts may simply be an indication of pre-wedding 'nerves'. On the other hand, they may be real anxieties about the future. In a sense, the engagement is consciously devised to give the couple the opportunity to reflect on their decision, and to make really sure that they want to go through with the marriage. Admitting that you have made a mistake, especially after the news has been widely broadcast, can demand a great deal of courage. However, simply airing your fears, whether to your partner, your parents or a close friend, can often solve the problem in itself. Whatever the real nature of your feelings, however, it is vital to admit, above all to yourself, to their existence. Simply ignoring doubts will, regrettably, not make them go away.

The Engagement Ring

The engagement ring is thought to set a seal on the couple's betrothal. Its monetary worth is little indication of the depth of emotional feeling it symbolizes and common sense and practical considerations should be taken into account. Many young couples give a great deal of thought to the amount that will have to be spent on setting up home before estimating how much will be left over for the ring. While in the past it was generally the man who bought the ring and presented it to his lady love on bended knee, these days the choosing of the token is usually a responsibility shared between the two. Whatever its intrinsic worth, however, an engagement ring always possesses symbolic and sentimental value for the wearer.

The ring is a symbol. It can be chosen for the quality of the design or for some reason of sentiment, or, if the man wishes to make a traditionally generous gesture, for its investment value.

It was not until the nineteenth century and the exploitation of South African diamond deposits that jewelled rings became popular as engagement rings. Plain gold or silver rings, perhaps twisted into a lover's knot, were the usual choice. The sparkling diamond of legend is still a girl's best friend, and diamond rings are the most popular choice for an engagement ring. As long as they have existed, diamonds have exercised a strange spell over men and women. Fortunes have been spent, battles fought, frauds and even murders committed in their name. Their brilliance when cut, reflecting a spectrum of colour, has made diamonds the most valued and revered jewels in the world. The word diamond comes from the Greek word *adamas*, which means unconquerable.

But what is it that makes a diamond so precious? How can you recognize its worth? There are four factors which affect a diamond's cost: colour, cut, carat weight and clarity. It frequently takes an expert to detect the differences in quality, the delicate graduations of colour and the accuracy of cutting that make one diamond more expensive than another. So when you are searching for a good diamond, it is always advisable to consult a reputable jeweller.

Few of us can afford to buy really big diamonds, but recent advances in the skills of cutting and setting mean that small diamonds can be used to great advantage in jewellery. Whether it be a small solitaire or a cluster of tiny stones (a pavé setting) these rings put diamonds within almost everyone's reach.

There are many alternatives to diamonds including all the other precious and semi-precious stones, which modern designers often use with imagination. An antique ring, being second-hand and therefore cheaper, can often prove an attractive solution. One particularly appealing idea for an engagement ring is one in which the first letters of the names of the stones used in the design spell a word. These rings are now sought after in antique shops. They spell out such words as 'dearest' (diamond, emerald, amethyst, ruby, epidote, sapphire, turquoise) or 'love me' (lapis lazuli, opal, vermeil, emerald, moonstone, epidote). The fiancé's birthstone is supposed to bring luck. Birthstones vary from country to country, but common dedications are:

January: garnet *(constancy)*	July: ruby *(love)*
February: amethyst *(sincerity)*	August: peridot *(joy)*
March: aquamarine *(courage)*	September: sapphire *(wisdom)*
April: diamond *(innocence)*	October: opal *(hope)*
May: emerald *(happiness)*	November: topaz *(fidelity)*
June: pearl *(beauty)*	December: turquoise *(success)*

One ring for everything

An untraditional solution might be an ingeniously designed 'twin-set', which makes the most of the metal with less emphasis on the gem setting, or, alternatively, a gem-set wedding ring, based on the style of an eternity ring. One ring for everything combines the engagement and wedding ring in a single design, reminiscent of eternity rings, which have been worn for over 4,000 years; these rings eliminate the problem of trying to find two rings which look and feel good together. Another point in their favour is that choosing one ring for a dual purpose could be a way of cutting costs.

Jewellers are now realizing the problems involved in wearing two rings on the same finger, and are producing companion rings, which are specifically designed to be worn together, often fitting together like a puzzle.

Another idea might be to have a ring specially designed for you or to reset an old stone from an existing brooch or family piece. Having a ring specially designed for you is no longer a privilege reserved for the very rich. Many jewellery designers enjoy taking on personal commissions. Browse in any of the good shops and galleries selling young designers' work, and ask the gallery to put you in touch with the artist whose work you most like. From then on, it's between you two. Your ring will have its own sentimental value, as well as being a unique piece of jewellery.

Practical points

Whatever kind of ring you choose, however, there are certain practical considerations to bear in mind before getting carried away with some flamboyant design. Will the ring be worn every day or only on special occasions? Do you mind having to take it off in order not to tear the sheets or rip your tights? Will it clank against your typewriter or get in the way of any other occupation you may follow? Before deciding on one design, have a good look round several shops, bearing in mind that choosing a wedding ring is not unlike choosing a husband – both are picked for their qualities of endurance as well as for looks and character. In a small way, jewellery, like fashion, is less confined by rules and precedents today, and there is much more choice available. More and more designers are cottoning on to the fact that buying jewellery is little different from any other purchase – practicality and price come high up on the list of priorities, along with personal taste. So take advantage of all the possibilities and don't rush into buying a design you may grow to dislike in a few months' time.

A free choice

You are under no obligation to accept or wear an engagement ring at all. The custom of doing so dates from the time when the undertaking to marry was of greater importance than it is today. Under Roman law, the ring was the symbol of a solemn and serious contract, often involving large amounts of money and land. 'Returning the ring' is still a significant step in breaking an engagement today, although it is not legally necessary. The engagement ring also signified to other men that this girl was 'spoken for'. While the wearing of an engagement ring is a general custom, some women feel that it is an unnecessary, and even distasteful, hangover from less liberated days. It does seem curious that, while many men agree to wear a wedding ring, most would be totally thrown by the idea of wearing an engagement ring.

Choosing a wedding ring

Unless you choose a matching set or one ring for both purposes, you will have to bear in mind what kind of wedding ring you want when buying your engagement ring. Gold wedding rings are still the most popular choice, although there is a revival of interest in platinum. In all materials, however, there is a wide variety of choice. The most important point to remember when buying a gold ring is that, paradoxically, the lower the 'caratage', the more resistant the ring will be to wear and tear. 'Carat' can be a confusing word. When it refers to gems it denotes weight, but where gold is concerned it defines the proportion of gold to metal alloy. Twenty-four carat is pure gold so that an eighteen carat gold ring will be eighteen parts of pure gold and six parts of inferior metal. The colour of gold can also be changed by the addition of other metals so that the range extends from the palest moonshine through green-gold, pink and bronze. There are designs which attractively combine two or three different colours of gold.

The practice of engraving the inner side of a wedding ring with names or initials or the date of the wedding is of unchanging charm and sentiment.

Breaking an Engagement

From the legal point of view, an engagement was regarded, until January 1971, as subject to the rules applicable to the ordinary law of contract. An action for damages for breach of promise could therefore be brought if either party broke the engagement without the other's consent.

Today, a broken engagement cannot give rise to legal action to compensate for wounded feelings or monetary loss. Even though money may have been spent in preparing for a wedding that will not take place, or in buying things for a home that will not be set up, none of it is legally recoverable.

As far as engagement presents are concerned, the law since 1971 states that any presents that are given conditionally upon a wedding taking place should be returned; otherwise, the recipient may keep them. Since engaged couples are generally not in the habit of giving each other presents with an eye to what is likely to happen if they break off the engagement, in most cases presents exchanged between the couple are not returned. Whether to retain or keep the engagement ring is a vexed point. There is no legal obligation to give it back, unless it is a family heirloom, and in practice everything depends on individual circumstances – but if you are to blame for the break-up you should at least offer to return the ring, the token of togetherness.

Wedding or engagement presents are given to the couple on the understanding that the recipients of the gifts will marry. These should be returned to the donors if the marriage is not to take place. In general, the good sense of the parties and their families will ensure that any disputes will be contained. If, however, this should prove impossible, it may be necessary to consult a solicitor.

Sometimes the engaged couple have bought joint property – a house in which they intend to live after they are married, for example, or a car. If no marriage takes place, and the couple cannot decide between themselves on a fair division, a court will have to make the decision for them and will apply the same principles to determine their rights as if they had been actually married.

Ends and Beginnings

An engagement is in a sense a transitory stage marking the end of one life and the beginning of another. As such, it is characterized by certain rites of passage. The announcements in the press, the giving of presents, engagement and stag parties to celebrate (or bemoan) the ending of celibacy, all recall the fact that marriage still means the leaving of one family group and the joining of a new one. The rituals and customs surrounding betrothal are today less widely practised, partly due to the fact that an engagement is no longer a legally binding contract. Nevertheless traces of old traditions survive even late in the twentieth century.

The meaning of the betrothal has changed, not so much in its implications, but in its emphasis. A betrothal is still a public declaration of an intention to marry, but it no longer carries the same weight. Under Roman law, for instance, the bridegroom was expected to furnish security for the completion of the bargain. Guernsey betrothals were marked by 'flouncing', a party at which the pair met friends of their parents-in-law-to-be. From this point on, if the girl changed her mind, her fiancé could lay claim to half her property; if he recanted, she could do likewise. In imperial China, the engagement was so significant that if either partner should die, the wedding ceremony went ahead as if nothing had happened and the survivor was treated thereafter as a widow or widower.

Nowadays marriage is no longer bound up with contractual agreements
between parents or the payment of bride-price or dowry, and the engagement
has therefore all but lost its original solemn and binding character. Many
marriages take place these days without any preceding formal engagement at
all, and the significance of the engagement is largely a matter of personal
commitment based on love and friendship rather than on money and
businesslike negotiations.

LEPAPE 1923

2

RELIGIOUS AND LEGAL MATTERS

Who May Marry Whom

Although the marriage contract is by no means a contract in the sense that businessmen use the word, it nevertheless carries with it certain legal rights and obligations. English law puts few obstacles in the way of marriage, providing various conditions are observed. In order to marry legally, a person must be over sixteen years old, and if under eighteen, must obtain consent from his or her parents or legal guardian (if consent is refused, the person can apply for a magistrate's permission through the courts); both parties must be single, one male and one female. Certain blood relations, or those related by marriage, for biological, social and psychological reasons, may not marry. A man cannot marry his: mother, mother-in-law, aunt, grandmother, step-grandmother, grandmother-in-law, stepmother, adoptive mother, sister, half-sister, daughter, niece, daughter-in-law, stepdaughter, granddaughter, granddaughter-in-law, step-granddaughter. A woman cannot marry her: father, father-in-law, uncle, grandfather, step-grandfather, grandfather-in-law, stepfather, adoptive father, brother, half-brother, son, nephew, son-in-law, stepson, grandson, step-grandson, grandson-in-law.

Marriage Ceremonies, Religious and Civil

The religious rules and rites can vary with each denomination, so it is essential to make an appointment to see the minister concerned as soon as possible. Among the Christian churches most would like at least one of a couple to be baptized.

You will have to fill in a form giving details about yourselves and your respective fathers. Those who are adopted or illegitimate will have to impart this information and it will be recorded on the marriage certificate, as it was on the birth certificate, unless preventive steps are taken.

A Church of England marriage

Once you have decided on the church in which you wish to be married, you should make an appointment to see the vicar who will be officiating at the marriage. You should both go along to see him. He will explain the system of 'calling the banns', which is the publication, in the church of the betrothed, of their intention to marry. The couple's names are read out in church in order that anyone who knows of any 'just impediment' to the marriage can report it to a church officer. The banns must be published on three successive Sundays before the marriage can take place.

It is important to note that if you and your future husband live in different parishes, the banns must be called in both churches. Application for the publication of banns must be made to the clergyman of the parish in which each person lives. These requirements apply to the marrying couple, irrespective of where each set of parents may reside.

The wait and the publication of banns can be avoided if you apply for a Common Licence. This can be obtained from the superintendent registrar or from the surrogate to whom you will be referred by the vicar. A Common Licence is conditional upon a minimum fifteen-day residential qualification for one partner, and the marriage may take place after one clear day (other than a Sunday, Christmas Day or Good Friday) from the date on which notice was given to the superintendent registrar and entered in the marriage notice book.

A Special Licence may be issued on behalf of the Archbishop of Canterbury in special cases. This enables a marriage to take place according to the rites of the Church of England at any time or place. The Special Licence is more expensive than the other methods referred to.

A fairly common exigency is when a couple wish to marry in a church outside either of their own parishes. In this case, you must apply to be put on the electoral roll of the parish in which you wish to be married or take up residence in the locality. It is part of the church law that if a non-parishioner wishes to have his name entered on the electoral roll the following conditions must apply. One of the couple, as part of normal practice, is expected to sign an application form declaring that he or she has attended church services for six months. Marrying in a church outside either of your parishes therefore requires fulfilment of the fifteen-day residential qualification or regular attendance at the services of the church for six months.

The wording

The vicar will probably ask if you would like to have the revised wording in the marriage service. The wording differs only slightly from the original version of 1662 and both versions can be found in the 1928 Book of Common Prayer. The service is published in the Book of Common Prayer under the heading 'The solemnization of matrimony'. This gives the order of service, setting out the exchanges and rites in the familiar, and beautiful, seventeenth-century version.

Church of England churches may well be using a modern-language version of the revised wording. The Alternative Service Book has already found favour among clergymen and marrying couples. The language is more direct and accessible than that of the revised version. Also, its advocates hold that the wording is attuned to an understanding of the meaning of modern matrimony, whereas the old liturgy, if taken literally, embodies a past picture of marriage.

The vows taken by the bride and groom in the new wording can be the same, or differ by a degree. It is not permissible, although the contrary is widely held, to write your own vows in the Church of England.

Nearer the day, the minister will probably want to discuss final details and explain the meaning of the vows, and may, if it is to be a large formal wedding, want to have a dress rehearsal, going through all the procedures in the church itself.

Baptism

Strictly speaking, a denominational marriage service in the Church of England or the Roman Catholic Church requires evidence of baptism. In practice, the minister concerned may simply ask for a verbal assurance that you have both been baptized. If written evidence is required, this can be obtained by applying to the present minister of the church where the christening took place. A small fee is involved.

When one of a couple has not been baptized, the practice adopted by local churches varies considerably. The minister's agreement will largely depend on his own attitudes. He may believe in abiding by the exact prescriptions of church propriety on this matter or he may take a more independent line.

There are precedents proving that it is possible for a couple in these circumstances to have a denominational marriage service in the Church of England or the Roman Catholic Church. However, aspirants should be prepared for time-consuming and perhaps technical negotiations. It is best to seek the advice of a competent clergyman at the earliest opportunity.

When neither member has been baptized the chances of a marriage service in church are very slim.

Fees

Certain basic costs are statutory and cannot be amended at the discretion of the local church. Others, such as fees for bell-ringers, the choir or organist are a local matter and may vary widely from church to church.

Special cases

When someone does not wish to disclose their full parental origins on the marriage documents they should apply to the Registrar General's office for guidance or take the advice of a solicitor. It may be of interest to know that there is no legal requirement that binds the individual to disclosure.

The Church of England

The foregoing information should be read as guidelines only to procedures and usual arrangements. As in most things to do with the Church of England it is almost heresy to write of absolutes and uniform rules, and this wide diversity of practice applies especially to the conduct of the marriage service. The vicar may be a man with strong views on one or more aspects of church marriage, as the Church of England harbours many different shades of opinion. Local custom, the views of the bishop, and the changing attitudes of the mother Church itself – one way or the other – may have a bearing in your case. Whereas the diversity of viewpoint and practice may give a considerable degree of latitude to individual couples with ideas of their own on marriage, it by no means follows that the local vicar will go along with these. If he is unwilling or unable to accede to your request, and this is within the proprieties of church marriage, there is the possibility that somewhere there may be some other clergyman who will take a more sympathetic view.

The Roman Catholic marriage

When both bride and groom are Roman Catholic, the banns are published at their local churches on the three Sundays before the wedding. Usually, the brief wedding ceremony is incorporated into the Mass, which then becomes known as the Nuptial Mass, during which the couple receive Holy Communion.

Other Christian denominations

In the Free Church banns are not called, so the couple must obtain a certificate of marriage or licence. The service is similar to that of the Church of England.

Marriage in the Church of Scotland differs from that in the Church of England in that the banns need only be read twice, sometimes only once. Scotland is still popular with young elopers because of the low age of consent – couples over sixteen and under eighteen years of age do not need to obtain parental consent, and the famous Gretna Green, just over the Border, still welcomes many couples each year.

A Quaker marriage is different from most other wedding services. Its appeal lies in its extreme simplicity and lack of ceremonial. Only one of the couple has to be a member, and the other is acceptable so long as he or she is in sympathy with the testimony and the nature of the marriage, and can produce two recommendations in writing from full members. Wedding rings play no formal part in Quaker marriages, although some couples like to give each other rings after making their declarations.

The Orthodox Jewish marriage

An Orthodox Jewish marriage need not take place in a synagogue but can be celebrated almost anywhere indoors or out of doors, at any time of the day or night, under a *chupah* (canopy). The rabbi or minister who is to perform the ceremony should be contracted at the earliest opportunity.

The Jewish bride and her future husband should both attend at the office of the chief rabbi in order to apply for the chief rabbi's authorization of marriage. A parent from both sides is usually present as well. Outside London, the local minister or secretary for marriages will usually arrange for the chief rabbi's authorization. Apply as early as possible and not later than three weeks before the date of the wedding.

When applying for authorization the following information will be required; the superintendent registrar's certificate or licence (see 'Register Office marriage'); the Jewish marriage lines of your respective parents or, if these are not available, the date and place of their respective marriages; your respective birth certificates; the Hebrew names of yourselves and parents; and information as to whether each respective father is a 'Cohen', a 'Levite' or an 'Israelite'; a fee.

A ring is an essential part of the ceremony. As in other denominations, the Jewish bride usually wears traditional white dress and headdress. The men wear hats.

In case of query, doubt, absence of documents, previous marriage, divorce or where one party is coming from abroad, advice should be sought at the earliest opportunity from the Office of the Chief Rabbi, Marriage Authorization Office, Adler House, Tavistock Square, London WC1H 9HN.

Etiquette can vary from synagogue to synagogue and may be dependent on the practice of the officiating minister or rabbi. At an Orthodox Jewish marriage, the bridal party can take the following order on entry; the bride on the arm of her father, followed by the bridesmaids, the groom's parents and the bride's mother on the arm of a male relative. After the marriage, the bride and groom walk out together, followed by the bridesmaids and parents.

A Jewish wedding is both a civil and a religious ceremony. The couple get married in the eyes of both Jewish law and the law of the country where they are married, which means that the requirements of both must be satisfied. Two separate applications for permission to marry are needed.

The couple must obtain a certificate of marriage from the superintendent registrar of the district in which they live. They must also obtain permission from the chief rabbi. Ask your local minister for details of how this is done.

According to Orthodox Jewish tradition, the bridegroom should attend the service on the Sabbath before the wedding, during which a blessing may be given for the future happiness of the bride and groom.

It is customary for the bride and groom to fast on the day of the marriage until after the ceremony. The service itself is known as the *kiddushin* and consists of two parts: the act of betrothal (*erusin*), which establishes a legal bond between the couple, and the celebration of the marriage proper (*nissuin*). Before the bride comes to the *chupah* (the canopy under which all Jewish marriages are performed) the bridegroom is formally requested by the minister to approve the two witnesses to the *ketubah* and to accept the terms and conditions of the *ketubah*, whereby he undertakes a number of basic obligations and responsibilities towards his wife.

The ceremony is often introduced by the singing of a psalm, followed, as the bride enters, by a traditional chant of welcome. The bride stands under the canopy at the groom's right. On each side of the couple stand their parents. Then come the blessings of betrothal, known as such because originally the betrothal and marriage services were separate, with sometimes an interval of up to a year between them. These days they are combined in one ceremony. The couple become man and wife in the eyes of Jewish law when the bridegroom puts the ring on the bride's finger, saying the words 'Behold you are consecrated unto me by this ring according to the law of Moses and Israel.' The *ketubah* is then read, and subsequently handed to the bride. This is followed by the seven blessings of marriage. The couple take a sip of wine from the same glass, to symbolize the fact that from now on they must share the same cup of life, and then the glass is broken by the bridegroom as a reminder of the

The line-up of the bridal party in front of the rabbi or minister at a Reform Jewish marriage

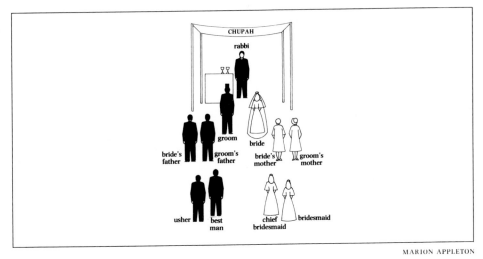

destruction of the temple at Jerusalem and the social responsibilities of the new couple to share in the trials of their people. The ceremony ends with a blessing on the couple recited by the minister.

Members of a Reform synagogue are able to interpret religious practice in a more liberal way than those of the Orthodox faith, and this approach also applies to etiquette and social procedures at a marriage. Much depends on the views of the individual minister as attitudes vary.

To marry according to Jewish law the couple must both be of the Jewish faith and free from any religious or marital impediment. While commending the ideal of keeping the same partner, Jewish law does not consider marriage to be a contract binding until death. If the marriage breaks up the rabbis may administer a bill of divorce. It is not possible to be remarried in the Jewish faith unless this dispensation is done.

Religious Differences

Some people who wish to marry with the rites of their religion run into all kinds of complications, because their position puts them at odds with the religious authority concerned. The reasons are legion, but two special cases cause a great deal of pain: mixed marriages (between partners of differing religious convictions) and marriages where one, or both, of the partners has been divorced and there is a former spouse still living.

As a background, it must be remembered that the major faiths and denominations exercise strict regulations on marriage. Worshippers whose circumstances fail to accord with the prescriptive customs of their faith are in for a hard time if they hope to find an acceptable way through the rules.

However, the modern spirit of religious toleration and the ecumenical movement, which seeks to bridge differences between the various theologies, have both encouraged a more flexible attitude. The individual needs good advice on his or her special problem. The first person to consult is the minister concerned, who may well have strong objections to what is being proposed. It may be necessary to take your case to a higher authority and it will certainly help if you or your partner show some initiative in pressing the merits of your cause in the right quarters. Where there is an attempt to combine a religious service with a marriage between members of differing faiths it will probably be found that each denominational authority knows its own rules but has an unsure grasp of the canons of other religions. Almost as great a source of confusion, according to the authorities in these matters, is that the powers that be may think they know all the answers, but may turn out to be misinformed.

Arranging an interdenominational marriage service
A point to be considered when arranging an interdenominational marriage service is that many members of the congregation are likely to be unfamiliar with the religious observances involved and, in the case of some dissenters, the procedures may stir reactions of dislike. In general, most people are prepared, in the interests of the day, to park their personal beliefs and to go along with the order of service. However, it is as well not to press tolerance too far in this direction. If a shorter, simpler observance is an option, it might be a good idea to choose this in preference to the full form.

Marriage between a Roman Catholic and a non-Catholic
At one time it was an invariable rule that 'mixed marriages' were permitted by the Church of Rome only in very rare cases, and with strict provisos attached. However, the Roman Catholic faith has considerably relaxed its attitudes. Two of the most contentious issues, for example, on birth control and the upbringing of children, are now closer to being considered as matters of individual conscience. A written promise from a non-Roman Catholic partner about the religious upbringing of children is no longer required. Very many Roman Catholics use artificial contraceptives and have no difficulty with their church in so doing. The couple may have a Nuptial Mass, but the non-Catholic partner is not usually permitted to take Communion.

On becoming a Roman Catholic

It cannot be stressed too strongly that this is a serious undertaking, which should only be pursued for its own sake as a matter of individual belief, and not as an expedient to facilitate a full Nuptial Mass at the marriage.

Assuming sincere belief, the first step is to talk the matter over fully and seriously with your priest. You may be referred to the Catholic Enquiry Centre which will supply postal courses giving religious instruction. At some stage, the convert will be taught the rudiments of the faith by a priest or catechist, and when he considers the time to be right, there will be a ceremony of reception into the church. If the person has not already been baptized, the principal rite of Christianity, a baptism, will be part of the ceremony.

Marriage between a practising Jew and non-Jew
Judaism does not accept the principle of mixed marriage. There is little indication that the traditional attitudes of either the Orthodox or Reformed branches of Judaism have changed on this fundamental point. A few rabbis of the liberal branch of Judaism may be prepared to help, but it would be misleading to indicate that this is a probability.

Converting to Judaism

If one partner wishes to convert to the other's Jewish faith, the process is long, heart-searching and rigorous. Nor is there any initial undertaking at the beginning of conversion that a non-Jew will be admitted to the faith.

There is, as yet, no ecumenical movement in Judaism. Marriage within the Jewish faith requires that both partners should be accepted by the religious authorities as Jews.

The process of conversion, for the few that undertake it, varies according to whether the non-Jew wishes to convert to the Orthodox or non-Orthodox faith. Either way, Judaism does not encourage conversion, and it would be futile to attempt it for the sake of convenience or expedience.

The rabbi will advise on all particulars, which certainly will involve a lengthy period of religious instruction and evidence on the part of the applicant that they intend to live a full and complete Jewish life. The applicant will be allocated to a private tutor for instruction. After they have satisfied their tutor of their understanding of the faith, they will be expected to appear before the authorities who will examine the knowledge and attitudes of the applicant. If they are satisfied that he or she is ready to join the faith, there will be a formal ceremony of admission, with a ritual bath.

The non-Orthodox, or Reformed, branch of Judaism is held to be more liberal in its attitudes but nevertheless demands evidence that the applicant's interest is serious. The process of conversion may take up to two years – the authorities stress that it is difficult to give guidelines – after which the non-Jew may be formally admitted to the Jewish faith. However, the ecclesiastical courts must first be satisfied of the applicant's suitability.

Marriage between partners belonging to different Protestant denominations

In general, this is not a problem area except where individual believers wish to raise difficulties. The Church of England, the Church of Scotland, the Church of Wales and the Nonconformist Protestant Churches accept that their members may wish to intermarry, and only in very rare cases are there any obstacles.

Remarriage When a Partner has been Divorced

In the Church of England

The official position is that the Church of England does not permit marriage in church of a couple when one or both partners are divorced and there is a living spouse (or spouses). However, if you know where to go with a case that might be an exception to the rule options may open.

The law in England permits the Queen's subjects to be married within the Established Church. However, the 'established custom' of the Church of England is at variance with this constitutional right. Many members of the clergy have understandable objections to administering the vows 'till death us do part' to the same person in a repeat performance.

The divorced individual who wants to remarry in church has little option but to seek out a sympathetic ear among the clergy. Some ministers are prepared to take a stand against church orthodoxy in this matter. Should assistance be found further difficulties may loom, however, and, unless you have the good luck to find a sympathetic minister locally, some way will have to be found of fulfilling the usual residential qualifications.

The Church of England Service of Blessing

The acute difficulties encountered by divorced couples who wish to remarry in the Church of England have led to the acceptance of a compromise ceremony, 'a Service of Blessing'. This customarily follows a register office marriage, but can be held at a later date. The exact form of it depends, like so much else to do with remarriage and the Church of England, on the views of the individual minister concerned. Some are prepared to allow the traditional appurtenances of the service of the solemnization of matrimony with a wedding dress, bridesmaids, a choir and wedding bells, but the general tendency is to keep the observances low-key and discreet.

The service usually consists of hymns, a gospel reading, prayers and a blessing. The religious function is, as the name of the ceremony suggests, simply to bless the marriage of the bride and groom. It is not usual in the Church of England for marriage vows to be taken in the usual Service of Blessing, but you may find a minister who permits this.

Remarriage between divorced partners in the Nonconformist denominations
The Nonconformist Churches, the Methodists, the Baptists, the Orthodox Church, the United Reformed Church, allow marriage in church when there is a divorced partner with a living spouse. However, in each case, the minister concerned will wish to satisfy himself that the request is sincere.

Recently, the liberal attitudes of the Nonconformist Churches towards this sensitive matter have offered a spiritual harbour to many divorced couples.

Remarriage in the Roman Catholic faith
A Roman Catholic who is divorced has some hope of remarriage in church. The Church of Rome has traditionally dissolved marriages on grounds of nullity, which means that the marriage did not exist in the eyes of the Church despite outward appearances.

The subject of grounds on which nullity is granted is far too specialized to enter into here in any detail. One point, however, may be of special interest. The position of the person who wishes to remarry, and whose first marriage was in a register office, may be able to have the first marriage declared null and void. The position of a Roman Catholic who wishes to remarry and whose marriage does not take place under the auspices of the church is regarded in canon law – church decree – as not having been married previously.

These, and other conditions under which a marriage can be dissolved by the Roman Catholic church, are said to be easier and less costly than in the past. The advice of a good canon lawyer is an important first step.

The Remarriage of Widows and Widowers

In the eyes of the major denominations, the position of a widow or widower who wishes to remarry is comparable to that of anyone who is getting married for the first time.

The Register Office Marriage

The marriage that takes place in a register office is a simple, brief, legal commitment with a short ceremony. A civil ceremony is statistically the most popular way of marrying; just over half of all marriages in England and Wales take place in a register office, and about a third of first marriages.

A register office wedding is the obvious course for many people including those who have no religious beliefs, those who are arranging a second marriage, and those who for one reason or another are unable to marry with the blessing of their faith.

Relative speed and simplicity may be considered as advantages and a civil ceremony can be the least costly path to matrimony, as many of the traditional wedding embellishments can be dispensed with. However, many people want to make a memorable occasion out of a civil marriage and do so. In general, the services offered by the superintendent registrar have improved considerably in recent years, and recognition is given to the need to provide dignified and civilized surroundings in which marriages can take place. As ever, much depends here on the individual local authority.

The procedures and documents

The first move is to go to the superintendent registrar and for you or your partner to give notice that you are going to be married. Whoever gives notice will be asked to sign the official declaration that the details are correct. The timing of the wedding will largely depend on whether you decide to be married by certificate or licence. In either case, residential qualifications are required. The superintendent registrar will answer your questions about the rules and regulations and the ceremony.

Marriage by certificate: the requirements are that you will have lived in the district for seven days immediately preceding your visit to the superintendent registrar to give notice that you are going to be married.

When you and your future husband live in the same registration district, only one of you need 'give notice'. Either of you may undertake this responsibility. Note that the marriage ceremony must take place, as a general rule, at the register office where notice has been given.

When you live in different registration districts it is necessary for the superintendent registrar in each area to be notified. Each partner may give notice that you are going to be married in his or her district, or either of you can give both notices. Note the residential qualifications. The regulations state, 'no superintendent registrar can accept notice until both parties have had their usual place of residence in their respective districts for the seven days immediately preceding'.

For marriage by certificate a period of twenty-one days must intervene between the day on which the notice is given and the earliest date on which the marriage may take place.

Marriage by licence: only one notice is required. This can be given by you or your future husband provided that it is given to the superintendent registrar of the district in which one of you has resided for the past fifteen days. This is known as the fifteen days residential qualification. The marriage must take place at the register office where the notice has been given. The regulations for marriage by licence stipulate that both of you must be in England or Wales, or have your usual residence in these places, on the day that notice is given.

One clear day must pass between the date of the notice and the first date on which the marriage may take place, and this may not be a Sunday, Good Friday or Christmas Day. For anyone with the required residential qualifications marriage by licence facilitates short-notice marriage.

In all cases, if the pair are under eighteen they will both have to obtain the consent of their parents or legal guardians, and both will have to produce their birth certificates. Divorced persons must produce their decree absolute and widows and widowers will need to produce a death certificate of their spouse or spouses. A foreign national will need a passport or identity card.

The event

Register office marriages take place between 8 a.m. and 6 p.m., usually on a weekday; the majority of offices do not stay open all day on Saturday.

If you are hoping for a Saturday morning booking during the popular spring and summer months you will probably have to move smartly. Notice cannot be given more than three months in advance of the wedding, however.

Two witnesses are a legal requirement but many couples may wish to share their marriage with relations and friends. Before deciding on how many to invite to the civil ceremony, establish in advance the facilities that are available at the register office. Some are equipped to handle quite a large party; others have only limited resources.

The superintendent registrar can tell you about the usual arrangements for flowers. If you wish to provide your own, ask how this can be done. Normally, photographs may be taken after the marriage but photography is not permitted during the ceremony. Some people like to be photographed during a mock signing of the register.

On the day

On the day of marriage, the bride and groom, the two witnesses and everybody else in the party assemble at the register office. It is inadvisable to arrive too early as you will almost certainly get mixed up with the preceding wedding group. The usual timing is to arrive ten minutes or so ahead of schedule and to await your turn in the waiting-room.

The marriage ceremony, which takes about fifteen minutes in all, is supervised by the superintendent registrar and the registrar. You and your partner will be reminded that the vows you are about to take are binding and solemn. You will both be asked to declare that there is no lawful impediment to your marriage. A ring may be given at this point or rings exchanged, but there is no legal obligation to have a ring.

You will then call on the attendant audience to witness the marriage. The signing of the register follows, in which you and your partner both sign your usual signatures. The two witnesses add their signatures and so do the two officers, the superintendent registrar and the registrar. That completes proceedings. A marriage certificate can be handed over at this point.

The fees

Whichever way you get married you have to pay for each notice of marriage and the attendance of the registrar; the copy of the marriage certificate is an optional cost.

If you choose to marry by superintendent registrar's licence there is an additional fee. Details of fees are available at the register office. Those who want to know about procedures in Scotland and Northern Ireland should contact one of the following national register offices: General Register Office for Scotland, New Register House, Edinburgh EHI 3YT, telephone 031 556 3952 or, for Northern Ireland, General Register Office, Oxford House, 49–55 Chichester Street, Belfast BTI 4HL, telephone 0232 35211.

Clothes for a register office wedding

The custom is to look your best for marriage, here as anywhere else. In practice, the style of dress for the bride tends to depend on the arrangements that follow the wedding. The general tenor of register office wedding fashion is to show respect for the occasion. Women wear hats or flowers in the hair or go hatless, according to taste and the chosen clothes. Sometimes a bouquet is carried. The witnesses dress as they please.

The bride in white

Sometimes the bride wants to wear wedding white, and there is no reason why she should not, with the proviso that the effects should be appropriate for a civil ceremony. It has to be remembered that many aspects of traditional bridal attire have their roots in religious tradition and, if carried to extreme, may look anachronistic in the atmosphere of a municipal office. However, it is by no means unusual for a register office bride to be accompanied by bridesmaids.

The groom usually wears a lounge suit and a buttonhole but he should key his level of dress to that of the bride. If she is wearing white, and there is to be a formal wedding reception, he may prefer to wear morning dress. Some men like the idea of following tradition and wearing morning dress at their marriage especially if they have not been married before. In this case, the bride should perhaps pay him the compliment of relating her style of dress to his and opting for whatever looks right with a partner who is formally attired.

Changing Your Name

At the end of the marriage ceremony, the bride signs her birth name in the register. For most, it will be for the last time; since from that moment on the bride traditionally assumes a new state. The renunciation of a maiden name, and the acquisition of a new married name, has for centuries been one of the most tangible signs of a woman's new married status.

Not many people realize, however, that there are surprisingly few laws or regulations governing a change of name, and that the decision to become Mrs A or remain Miss B is entirely a matter of individual choice. Legally, there are only two documents that matter as far as your identity is concerned. One is your birth certificate, which remains unchanged for life, whether you marry or change your name in any other way. The other is your marriage certificate, which is stored separately from the birth certificate. Either is a legally acceptable means of identification. You are under no legal obligation, however, to adopt your husband's name. English law takes 'common usage and reputation' as the deciding factor in determining a person's name. You may, in fact, adopt any name you please as long as there is no fraudulent purpose in doing so. No forms have to be filled out, and no written evidence is needed, because a person's name is that by which he or she is known, and which is acquired over the years by continuous use.

Despite the lack of legal formalities, however, the majority of married women do adopt their husband's name. The reasons for doing so are as much social as they are emotional. For while most women find taking their husband's name an integral part of getting married, it is also true that social custom, built up over the centuries, dictates that a woman be known by her husband's name rather than by her father's.

Retaining your maiden name used to be a privilege of the rich and famous, but along with the independence of women, came the recognition that anyone could do it, and many do. Such people have their own reasons for doing so, although many confess that the reasons had to be strong enough to compensate for all the aggravations implicit in the decision. Government departments, employers, banks and a host of other official bodies have developed such an entrenched resistance to such a change from the norm that many women often feel that they are breaking the law in using their maiden name after marriage. Whilst this is emphatically untrue, it is well to be forewarned that there are thorny problems attendant on retaining your maiden name. These are primarily social and depend more for their resolution on changing attitudes than changing the law. The use of the designation Ms, for instance, is undoubtedly on the increase, but it is not yet the accepted form of address for a female except in business correspondence. Abolishing this distinction between a married and single woman has its uses, but Ms cannot be said to sound like sense or read well.

The reasons for deciding to retain your maiden name often concern work. If a person is, for one reason or another, well known in their profession by one name, then it may be easier, and more desirable, to retain that name for professional purposes. Sometimes, however, the reasons are more emotional than practical. Some women feel that to assume the name of their husband implies a loss of identity, and prefer to keep their own name for that reason.

A compromise is to be known by your maiden name or present name in one sphere and by your married name in another. Those who opt for a two-name identity find, however, that there are disadvantages and recommend going by one or the other.

There are, of course, alternative options. The husband can take the wife's surname, or they can both choose a completely different name. There is also the American practice of combining the husband's and wife's surnames, so that when Miss Smith marries Mr Jones they become Mr and Mrs Smith-Jones, or vice versa.

It is up to you to inform the rest of the world how you wish to be known.

Who should you tell?

So if you do wish to change your name, who should you tell?

First, your tax inspector should be informed of the marriage as your tax allowances will be altered. Unless you indicate that you wish to be taxed separately, all correspondence will be addressed to your husband and you will automatically be referred to by your married name. HM Inspector of Taxes does not mind which name you are called by, but if you wish to retain your maiden name you must make sure that this is made clear to him.

It is not necessary to have your passport altered to your married name, although it can undoubtedly avoid complications in certain countries when you are travelling together with your husband. If you do want the document changed, the Passport Office in Petty France, London, can do this for a small fee. It does, however, take at least six weeks, so if you are going off on honeymoon straight after the wedding, remember to send it off in time.

You should also instruct your bank manager if you intend to set up a joint account or keep your own but change your name. Any credit cards you hold should be returned to the respective companies with a covering letter explaining that you have changed your name. They will issue you with new cards. The same goes for any savings or shares you own, which should also be re-registered in your married name. Any insurance policies held in your maiden name should be changed by writing to the insurance company. If you have a driving licence, this too should be sent away to be altered. There is a section on the licence itself which should be filled in. If you own a car, the registration document should also be altered.

Make a list of the people to be told, and write to all of them at the same time. This ensures that the whole operation takes place with minimum fuss and maximum efficiency.

Apart from informing the various authorities it is also necessary to inform yourself. This is not as ludicrous as it sounds. It is not easy to become accustomed to an unfamiliar name overnight, when you have thought of yourself by another name for so long. You have to become familiar with the practice of signing a strange name on cheques, letters and forms.

1929

3

TELLING EVERYBODY

Communication is an important part of organizing a wedding. There are three approaches to the task: to follow custom, to adapt it, or to make your own rules.

A considerable amount of etiquette attaches to the wording of announcements, the style of the wedding invitation, the writing of guest names on cards and envelopes. Decisions here depend on how formally correct everything is to be, and your own attitude and your family's to the importance of such points. In favour of following the established pattern is that it is at least known to work. In favour of writing your own lines is that these may suit your own circumstances better than the old order, quite apart from considerations of originality.

Announcements of Engagement

Announcements of engagement in the local press or national newspapers are a useful way of spreading the news. The classified advertisement department of the publication concerned will have the cost per line of an insertion and will advise on wording. Announcements are usually brief: 'The engagement is announced between Ian Peter, son of Mr and Mrs J.J. Green, of Bridstow, Wessex, and Patricia Jane, daughter of Mr and Mrs L. White, of Brighton.'

The information can be as full as is wished, bearing in mind the cost per line. To help to identify the subjects details can be given: 'younger son', 'only daughter', 'twin son', or 'daughter to' in the case of adoption, and so on. When one or the other is generally known by a nickname, this is sometimes given in brackets after the given name, 'Joanna (Dana) Brown'.

Specific cases
The announcement of an engagement from abroad: 'The engagement is announced in Australia between . . .'; *the announcement of an engagement when a parent has*

died: 'Ann, daughter of the late Mr B. White and Mrs White'; *when both parents have died:* 'son of the late Mr and Mrs S. Black'; *when parents are divorced:* 'daughter of Mr A. Smith and Mrs Barbara Smith'; *where the mother has remarried:* 'daughter of Mr B. Smith and Mrs E. Hill'.

The national newspapers noted for their announcements of engagement and marriage are *The Times* and the *Daily Telegraph*. In the 'Forthcoming Marriages' columns titles and professional styles are given – Sir, Doctor, Captain – and the prefixes Mr or Miss or Mrs.

Announcements of Marriage

The style of engagement announcements applies to announcements of forthcoming marriages. When an engagement and marriage announcement is combined, the final line can read, 'The marriage will take place shortly', or more facts can be given if wished as to when and where.

A brief marriage announcement runs, 'WHITE : BLACK The marriage took place at Temston, Wessex, on Saturday 10th June, between Andrew Brian White of Botherington and Miss Catherine Black of Pintstable.'

A fuller form of marriage announcement is, 'Mr E.F. Gonnard and Mrs J. Branch: The marriage took place quietly in Wessex Cathedral on September 1st between Mr Edward Frederick Gonnard of Alsley and Mrs Jacqueline Branch of Kentish Avenue, Uppington.'

A full announcement of marriage such as is run in the marriage columns in the national or local press:

DR W.N. SAND AND MISS O.P. LAKE
The marriage took place on *(date)* at *(name of place of worship)* between William Nigel Sand, son of Mr and Mrs Michael Sand of Knapstock, and Olivia Patsy Lake, only daughter of Dr and Mrs Patricia Lake of Torrige Hill, Sudford. The Reverend John Fairhall officiated. The bride, who was given in marriage by her father, was attended by *(names of bridal attendants)*. A reception was held at *(name of hotel)* and the honeymoon is being spent in *(destination)*.

A brief description of the bride's effects can be included: 'the bride wore a dress of cream voile and carried a bouquet of cream roses and stephanotis'. In the event, 'a reception was held at the bride's home'.

An announcement of a Service of Blessing could read, 'A Service of Blessing took place on *(date)* at *(name of church)* of the marriage of Robert Simon Cornforth, son of Mr and Mrs W. Cornforth of Toronto, and Tricia Grove, daughter of Mr and Mrs Tom Grove of Polston, Bridgely.' The name of the officiating minister can be added.

Cancellations

When a formal engagement of marriage is broken off, or a marriage cancelled, the news is usually relayed by word of mouth or by letter. However, a formal announcement to the effect may have its purpose. The wording can read, 'The marriage arranged between Mr Martin Snow and Miss Ingrid Stalk will not take place.'

If a wedding has to be postponed and a formal card of announcement is sent to guests, the wording can read, for example, 'Owing to ('unforeseen circumstances', 'her recent bereavement', 'her' or 'her husband's' appointment abroad'), Mrs Joseph Miles regrets that she is obliged to cancel the invitations to the forthcoming marriage of her daughter Lucy to Mr Harry Field, which will now take place quietly in Bath.'

The Wedding Invitation

There are many different styles of wedding invitation – plain, jolly, decorated, formal and personal. By custom, the invitation card is specially printed or engraved on plain white paper folded in two with a standard measure of $5\frac{1}{2}$ × 7 in (14 × 18 cm). Black or silver lettering is usual.

Except in the case of a very small wedding when the invitations can be handwritten, it is a considerable convenience to send printed invitations. A good stationer should supply specimen invitations showing different sizes, styles of lettering, and design, and will probably be able to advise on the wording if there are doubts. Notice the difference between engraved and printed script. The former is a more expensive process but the lettering stands out elegantly on the page and is considered correct.

Allow plenty of time for the order which should include envelopes remembering that where parents with young children are invited only one card need be sent. Ready-printed wedding invitations can be bought at a stationer with spaces for names, addresses and details to be filled in by hand. Decorations such as silver bells on the card are a matter of taste and the traditions of the community.

Invitations are sent out about six weeks in advance of the wedding date in theory, but many people work closer to the deadline these days. The bride and her family are responsible for the costs and organization of the invitations.

The wording of wedding invitations

The wording of wedding invitations can follow a set pattern which is related to the lay-out of the lettering on the page and the general style. The wording depends on the relationship of the host or hosts to the bride. Some invitations covering different relationships are given below and on the following pages, and specimen invitations are illustrated.

In all cases a wedding invitation should carry the names of the host and/or hostess, the marrying pair, the date, the time, the place and an RSVP address to which guests can reply. In the example given here and in those on the following pages, 'honour' can be used in place of 'pleasure'.

The bride's parents as hosts

Mr and Mrs John Budd
request the pleasure of
your company at the marriage
of their daughter
Elizabeth
to
Mr James Edward Cave
at St Michael's Church, Mexforth
on (date, month, year)
at (time)
and afterwards at
The Grand Eagle Hotel

RSVP
12 Green Avenue
Nottingham

The bride's mother as host

'Mrs James Matthews requests the pleasure of your company at the marriage of her daughter . . .' If the mother is divorced she uses her forename and surname, 'Mrs Ann Matthews', if she has remarried, 'Mrs William Dale'. If she is unmarried she can use the designation 'Ms'.

The bride's father as host

'Mr Jack Wood requests the pleasure of your company at the marriage of his daughter . . .'

The bride's father and stepmother as hosts

'Mr and Mrs Robert Beech request the pleasure of your company at the marriage of his daughter . . .'

The bride's mother and stepfather as hosts

'Mr and Mrs Nigel Roland request the pleasure of your company at the marriage of her daughter . . .' Sometimes the bride's surname is given in the interests of clarity, 'request the pleasure of your company at the marriage of her daughter, Jane Harris'.

The bride's parents as hosts

The bride's mother as host

Mr and Mrs Edward Smith
request the pleasure of
your company at the marriage
of their daughter
Joanna
to
Mr James Julian Nott
at St Margaret's Church, Haslemere
on Saturday, 14th July
at 3 o'clock
and afterwards at
Woodlands

R S V P
(address)

Mrs James Matthews
requests the pleasure of
your company at the marriage
of her daughter
Jane
to
Mr Christopher Collins
at St Michael's Church, Staveley
on Saturday, 13th June
at 2 o'clock
and afterwards at
The White Swan

R S V P
(address)

The cards shown above are reduced from the original size

The bride's stepmother as host

'Mrs Michael Baker requests the pleasure of your company at the marriage of her stepdaughter . . .' The bride's surname can be given if wished.

The bride's divorced parents as hosts

'Mr Christopher Brown and Mrs Fiona Brown request the pleasure of your company at the marriage of their daughter . . .'

The bride's divorced parents as hosts – mother remarried

'Mr John Sadler and Mrs Michael Jackson request the pleasure of your company at the marriage of their daughter . . .'

The bride's remarried father and remarried mother as hosts

'Mr Peter Whittle and Mrs Patrick Neale request the pleasure of your company at the marriage of their daughter . . .'

The bride as host

'Miss Polly Miller requests the pleasure of your company at her marriage to Mr Kevin Farr at *(address)*, on *(date)*, at *(time)* and afterwards at *(address)*'.

The bride's mother and stepfather as hosts

Mr and Mrs Nigel Roland
request the pleasure of
your company at the marriage
of her daughter
Jane
to
Mr Mark Anthony Green
at All Saints Church, Burnham
on Saturday, 13th June
at 4 o'clock
and afterwards at
The White Swan

RSVP
(address)

The bride's divorced parents as hosts

Mr Christopher Brown
and Mrs Fiona Brown
request the pleasure of
your company at the marriage
of their daughter
Jane
to
Mr Michael Stevens
at All Saints Parish Church,
Stow-on-the-Wold
on Saturday, 6th June
at 2.30 pm
and afterwards at
The White Swan

RSVP
Mrs Fiona Brown
(address)

The bride and groom as hosts

'Mr Jeremy Clarke and Miss Clare Hammond request the pleasure of your company at their marriage at *(address)*, on *(date)*, at *(time)* and afterwards at *(address)*'.

The bride's relations, guardians or godparent as hosts

'Commander and Mrs Henry Pottington request the pleasure of your company at the marriage of their niece (ward, his/her goddaughter, cousin), Jane...' The bride's surname can be included, if wished.

Proxy parents as hosts

'Mr and Mrs J. Scott request the pleasure of your company at the marriage of Susan, daughter of the late Mr Chuck Kraft and Mrs Kraft of Minneapolis, to Mr Maxwell Dodd...'

The bride's close relations as hosts

There are so many permutations in the class of family relationships that it is impractical to try to cover all of them. Some likely relationships are covered in the following wording:

The bride's divorced parents as hosts – mother remarried   *The bride and groom as hosts*

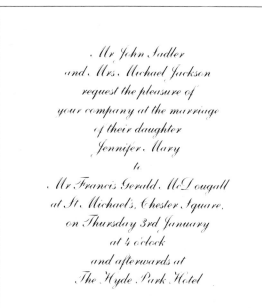

Mr John Sadler
and Mrs Michael Jackson
request the pleasure of
your company at the marriage
of their daughter
Jennifer Mary
to
Mr Francis Gerald McDougall
at St. Michael's, Chester Square,
on Thursday 3rd January
at 4 o'clock
and afterwards at
The Hyde Park Hotel

RSVP
(address)

Mr Jeremy Clarke
and Miss Clare Hammond
request the pleasure of
your company at their marriage
at All Saints Church, Romford
on Saturday, 14th November
at 3 o'clock
and afterwards at
The White Swan

RSVP
Miss Clare Hammond
(address)

The brother of the bride is host: 'Mr Frederick Bisley requests the pleasure of your company at the marriage of his sister Deborah ...'

The brothers are hosts: 'Mr Frederick Bisley and Mr Samuel Bisley request the pleasure ... their sister Deborah ...'

A brother and unmarried sister are host and hostess: 'Mr Frederick Bisley and Miss Ann Bisley request the pleasure ... their sister Deborah ...'

An unmarried sister is hostess: 'Miss Bisley (or Miss Ann Bisley) requests the pleasure ... her sister Deborah ...'

Two unmarried sisters are hostesses: 'The Misses Bisley request the pleasure ... their sister Deborah ...' or 'Miss Ann Bisley and Miss Kate Bisley'.

A brother and his wife are host and hostess: 'Mr and Mrs Frederick Bisley request the pleasure ... his sister Deborah ...'

A married sister and her husband are host and hostess: 'Mr and Mrs E.P. Turner request the pleasure ... her sister Deborah ...'

A married sister and an unmarried sister are hostesses: Mrs E.P. Turner and Miss Ann Bisley request the pleasure ... their sister Deborah ...' By custom, the married sister takes precedence whether she is older or younger than her unmarried sister.

Proxy hosts

A reply card enclosed with an invitation

Owing to the absence in Australia of
Mr and Mrs Herbert Latham,
Lieutenant Colonel and Mrs John Trillon
request the pleasure of your company
to celebrate the marriage of
Linda and Adrian
on Saturday, 20th April,
at Powers Hall

RSVP
(address)   6.15 pm

Thank you for your kind invitation
which I/we will be able/unable to accept

....

No. of persons...

Please reply on or before 15th June

The brides' parents are host and hostess at a double wedding of sisters

Mr and Mrs P. Knowles
request the pleasure of your company
at the marriage of their daughters
Gillian
to
Mr Robin Pickett
and
Helen
to
Mr Ian Gimble
at __ on __ at __ and afterwards at __.

RSVP

Other traditional wedding invitation styles

Europeans and the practising Jewish community traditionally send out
wedding invitations in the names of both sets of parents,
'Mr and Mrs Lawrence Starr request the pleasure of your company at the
marriage of their daughter Sheila to Benjamin, son of Mr and Mrs (*names*) . . .'

Formal invitation card in English and Hebrew

*Aaron & Frances Winegarten
and Mina Hager*
request the pleasure of your company
at the marriage of their children
Louise
to
Freddy
Son of the late Michael Hager
on Sunday, the 25th of February
at the Brent Town Hall,
Forty Lane, Wembley, Middlesex.

Reception - 12 o'clock
Chupah - 12.45 o'clock
Luncheon - 1.30 o'clock

R.S.V.P.

בעזהי"ת

אנו מודים לד' על כל הטוב אשר גמלנו ובחסדיו הגדול
זכנו בנשואי צאצאינו החתן

אפרים שאלתיאל שי'

עם בת הכלה המהוללה מרת

לאה תחי'

החופה תהיה בעזהי"ת למזלט ביום א' כ' לחדש אדר א' תשכ"ג
הבא עלינו ועל כל ישראל יחיו לטובה ולברכה
בחצר ברענט טאון האלל שבעיר לונדון
בשעה 12.45 בשעה טובה ומוצלחת

בשמחה וטוב לבב נקרא לידידינו ומכירינו אשר ביום
שמחת לבבנו יאילו נא לשמוח אתנו יחדיו ולברך את
הזוג יחיו ואותט כלנו בברכת טוב וחיים מאושרים
בגשמיות ורוחניות

הא-ל הטוב הוא יתברך יברך את כבודו ואנשי ביתו יחיו
בתוך כללי אהבי יחיו בברכות מאלפות מנפש ועד בשר —

הורי הכלה: הורי החתן

מינצא האגער   אהרן ווינערטן ורעיתו
לונדון   לונדון

*Work on this invitation took
some planning but almost
everything is possible provided
that you allow the stationer
and printer enough time to do
the job properly.*

Conventional Forms of Address

As you may want to follow convention in even the smallest details, the following procedures set out the forms of address established by custom.

All wedding invitations bear the handwritten name of the guest to whom they are addressed placed in the top left-hand side of the card. The groom's family (but not the groom himself) and the officiating minister are sent invitations as a record of the occasion. All the star participants such as the bridesmaids, best man and ushers, receive invitation cards despite the fact that the information on it is likely to be engraved on their hearts. Cards are often sent as a matter of courtesy to friends and relations who are unlikely to be able to accept. In general, an individual card is sent to everyone who is invited, but one card is sent to a husband and wife. See the following pages for details. Invitations are placed in envelopes, sealed, addressed and mailed, except where hand delivery makes sense.

How to address the guests on invitation cards

Usually the prefix 'Mr' or 'Mrs' or 'Miss' is used with a forename, or initials, and surname. Usually names are written in full but in the case where people are

Invitation in English and Hebrew, to a Jewish marriage

עוד ישמע בערי יהודה ובחוצות ירושלים

קול ששון וקול שמחה

קול חתן וקול כלה

Mr. & Mrs Gabriel Diner
request the pleasure of the company of

at the marriage of their daughter
Valerie
to
Stephen
son of Mrs Deborah Alexander
at Marble Arch Synagogue
Gt. Cumberland Place, W.1.
on Tuesday 11th June 1974 at 5 p.m.
and afterwards at
The King David Suite.

R.S.V.P
42 Biddulph Mansions,
Elgin Avenue,
London, W.9.

Reception 5.45 p.m.
Supper Dance 7 p.m.

Invitation to a Jewish marriage

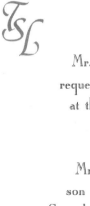

Mr. and Mrs. Wesley Alan Miller
request the honour of your presence
at the marriage of their daughter
Terri Edda
to
Mr. Lawrence Gordon Shulman
son of Dr. and Mrs. Alex Shulman
Saturday, the twenty-seventh of October
at half after six o'clock
Temple Emanuel
Denver, Colorado

Dinner at the Fairmont Hotel

known by an acceptable or shortened version of their forename, there seems every reason to use it.

A single man: 'Mr Joseph Grey'.

Brothers: 'Mr Joseph Grey and Mr William Grey'.

Children: 'Sally and Ian'.

A husband and wife: 'Mr and Mrs Jack Bean'.

A family: it has become acceptable to send one card where the parents and young children are invited – 'Mr and Mrs Jack Bean and Sally and Ian'. Older children however will appreciate an invitation of their own. The designation 'Master' as in 'Master John Grey' for a young boy is sometimes used.

A single woman: 'Miss Shulman' or 'Miss Alexandra Shulman'.

Sisters: the eldest takes precedence – 'Miss Alexandra Shulman and Miss Nicky Shulman', or 'The Misses Shulman'.

A brother and sister(s): separate invitations are usually addressed to brothers and sisters. An alternative style could be simply 'Ian and Sally'.

A couple who are not husband and wife: one option is to address separate invitations to the couple; or an informal style is to write 'Roddy and Tessa' on a single card to both.

A couple where the wife is known by a professional name of her own rather than her married appellation: much may depend on the known sensitivities of the guest on this matter. The custom is to use the married style of address: 'Mr and Mrs Stanley Watkins', but you could write the names of both, 'Mr Stanley Watkins and Miss Muriel Sweep', or dodge the issue by addressing the card to 'Stanley and Muriel'.

A woman whose marriage has been dissolved: 'Mrs Sarah Smith'.

A widow: use her late husband's forename or initials, 'Mrs I.I. Lewis', unless she is generally known as 'Mrs Maria Lewis'.

A medical practitioner or a PhD, etc: 'Dr Michael Hunt' or, if married, 'Dr and Mrs Michael Hunt'. If the doctor is a woman 'Dr Ann Grey' and, if married, 'Mr Peter Grey and Dr Ann Grey'. Strict etiquette would require that the last example read 'Mr and Mrs Peter Grey'. Consultant practitioners are addressed as 'Mr', 'Mrs' or 'Miss'.

NOTE: the non-specific prefix 'Ms' can be used on invitations where this suits, but the widespread use of this designation in business correspondence does not seem to have caught on in this country in social correspondence.

Ecclesiasticals

A vicar or rector: 'Mr Trevor Godley'; if he is married, 'Mr and Mrs T. Godley'.

A canon: 'Canon John Brown and Mrs Brown'.

A bishop: 'Dr Hughes'; if married, 'Dr Hughes and Mrs Hughes'.

An archbishop: 'The Archbishop of __'; if married 'The Archbishop of __ and Mrs Thomas'.

A Roman Catholic priest: 'Father Smith'.

A clergyman carrying the designation 'Dom': 'Dom Andrew'.

A Jewish minister: 'Mr Cohen' or 'Dr Cohen', according to degree.

A rabbi: 'Rabbi Cohen'.

The wedding-invitation envelopes

A single man, brothers, a single woman, sisters, a divorced woman, a widow: in these cases the envelope is addressed in the same way as the card itself. In the case of a single man, however, there may be a choice between the older form, 'J. Teesdale, Esq' or the plainer 'Mr J. Teesdale'. You can't go wrong if you use the formal style, but few people would object to plain Mr.

A husband and wife: the custom is to address the envelope to the wife only, 'Mrs Jack Bean', though many people prefer to include the husband's name as well – 'Mr and Mrs Jack Bean'.

A husband and wife with young children who are also invited: the names of the children are by custom omitted from the envelope.

Ecclesiasticals

Vicar or rector: 'The Reverend Eric Church'; if he is married, 'The Reverend Eric and Mrs Church' – or to the wife alone, 'Mrs Eric Church'.

A canon: 'The Reverend Canon __'.

A dean: 'The Very Reverend —'.

A bishop: 'The Right Reverend the Lord Bishop of __'; if he is married the envelope is addressed to the wife alone.

An archdeacon: 'The Venerable the Archdeacon of __'; if he is married, 'The Venerable the Archdeacon of __ and Mrs Stratton' __ or to the wife alone.

An archbishop: 'His Grace the Lord Archbishop of __'; if he is married the envelope is addressed to the wife alone.

A Roman Catholic priest: 'The Reverend R. Connor'.

A clergyman carrying the designation 'Dom': 'The Reverend Dom P.J. Smith'.

A Jewish minister: 'The Reverend A. Cohen' or 'The Reverend Dr. A. Cohen' according to degree.

A rabbi: 'The Reverend Rabbi A. Cohen'.

Europe

Information on continental wedding procedures can be obtained from the appropriate embassy. A very brief note on forms of address for correspondence

LEPAPE   1925

is given here. All are written in full, followed by a forename or initials and surname. Envelopes are addressed to both husband and wife.

French: a man is addressed as 'Monsieur', a married woman as 'Madame', an unmarried woman, 'Mademoiselle'. A husband and wife are addressed as 'Monsieur et Madame __'.

German: a man is addressed as 'Herr', a married woman as 'Frau', an unmarried woman as 'Fräulein'. A husband and wife are addressed as 'Herr und Frau __'.

Spanish: a man is addressed as 'Señor', a woman as 'Señora', an unmarried woman as 'Señorita'. A husband and wife are addressed as 'Señor y Señora'.

Italian: a man is addressed as 'Signor', a married woman as 'Signora', an unmarried woman as 'Signorina'. A husband and wife are addressed as 'Signor e Signora __'.

People with titles and ranks

Correct styles of address in the case of people with titles and ranks is a whole subject of its own. The fullest information can be found in reference works such as Debrett's *Correct Form*, available at the public library. Note that there is a distinction between the style in which a guest is addressed by custom on invitation cards and envelopes. Full titles are usually given on envelopes. When a married couple is invited, the envelope is by custom addressed to the wife alone, but the husband's name can be included as well if this is preferred.

Dukes, earls and viscounts are given their full title on the envelope, thus: 'His Grace the Duke of Wessex', 'The Earl of Wessex', 'The Viscount Wessex'; but if he is married, the envelope is by custom addressed to the wife alone, thus: 'Her Grace the Duchess of Wessex', 'The Countess of Wessex', 'The Viscountess Wessex'.

The invitation cards are addressed thus: in the case of a duke, if unmarried, to 'The Duke of Wessex' or, if married, to 'The Duke and Duchess of Wessex'; in the case of earls and viscounts, if he is single the card is addressed to 'Lord Wessex' or, if married, to 'Lord and Lady Wessex'.

In the case of knights and baronets, if he is single the envelope and card are addressed to, for example, 'Sir George Swell'. If he is married, the envelope is addressed to 'Lady Swell' and the card is addressed to 'Sir George and Lady Swell'.

When a guest has a double handle such as a service rank and a title, 'Major General Sir Robin Beagle', he is addressed on the invitation card, 'Sir Robin Beagle'. His full title and rank are given on the envelope.

When a commoner marries the daughter of an earl the couple are addressed on the invitation card 'Mr Jasper and Lady Eleanor Porchester'. The envelope is by custom addressed to the wife alone, 'Lady Eleanor Porchester'.

The designation, 'Honourable', denoting the son or daughter of a peer, is not given on invitation cards but is usually used on envelopes. When a single man or woman holds the Hon., he or she is addressed 'The Hon.' (or 'the Honourable') 'James/Caroline Forbes'. If a man is the Hon., married to a commoner, his wife holds a courtesy title and the envelope is addressed to 'The Hon. Mrs Charles Black'.

Senior ranks in the armed services are given on cards and envelopes.

Invitations to the Reception Only

Everyone who is invited to the marriage ceremony is invited to the reception. However, for a number of good reasons, more people may be asked to the reception than are included in the guest list for the wedding ceremony.

If family and a few friends only are attending the marriage – as at a register office wedding, for example – invitations to the ceremony can be handwritten, and the formal invitation card can be the one to the wedding reception.

An invitation to a reception alone can resemble the style of a traditional wedding card in its presentation and lettering and design. The wording depends on the particular details of the occasion. Some examples are quoted below.

Mr and Mrs John Black
request the pleasure of
your company at a reception
following the marriage of their daughter
Paula
to
Mr Francis Wheeler
at the Hind's Head Hotel
on Wednesday 13 September 1980
at 12 o'clock
RSVP
(address)

An alternative form:

Mr and Mrs Charles Black
at home
to celebrate the marriage of their daughter
Violet
to
Mr Victor Smart
on *(day, month, year)*
at *(time of day)*
RSVP
(address)

A ready printed or engraved 'at home' card is an option in which the name of the hostess, her husband, and all the particulars of when and where are filled in by hand.

At a second marriage, when the bride is host at her own wedding reception, the wording can read, 'Mrs Angela Morell at home following her marriage to Mr Stephen Hills on *(date)* at *(time)*. RSVP *(address)*.'

Invitation to reception only – bride's parents as hosts

Mr and Mrs Philip Clarke
request the pleasure of
your company at a reception
following the marriage
of their daughter
Jane
to
Mr Michael Matthews
at The Water Wheel,
Park Langley
on Saturday, 13th June
at 4 o'clock

RSVP
(address)

Invitation to reception only – bride as host at her remarriage

Mrs Jim Matthews
requests the pleasure of
your company at a reception
following her marriage
to
Mr David Ellis
at The White Swan,
Beauchamp Park
on Saturday, 20th June
at 4 o'clock

RSVP
(address)

Invitation to reception only – bride's mother as host

Lady Brown
At Home
following the marriage
of her daughter
Vanessa
to Mr John Phillips
at 30 Pavilion Road, SW1
on Friday, 11th July

RSVP
(address)

10 pm
Black Tie

Invitation to reception only – proxy parents as hosts

Mrs Charles Brown
At Home
to celebrate the marriage of
Amelia Jane Howard
to
Mr Christopher Reynolds
on Saturday, 13th June
at 3 o'clock

RSVP
(address)

Informal Wedding Invitations, Personal Announcements and Messages

The interest in putting a more personal imprint on wedding proceedings can be shown in the design of the wedding invitation. There are many attractive alternatives to the conventional form, with design, lettering and wording reflecting a more personal approach. The Americans have all kinds of upbeat ideas for wedding stationery far removed from our own sober conventions and these are becoming accepted alternatives in this country.

Unusual invitation cards can be bought at specialist shops, or designed to order, or hand made at home. Lettering on a coloured card, handwritten scripts, informal wording, decorated and illustrated cards are all lively possibilities. When a card design is commissioned from an artist or calligrapher, the design can be reproduced by a printer. Decorative emblems or images signifying the interests or hobbies or associations of the couple are used as part of a personal design. Students of graphic design or painting at art colleges are among those prepared to accept commissions on this account.

A wedding is an occasion which can call for special stationery orders. Among the options are matching and/or coordinated sets of stationery such as wedding

A modern wedding invitation

A do-it-yourself invitation

Mr & Mrs Robert Cook
would like you to join them
to celebrate the Marriage
of their daughter Sally
to Barry Weaver
at All Saints Church
Appletreewick Yorkshire
on Saturday May 1st at 2pm
the reception afterwards
will be held at the
Royal Hotel Appletreewick

RSVP
7 Meadow Lane, Appletreewick

SCOTTY

SUE AND CHRIS

INVITE YOU TO THEIR

WEDDING PARTY

AT RASPUTIN'S CELLAR,

THE PARADE, HARROW

ON SATURDAY 2ND MAY

AT 8 O'CLOCK

RSVP

24 BECMEAD ROAD

HARROW

Left: If your budget is really tight, there is nothing wrong with a short note giving all the details about the wedding. This card is made by cutting coffee-coloured background paper into a wedge shape and then typing on creamy-coloured Indian writing paper all the relevant details of the wedding party. The writing paper is glued on to the background, which can be folded up like an envelope, sealed and mailed.

invitation cards, change-of-address cards, announcement of marriage cards, correspondence cards. However, printed thankyou cards for presents and messages of goodwill are too chilly and impersonal; a handwritten letter or card will give much greater pleasure. Wordings for informal wedding parties and celebrations simply say what has to be said in the simplest terms; for example, 'Mr and Mrs Peter Jones hope you will join them at a party to celebrate the marriage of their daughter Janice to Ron Freen at __ on __ at __ RSVP *(address)*'.

When the bride and groom are acting as hosts at their own wedding party the invitation can read, 'Merry Blackett and Geoff Baynes invite *(name of guest to be filled in by hand)* to a celebration following their marriage at *(address)* on *(date)* at *(time)*. RSVP *(address if different from the party address)*'.

An informally worded invitation from the bride's parents: 'Mr and Mrs R. Teague are happy to announce the marriage of their daughter Sandra to Dave Croft and invite you to the ceremony at *(address of place of worship)* on *(date)* at *(time)* followed by celebrations at *(address of reception location)*. RSVP *(address)*.'

One of the main points in departing from tradition is to come up with a good idea on the subject. It is important that any innovatory design should convey the basic invitation information in a clear, unambiguous manner. See examples in the illustrations.

Folded designer white card with handwritten lettering on the front (below left) using forenames only for the couple concerned. Inside – surprise! – a pop-up paper dove repeating an illustration of a dove on the card (right).

Fay and Thomas
invite you to their wedding
at Kensington Register Office, W.8
on Saturday 8th June 1974
at 2.30 pm
and afterwards at
The Royal Oak, Cranbourne Gardens
London S.W.7

R.S.V.P. to 17 Wilmington Mews
London S.W.3

MANN AND WIFE

Printed Personal Services

There are various accessories that can be specially printed and ordered from a stationer. Most people like to supply Order of Service sheets to the congregation when they arrive at the place of worship. This is a folded card setting out the titles of the pieces of music to be played during the service and giving the names of the composers and perhaps a note about the pieces. Sometimes the hymns and psalms are set out in print for the congregation to follow.

The 'sheets' can be single or double, and are usually printed in black or silver on a plain, white, good textured paper. The front page carries the forenames of the bride and groom 'Justin and Maureen', or 'The Marriage of George and Alice', or their initials, or some personal emblem. The day, date, month and year of the marriage are always given and perhaps the name of the place of worship. Sometimes, 'Order of Service' is printed on the card.

An Order of Service sheet – cover

An Order of Service sheet

Carmelite Church
KENSINGTON

Order of Service

Marriage

OF

Flora

AND

Robert

Saturday, 29th March, 1980

Order of Service

Air Suite in D	*Bach*
Water Music	*Handel*

ENTRY

Trumpet Tune	*Purcell*
Mass in B Flat	*Schubert*

MOTET

Ave Maria	*Schubert*

COMMUNION

Panlis Angelicus	*Cesar Franck*

SIGNING OF THE REGISTER

Laudate Dominum	*Mozart*

RECESSIONAL

March from "Aida"	*Verdi*

When ordering numbers, arrange for one sheet for every invited guest at the place of worship. There are no firm guidelines on style, and some musically minded people like to devise original Order of Service cards to match a particularly interesting selection of music, using specially textured papers, unusual scripts and lettering and other embellishments.

Among the accessories that can be printed with a personal emblem are table napkins which can be printed with the names of the married couple, their initials or a monogram; books of matches with the flap printed with the date or names or initials; place cards for the table. Drawn maps giving directions to the place of worship or reception location can also be printed.

TAKE CARE: The watchword when ordering printed stationery for a wedding in which every letter and comma counts, let alone the accuracy of the date, is to work ahead of time. Keep a note of numbers, costs, the wording, the lay-out, the script, the paper, the envelopes, the colours, and all stipulations and specifications. If an error occurs by the wildest chance in the type and time is short, the remedy lies in your hands – add a fine, handwritten, corrective touch of your own.

A card announcing a marriage – actual size

Miss Gloria Taylor and Lord Birkett
beg to announce that they were married
on 4th December 1978 and are living at
7 Cambridge Place London W8

4

PLANNING THE WEDDING

Getting married in the traditional way can be an exhausting and time-consuming process. Although the rituals, customs and procedures surrounding marriage are infinitely less rigid these days, organizing a wedding, on whatever scale, is still a demanding task. However formal or informal, and however much or little you have to spend, there are a thousand and one details to attend to, decisions to be made and things to be done. Even the best laid plans can go astray, so it is essential to check and re-check, right up until the day itself. This can all be needlessly tedious and nerve-racking, and tensions and rows between those involved have become almost part of the tradition. Everyone will have their own way of organizing a wedding, but this chapter sets out to help you avoid some of the small frustrations and bigger problems in planning one of the most important days of your life. Despite rising divorce rates, it remains true that most people only get married once, and everyone indeed wants the day to go as smoothly as possible.

Attitudes to weddings, and to getting married in general, have changed considerably in recent years in accordance with the changing social climate. The word 'etiquette' – for so long considered the heart of the matter – has lost its strict meaning. It should be noted, however, that whilst there is increasing flexibility as regards the social side of the day, most weddings at a place of worship involve certain traditional procedures which almost always have to be observed, at least to some degree.

The dream of the perfect wedding – unlike most dreams – can be realized, but it takes more than the wave of a magic wand. It should be planned with the precision of a military campaign. If that sounds daunting, take heart. With foresight, fortitude and a fair amount of good humour, the organization of the wedding can be as enjoyable as the day itself. Some people are born organizers and will find it easy to deal with the seemingly endless list of preliminaries; others can use the following blueprint for planning a wedding.

These guidelines are designed principally for the bride who is planning a formal, traditional white wedding with a reception afterwards. They can, however, be adapted to fit most needs by simply omitting those aspects that do not apply to your wedding plans. Many of the points outlined here are covered in greater detail in subsequent chapters.

Where and When?

One of the first things to be decided is the question of where and when your wedding is to take place. All the other arrangements are dependent on this, so it is vital to make this decision as soon as possible. If you are planning anything more than the most basic register office wedding, you will need at least two to three months to make all the necessary arrangements. Great care should be taken over the choice of date, and there are various factors that may influence it. You should bear in mind any religious regulations. Some churches and chapels do not allow formal weddings at various times in the religious calendar – Lent or Advent, for instance, in the case of the Christian church. Sundays, too, can be a problem since, although it is not forbidden by the Church, most ministers will be too busy to perform the wedding ceremony on that day. Similarly, certain times of year are extremely popular for weddings – the summer, June in particular, Easter and Whitsun – and Saturdays are usually reserved months in advance. Another consideration that may have some bearing on the decision is the tax year. A mercenary consideration depending for its importance on your and your partner's financial circumstances is that there may be benefits in marrying either at the end or the beginning of the tax year which commences on 5 April. If in doubt, an accountant will advise on a matter which may be straightforward but may require professional judgement. There are also family circumstances which may affect the choice of date; relations who are abroad, or who have previously arranged commitments that for one reason or other cannot be changed. Highly personal factors may play a part such as the bride's monthly cycle and her response to it.

Once you have decided on a certain day, you should give some consideration to what time of day you would like to hold the wedding. Common times are midday and three in the afternoon, to be followed by a meal. However, any time between 8 am and 6 pm is permissible, and late afternoon weddings, followed by an evening party, with dinner and sometimes dancing, are becoming increasingly popular.

Where to get married is, within certain regulations laid down by some denominations, a matter of individual choice and circumstances. Most couples tend to get married at the place of worship nearest to the woman's home or where they are parishioners. Like most traditions, this one has become common usage for essentially practical reasons; the proximity makes for greater ease in completing the arrangements and cuts down on the time you have to spend travelling to and fro.

It may be customary for the couple to marry in the bride's home town, but it is not, however, always practical. If you live in a city far from both sets of parents, it may make sense to be married there amongst your own friends. As the bride, it is your choice, but it is wise to consider the parents' feelings. Unlike America, however, where it is possible to get married literally anywhere, on the top of a mountain or in a small city garden, almost all weddings in Britain must be conducted in a place of worship or a building registered with the Superintendent Registrar of Marriages.

What Kind of Wedding?

Once you have set the date and place of your wedding, you should think about the type of wedding you want. There are as many styles of wedding as there are people getting married. It should, of course, fit with your dreams, but must also be in keeping with the financial circumstances. The costs can be considerable if you want a formal white wedding, and while most people want 'nothing but the best' on their wedding day, it should be only the best that you can afford. There is no need to feel that spending a large sum of money is essential for a successful wedding. Like everything else, weddings can cost as much or as little as you want them to. It is important, though, to keep financial limitations firmly in mind before deciding on the style of wedding for you.

Within the traditional white wedding there is a great deal of room for variation. No two weddings are the same, nor would anyone want them to be. All the details and decisions will add up to an individual style, and everything down to the minutest detail will reflect your tastes and preferences. It is these tastes and preferences that should be the first to be sorted out.

The Decision-makers

The problem of exactly who is going to make all these decisions can, however, be the cause of much controversy. Traditionally, it is thought that whoever is paying for the bulk of the wedding costs should be in charge, and it is usually the bride's mother who shoulders most of the responsibility. These days, however, attitudes have greatly changed, and the traditional arrangement of the bride's mother doing all the work, in varying degrees of collaboration with her daughter, is by no means the only option.

If the bride's mother and her daughter are both working full-time, neither may be able to devote the time they would like to the planning of the wedding. In this case, it seems only fair and sensible that some of the chores should be shared out amongst other members of the family. The groom, who is traditionally the least involved in the preparations, may be drawn into the discussions. It should be remembered, too, that misdirected communication, or none at all, with the groom can be a source of tension. It is important that he should at least feel involved, and although some men would rather be presented with a *fait accompli* on the day, most will waste little time in giving their views on the subject.

It is by no means uncommon these days for the bride and groom to undertake all the planning, and even all or part of the financing of the wedding. It is also quite common, too, for the groom's parents to contribute in some way, especially if their financial circumstances are healthier than those of the bride's parents. Care should be taken, however, to ensure that the bride's family are not offended or embarrassed by such an offer.

What Style of Party?

Determining the style of the reception is equally flexible. It can be of the same size and formality as the wedding or not. Some couples favour a large reception with all their friends and relations following a small, intimate family wedding; others prefer a large wedding followed by an informal, small party. It can be held at any time of day; it can be a sit-down or buffet party; you can have it at any location – at home, in a garden, village hall or grand hotel.

But whether you do the catering yourself, or have it done for you, whether it is formal or informal, traditional or not, the secret of a good party (and after all, that's what it is) is to plan methodically, according to your tastes and means.

New freedoms

There is no doubt that where weddings are concerned, the mood is changing to meet new social situations and is far more flexible. Should you take advantage of this, you may suspect that your friends and relations will be disappointed not to get a wholly traditional wedding, but certainly no one will be shocked. However, remember that most traditions have grown up for purely practical reasons. The traditional receiving line (where the couple and their parents greet the guests at the reception), for instance, is simply the best way of making sure that, however briefly, you do at least talk to everyone present.

Tensions and Tiffs

Planning a wedding can be a considerable strain on families, and tensions between parents and offspring may be heightened during the run-up to the wedding. This is all the more reason to be as organized as possible, so that the preparations may go smoothly. A certain amount of compromise, goodwill and patience is necessary even in the most harmonious of families. It should be remembered, too, that the people involved, particularly the bride and the all-too-often-neglected groom, are usually in a highly emotional state, and that disagreement over even the most trivial details may let loose all kinds of bottled-up resentments. There is no magic formula for avoiding the tiffs and tantrums, though good planning and allowing sufficient time for arranging everything are sensible precautions to take.

Step-by-step Guide

Three months is a comfortable time to allow for making all the arrangements, although it can be done in less. It is difficult to set out an exact list of priorities and procedures as they vary according to individual circumstances.

Three months beforehand

● Go and see the minister, priest or rabbi, who will explain about the church fees and the system of calling the banns, and will ask you to fill in a form with details of yourselves and your respective fathers. A register office wedding should also be booked well in advance if you intend to get married on a Saturday, particularly during the spring and summer. You should ask whether photography is allowed at the place of worship, if you would like it, and whether it is possible to have a tape-recording made of the ceremony. If you are getting married during one of the church festivals, your choice of flowers may be limited. Check this, and also ask if any other couples are being married on the same day, so that you can find out whether they would be prepared to share the cost of the flowers with you. Ask, too, what views the minister and the organist have about music at the wedding, whether they will accept secular music, so that you and your fiancé can choose what hymns and other music you want before, during and after the ceremony. It is important to get hold of a copy of the marriage service you will be using and read through it together. It is not necessary to learn the words and vows, although some people like to do this, as they will be 'taught' to you by the minister during the ceremony.

● Having decided what kind of reception you want, select your hotel or caterer – you should get at least three different estimates – and make a provisional booking for the day.

● Make a guest list with both sets of parents and your fiancé. This often poses problems where the families have many friends and relations. Other couples may find that the two families have lists that are heavily unbalanced, and in these cases a certain amount of tact and common sense is needed. It is often difficult, too, to know where to draw the line when cutting down on numbers, although most acquaintances will understand, whether your reasons for doing so are financial or personal. When ordering the invitations, which should also be done at this stage, note that you may need more than one per family. Service sheets and souvenir cake boxes – specially initialled mementoes such as table napkins, books of matches or place cards – should be ordered well in advance.

● Unless you live within walking distance of the church, you will need to arrange transport for the day. Again, car-hire firms are very busy during the summer months, so it is important to arrange this well in advance, particularly if you want something special, like a white Rolls-Royce or a carriage and four. Alternatively, make firm arrangements to borrow cars from friends and family.

● At this stage, book a photographer and arrange an appointment to meet him or her and discuss your needs.

● Your wedding cake should be ordered, if the hotel or caterer is not doing this for you. Remember to order a sufficiently large cake if souvenir pieces are to be sent. Families contemplating a christening service for the first-born sometimes like to keep a tier for this occasion.

● Bridesmaids, ushers and the best man should be chosen. This needs careful thought if jealousies are not to be aroused. Both relations and friends may feel they have a claim to be more than just guests at the wedding, though you may consider they are unsuited to the duties involved.

Two months beforehand
● Confirm food and drink arrangements with the caterers. They will be able to advise you about the possibilities, depending on seasonal availability, suitability and price.

● Organize the flowers. If you are going to employ a professional florist, make an appointment to meet her and discuss what you would like, and take her to the church and reception location so that you can decide what will be needed there.

● Shop for your wedding ring; if it is to be specially made for you, order it now. Wedding rings often sell out quickly in the popular summer months.

● Consult the minister about final decisions on the music for your wedding, and make an appointment to see the organist to discuss the music. Order your printed service sheets, and ask for them to be delivered to the best man at least a week before the wedding.

● Wedding-present lists are now becoming widely accepted. Some people find them an unappealingly mercenary idea, but there is no doubt that they do ensure that you get the presents that you want and need. Make a comprehensive list of everything you will need in your new home, making sure to include a number of relatively inexpensive items. The list can be circulated among the guests, who should cross off the item they intend to buy. Another way of coping with the present problem is to arrange to have a list at one or more shops. See pages 196–201. Many department stores and speciality shops run a wedding present service, and keep you informed of what has been bought by whom. Several smaller shops also run this service, and if there is a shop that you particularly like that does not, it is always worth asking the manager if he would consider the idea. Try to send thankyou letters for presents as they arrive, or you may find yourself with an enormous pile of letters to write after the wedding.

● Send out the invitations from four to six weeks before the wedding, and make a list of acceptances and refusals as they come in.

● There is no legal necessity to have the name in your passport altered, but if you wish to do so, allow at least six weeks. It will come postdated to the date of your wedding. Alternatively, Londoners can go to the Passport Office in Petty France where they will change it for you that day, but be prepared to wait.

● Check that the suppliers of cars, photography and flowers are correctly briefed.

● If the wedding is to be held at a distance from any station or big town, try to work out in advance who will need lifts and ask amongst your friends and relations whether they will be able to help.

● Work out, allowing for possible traffic delays, how long it will take you to get to the place of worship on the day.

● Arrange to have your going-away clothes (and honeymoon suitcase if you are leaving for the holiday immediately after the reception) sent to the hotel or wherever the party is to be held.

Two weeks beforehand
● Confirm final numbers in writing to the caterer or hotel.

On the day: who does what (Church of England)
When, after weeks of planning, the big day is suddenly upon you, it is important that everyone should know what they should be doing in order that the day goes as smoothly as possible and everyone can enjoy themselves. Timing is all-important. Leave plenty of time for everything, but not too much, as hanging about with nothing to do but wait can be equally nerve-racking.

An hour before the ceremony is due to start, the ushers should be at the church to cope with the inevitable early guests. Twenty minutes before, the best man should ensure that the groom is at the place of worship. They can then find themselves a quiet spot in which to sit and wait. As the guests arrive, the ushers should show them to their seats and hand out service sheets.

The usual seating plan is that friends and relations of the bride sit on the left-hand side and those of the groom on the right. The parents, brothers and sisters, and grandparents should sit in the front pews, with other guests behind them in descending order of closeness and relationship. This sounds all relatively simple, but in the case of divorced or separated parents the seating arrangements in the church, and at the reception too, can sometimes cause seemingly insurmountable problems. Each case will have its own individual variations, so the only guidelines are to use common sense and tact, and to realize that some sort of compromise will have to be reached in order to appease as many people as possible.

The vicar will probably tell the bridegroom and best man the appropriate time at which to arrive – usually about fifteen minutes beforehand. Together with the vicar they may check that the registers are entered correctly.

The chief bridesmaid and the other attendants should arrive about fifteen minutes before the bride is due. Shortly after, the best man and the bridegroom should go and stand at the chancel steps, with the best man on the groom's right. The bride's mother should also arrive at the church five minutes before the ceremony is due to begin, and be escorted to her seat by one of the ushers.

The bride and her father should arrive a few moments before the appointed time, in order that photographs can be taken without holding up the proceedings. It may be as well to leave home early to allow for traffic problems, even if it means driving round the block a few times.

The arrival of the bride will have been the signal for the organist to stop playing the introductory music and start the 'bridal march'. Then the bride, on her father's right arm, will start to walk into the church. If the service is fully choral, the procession will be as follows: the choir, the minister, the bride and her father, and lastly the bridesmaids. When the party reaches the chancel steps, the bride should hand her bouquet to the chief bridesmaid or, if there are no attendants, to her father, who will put it down near the front pew so that her mother can bring it into the vestry after the vows have been taken. If she is wearing a veil over the face, the bride can put it back when she wishes, and if there is a bridesmaid she should re-arrange it prettily. The bridegroom and best man should take their places on the bride's right.

The service can vary according to the couple's and the minister's views. The traditional sequence of events is that her father will give the bride's right hand

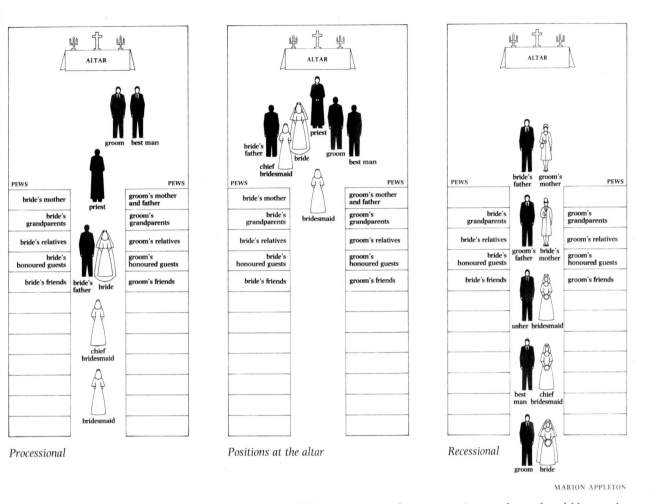

Processional

Positions at the altar

Recessional

The bridal party at a Church of England marriage service

to the minister, who will then pass it to the groom. A point here should be made about who can give the bride away. It is extremely rare for the father not to perform this duty if he is alive and physically capable of doing so. If he is not, however, the usual choice is a close male relation of the bride, such as her brother, or uncle or godparent or guardian.

After the vows have been taken, the bride's father, the best man and the bridesmaids may be asked to return to their seats at the front of the church. The couple will be led to the altar for the prayers, followed by the final blessing.

The bride and groom, the minister, the couple's parents, the attendants and the best man then go to sign the register. At least two witnesses are needed (usually the two fathers although mothers, friends or relations can fulfil this task), to sign the marriage registers with the bride and groom. If the bride is wearing a face veil and she has not already put it back, now is the moment to do so. While the bridal party are occupied doing this, it is customary for the choir to sing an anthem, or for the organist to play a piece of music. When these formalities are over, the bridal procession will leave the church in the following order: the bride and groom (the bride on the groom's left), the small attendants, the chief bridesmaid and the best man, the bride's father and the groom's mother, the bride's mother and the groom's father.

Outside the church, photographs are usually taken of the bride and groom and the rest of the bridal party. The couple should be the first to leave for the reception, with the guests following on behind. It is better, in view of the fact that most ministers object to the mess it makes, to reserve any confetti-throwing until later.

Double Weddings

A double wedding calls for precisely the same detailed prior arrangements. Each of the partners must have the necessary qualifications and each of them must give the same notice; each couple must be separately licensed and, of course, separate certificates of marriage will be issued to each of the couples.

Although any good friends or close relatives may have a double wedding, it is usually two sisters near to each other in age who choose to do so, or perhaps twins. The main appeal of a double wedding is the saving – emotional, as well as financial – to families facing two successive weddings. A girl who does not have to consider such factors may well be less inclined to share the spotlight on her wedding day.

Invitations to a double wedding are usually set out as shown on page 46. It is customary for each couple in a double wedding to have their own attendants, but the two wedding parties are usually the same size. The brides often serve as each other's maid and matron of honour, but this is optional.

Double weddings are usually formal and follow the same rules of dress as any other formal wedding. Both sets of ushers dress alike, while the bridesmaids wear dresses of the same length and formality. The styles and colours may be different as long as they harmonize. The brides, too, usually wear dresses in different styles, but their trains and veils should be about the same length.

When the two brides are sisters, the older sister takes precedence throughout. The order of the ceremony and the seating arrangements must be carefully worked out in advance. The ideal place to have a double wedding is a church with two aisles. This makes it possible to have simultaneous processionals and also recessionals – one on each aisle. It makes the seating arrangements simpler as well. When there is only one aisle, one set of parents must relinquish their right to the front row, or else the parents of both the grooms must sit together in the first pew.

In a single-aisle church the two grooms take their places at the front of the church – each with his own best man on his right. The future husband of the older (or first) bride stands in the centre of the aisle. The first bride enters on her father's arm, followed by her attendants, and the younger bride follows. A brother or other male relative may escort the second bride to the altar but he does not give her away.

On reaching the head of the aisle, the attendants usually separate so that those of the first bride are all on the left, those of the second on the right. The two couples stand side by side in front of the clergyman, with the first bride on the left. In a double wedding of sisters, the father stands beside the older bride until he gives her away, then moves over to give his second daughter away. A shared ceremony is usually divided into parts with the two couples completing each stage in turn. After the marriage vows are taken the final blessing may be given to both couples at the same time.

The recessional is led by the elder sister and her husband, followed by the younger couple. The two sets of bridal attendants come next, with the bridesmaids and ushers paired in appropriate order. The brides' father escorts the elder bride's mother-in-law and the mother is escorted by the elder bride's father-in-law. Close relatives or the appropriate best man stand in for the parents for the younger daughter.

A combined reception always follows a double wedding. Sisters receive in the same line, with the elder bride and her husband preceding the younger couple. The participation of parents may be omitted in order to keep the line at a manageable length. If there is a large wedding party the bridesmaids may also be excused from the receiving line. The size of the wedding party determines whether it is better to have a shared bridal table or separate ones.

Getting There

For the white wedding

A chauffeur-driven car with plenty of space is by no means a necessity for the bride on the wedding day, but it is extremely convenient, as the bride will wish to remain cool and uncrushed in every sense. A big car with a high roof is easy to get in and out of and minimizes the risk of disarrangement.

Usually, the car carries the bride and her father, or whoever is giving her away, to the place of worship. After the marriage, the car takes the bride and groom to the wedding reception. Two big cars may be required, one for the bride and her escort, and the other for her mother and the bridal attendants.

Among specialist ideas in transport at the wedding are: travelling in a white Rolls-Royce or vintage car or, where distances are short from the place of worship to the wedding reception, in a pony and trap or a horse-drawn carriage; departing from the reception in a helicopter. Not the least of the attractions of diversions of this kind is the extra interest they may bring to the wedding photographs.

The exact timings and costs, and any extras that may be required, such as white wedding ribbons on the car, should be confirmed in writing with the car-hire firm. Always book well ahead of the day. The drivers of hired cars usually expect to be tipped.

For the register-office marriage

Car arrangements for a register-office marriage depend on personal convenience only. 'White wedding' procedures in terms of who travels with whom are sometimes followed if this is the key to the style of the wedding. The bride may travel with one or both of the witnesses, which fits in well if she is not accompanied by parents, or everyone may arrange to meet at the registrar's. Where the couple leave from the same address, they obviously travel together.

The honeymoon car

When the newly-weds wish to drive off on honeymoon in their own transport someone may have to be detailed to get the car to the reception location if the bride and groom have used a hired car earlier.

TRANSPORT WATCHWORD: Always allow more time than seems reasonable for even short rides in a car. Check with the local authority, radio and police for roadworks and hold-ups *en route* on the wedding day.

The Cancelled Wedding

It sometimes happens that either the bride or the groom, or both, decide that they don't want to go through with the wedding. This is a difficult and painful decision for anyone to make, but if you do have doubts, it is best to express them at the earliest stage possible. That is not to say, however, that you should go through with the wedding simply because it is only a week away and you can't face the upheaval it would cause. It is far better to change course a week before than a week afterwards.

If you are feeling uncertain, the best plan is to talk it over with your parents or, if that is too difficult, with your minister or a close personal friend. They may be able to give you good, objective advice, and will probably help you break the news.

Once you have decided to cancel the wedding, there are several practical matters that must be attended to at once. First, all your guests must be informed. You can either telephone your guests, or write them a short note.

Probably the best plan is to telephone close family and friends and write to the rest. The note can come from the parents and should be brief; there is no need to give explanations. It might read:

> Mr and Mrs Charles Smith regret to inform you that the forthcoming marriage between their daughter, Jane, and Mr Michael Brown, at St George's Church, Waydown, on Saturday 4th June 1980, will not take place.

The wording of a published announcement might read 'The marriage arranged between Miss Jane Smith and Mr Michael Brown will not take place.'

All other arrangements that have already been made for the wedding – the cars, flowers, photographer, clothes and everything to do with the reception – must be cancelled. If you have set up a wedding-present list at a shop, it should be removed, and presents already received returned to the donors. Presents exchanged between the couple, including the engagement ring, need not be returned – but see page 19. It is unlikely that you will get back any deposits that have been paid, and there may be considerable financial loss on things which have already been bought. Don't expect to be able to re-sell your wedding dress easily, if already purchased, but newspaper advertisements, local dress-hire shops and the word of mouth are all worth trying.

Naturally, summoning up the courage to admit that you have made a mistake and that you have to cancel the wedding can be far from easy. On the other hand, everyone is likely to be sympathetic and understanding. It is possible that your doubts may only be pre-wedding nerves, but in any case it is better to postpone or even cancel the wedding before arrangements are too advanced rather than be faced with agonizing doubts two weeks beforehand.

BARBOUR 1930

5

MEMBERS OF THE WEDDING

The Bride's Mother

A cooperative mother who puts her heart into organizing the event can be a great asset to any daughter planning a wedding and is of irreplaceable value to a daughter who holds down a demanding job. Sometimes it can happen that her mother is keener on the whole affair than the bride, in which case, with the bride's connivance, the parent takes over the show.

By custom the mother acts as a stage manager, beavering away in the background to ensure the success of her daughter's wedding day. However, in practice, mothers (who may well have a full-time job of their own) and daughters sort out all the details between them, sharing the work load and relying on discussion and consultation to iron out any difficulties.

It may well take an inspirational touch of persuasion to get your own way, whatever this may be, when the parents are dead against it and they are paying. However, fathers tend to be more rigid than mothers as far as protocol and procedures are concerned, and it may be that your best friend in these circumstances is your mother. If you have serious objections to a decision, say so in no uncertain terms. There are few parents who cling to their traditional prerogatives and fewer daughters prepared to submit to authoritarian attitudes, particularly on matters of personal taste.

Her traditional responsibilities

A list of the bride's mother's duties along conventional job demarcation lines would include the following: deciding, in consultation with her daughter, on the size of the guest list; liaising with the groom's family on guests from their side; sending out the wedding invitations or arranging with the groom's family for them to handle their invitations; sending invitations to the groom's family and the officiating minister; keeping a record of acceptances and refusals;

Opposite: Marty, 1925
Overleaf left: Lepape, 1931
Overleaf right: Benito, 1930

VOGUE

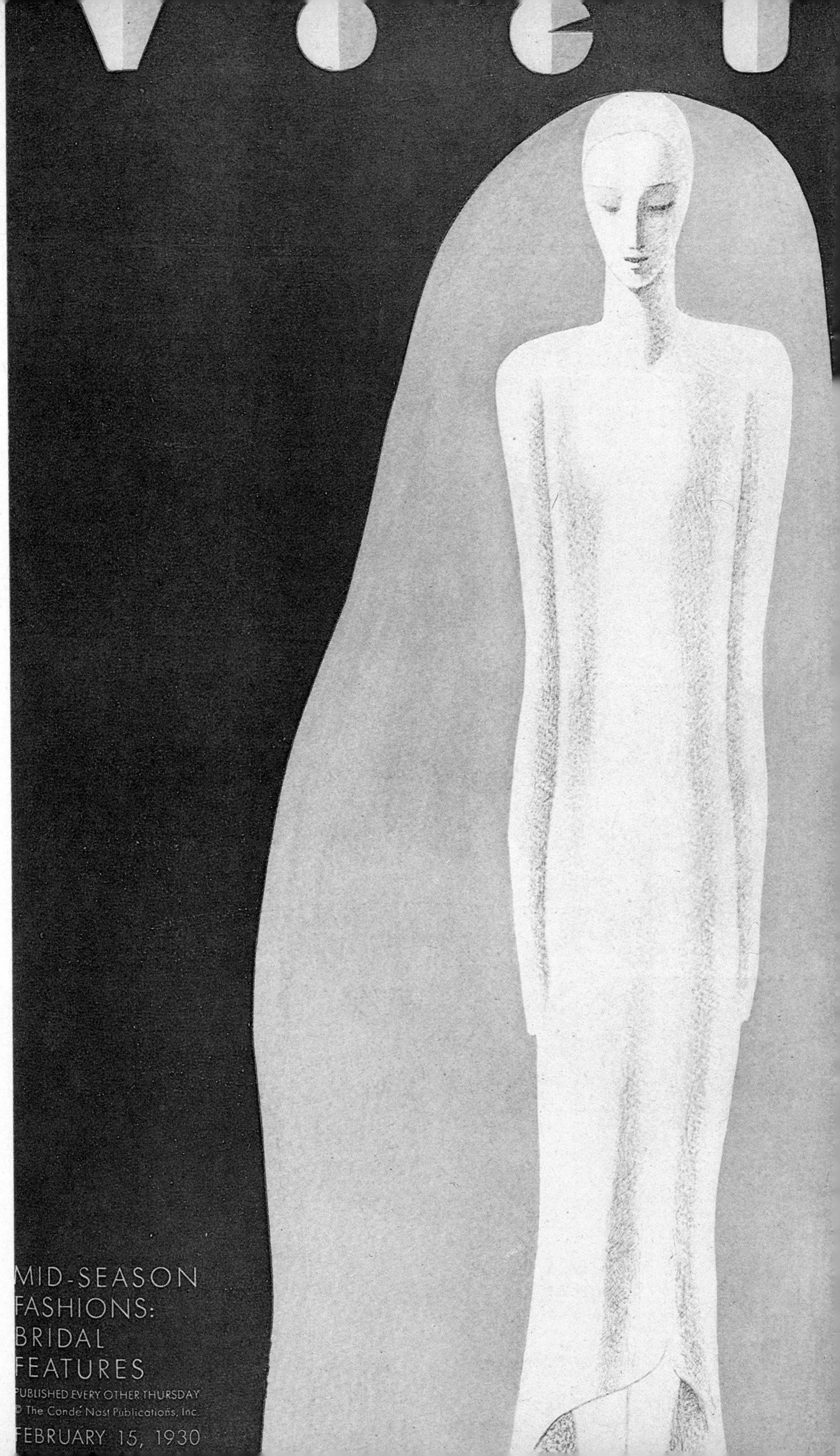
VOGUE
MID-SEASON
FASHIONS:
BRIDAL
FEATURES
PUBLISHED EVERY OTHER THURSDAY
© The Condé Nast Publications, Inc.
FEBRUARY 15, 1930

Vogue

SUMMER FASHIONS
PUBLISHED FORTNIGHTLY
JUNE 8 · 1929   PRICE 35 CENTS

choosing the flowers for the place of worship and the wedding reception; organizing the wedding reception; passing the word round when friends inquire about the wedding-present list; taking in wedding presents; keeping the groom's family informed of events; conferring with the groom's mother to establish a harmonious decision on questions of the style and colour of their wedding outfits, as the two parents will appear in close association as members of the bridal party.

Your mother may also be a good person to try to raise any extra help and support from friends and family. A wedding is an event with an honourable tradition of borrowing in the interests of goodwill: extra flowers from friends' gardens, spare beds to put up wedding guests, equipment for the party, extra cars for transport – these are services that might be put to good use – and your mother could also supervise the return of loans.

Shopping for the wedding dress

The dress is such an important decision that many people lose their nerve at the prospect of taking the final decision on their own, and find that a second opinion is almost always of value. Your mother will probably want to help you select your wedding dress. However, whether you or the family are paying for the dress, the family should be kept in touch with such an important decision. Those who are resistant to the idea of shopping with their mother could do all the reconnaissance work with a friend, bringing in parental opinion at the final stage. It may be worth mentioning that unless you have already canvassed your parents' views on the subject, you should not assume that they will favour the safe but dull. There is evidence that older people value innovation in dress and in some cases are surprised by their offspring preferring the security of tradition to the risk of the new.

The mother's role on the day

If the bride is leaving from home, her mother is expected to organize the domestic scene and act as a stage manager, making sure that everything goes, if possible, as planned.

However, she is also one of the principal members of the bridal party and the hostess at a formal reception, and she should be spared last-minute commitments and chores during the time before the party leaves for the wedding. She has to dress and get herself properly organized.

The bride's mother leaves ahead of the bride, usually with the bridal attendants. If no bridal attendants are included, she may prefer to be accompanied by a relative or friend. On arriving at the place of worship she is traditionally escorted by an usher to her seat. When the bride takes up her

Opposite: Bolin, 1929

position for the ceremony her mother is expected to take charge of the bride's bouquet if there is no adult bridesmaid or the attendants are too young to do so. The mother should carry this with her when the bridal party moves to where the bride and groom sign the register. It is also a good idea for her to take along a make-up repair kit in her handbag in case the bride wants to freshen up her face before the procession down the aisle and for the photographs.

Her place in the exit procession is behind the bridal attendants and on the left of the groom's father. The partnership of the parents of the bride and groom signifies the unity of the two families.

In formal wedding photograph sittings, portraying the family, the bride's mother is placed between the groom and the groom's father. Her traditional place at the wedding breakfast table is on the right-hand side of the groom, and the groom's father sits on her right.

Clothes for the bride's mother

The clothes of the mother of the bride will be determined by the time of the wedding service. Weddings take place during day time in the Protestant and Roman Catholic faiths, so day dress is required. Jewish weddings often take place in the evening and may precede a dinner and dance, so dress is long for women and black tie for men. As a register office marriage takes place during day time her clothes are of the kind that she might wear for a small wedding at a place of worship at that hour.

For weddings of all kinds, however, versatile clothes are preferable to fixed options. Outfits designed to combine with coats or jackets or tops provide flexibility on warmth, coolness, bareness, cover, formality, informality. Deciding factors should include the exact requirements of the day, expected weather conditions and personal ease and comfort, and of course, the approval of her offspring. A parent put neatly the way many women feel about their image on this occasion: 'I am pleased to be the mother of the bride, but I don't want to look like the Bride's Mother.' No doubt the mother had in mind the dull or overdone picture conjured up by the role set in the dignity of capital letters.

Perhaps the best approach is to invest in a few clothes which will not only fill the bill at the wedding itself, but also provide some useful wear after the event. If the wearer has little need for the kind of formal clothes called for, and if economies have to be made, the money should be spent on good-quality accessories, such as shoes or a handbag, which have a lasting usefulness.

The bride's mother's hat

The custom at weddings in church is for the mother to wear a hat, but this is not obligatory. She can dress her head with flowers or hair ornaments, and can enjoy the same freedom here as the bride. Hats are a question of fashion, and people who enjoy wearing hats do so with day dress or evening dress. When choosing a hat perhaps the most important aspect is that it should give a lift in every way to the wearer, visually and psychologically. A noted West End milliner gave this sound advice on buying a hat: 'The truth is, there are no rules. I believe, for example, that if you have a big nose, you should wear a turban and show it off. Never attempt to hide your features under a hat even if you consider that you are plain. There are no valid embargoes on style in relation to a woman's shape and size. It is a myth that short women should avoid big hats. Some little women can carry off a large hat with immense success. Do not choose a hat sitting down. Walk about wearing the hat and ask yourself if you feel happy and confident in it. Always consider the effect in a full-length mirror, and see yourself as others see you, back view. Confidence about choosing a hat comes from the heart but if reassurance is needed rely on the judgement of your daughter.'

If a big hat is chosen and the weather is blowy, it should be remembered that old-fashioned aids such as hat-pins, combs stitched into the lining, and elasticated linings are the best methods of anchorage.

Some women who wear glasses are concerned that these will not look well when worn with a hat, but this is nonsense. Presumably friends are already accustomed to the presence of spectacles; being able to see as clearly as possible is the essential priority. However, if the wearer goes in for flashy frames or coloured lenses, this should be taken into consideration when choosing a hat.

Handshaking and kissing

A prolonged stint of handshaking is a sound reason for wearing gloves, although these may be worn for fashion's sake too. If the mother is to receive the guests formally at the head of the line, a glove protects the hand nicely and eases pressures from hearty handshakes.

The general etiquette on gloves is that they can be carried or worn. If worn, they can be kept on for handshaking, drinking, and smoking, but should be taken off for eating. Long gloves are often made with wrist fastenings which enable the hand to be slipped out and the glove rolled back.

Social kissing is an integral part of the day for the mother and, pleasant as this is, it may present a problem if she hopes to present a groomed appearance in public. When there are many people to kiss, the gesture of bonhomie can be indicated by a brush of the cheeks without using the lips. This also precludes lipstick marks on the kissed. If the guest is a man, let him kiss the woman!

The mother's hat should enable people to see her face clearly and greet her with a kiss. If it has a veil, this should be worn off the face while she is welcoming guests or at any time when people hope to kiss her, or she is hoping to be kissed.

Good-byes and thankyous

Some brides like to say good-bye and thankyou to their parents during a private moment and others leave it all until later. If the mother feels low she should be allowed the privilege of expressing her feelings. Not every bride's mother sheds an emotional tear at the departure of the bride, but some do – it is an emotional moment.

Guests do not usually write formal thankyou letters to the bride's mother, but those who find good reasons for expressing their admiration for the way everything went are likely to be held in fond regard.

The gesture of thanks from the bride that is likely to be most appreciated is some form of communication – a telephone call, a telegram, a postcard – at the earliest practical moment. If some definitive token is called for, flowers or a house plant could be given as a present, or some favourite drink, to provide thoughtful recompense to parents who have been left to clear up afterwards and pay the bills.

The Bride's Father

Much is written, and spoken, about what actually happens on the day – what the bride does and says, what she should wear and so on – but little, if anything, about the role of the men, who are often considered to have little more than a walk-on part. The bride's father is, apart from the groom, the most important male character in the wedding scene, and the day will be a very significant one for him too.

The traditional role of the bride's father is simply to hand out the money and leave all the organizing, and all the fun, to the womenfolk. He is, however, just as likely, these days, to be as deeply involved in the planning and preparations as anyone else. Just as in other areas of life men are increasingly involved in the customarily 'female' tasks, chores and decisions, so they are in the wedding scene.

The bride's father has always had something of a raw deal at the wedding and during the weeks leading up to it, so it is important (as with the groom) to bring him more into the picture, and not simply to expect him to wait patiently, uncomplainingly and with open wallet, on the sidelines.

The role of the bride's father does, however, depend to a certain extent on how much he is contributing financially to the wedding. As has been suggested elsewhere in this book, it is by no means the norm nowadays for the bride's father to pay for all the wedding expenses. If, however, he is doing so (and the fact remains that many fathers feel an overwhelming desire or even compulsion to do so) then it is as well to remember that his views count for a great deal. He may well, for example, expect his daughter to look anachronistically bridal on the day, even if he has never lifted an eyebrow at unconventional attire before. This may accord with the bride's own ideas, but if not, either persuasion or compromise will have to prevail. It is, after all, hardly fair to expect someone to pay for something they hate.

The question of how far a father's authority goes in these decisions depends not only on the extent of his financial involvement but also on the nature of his relationship with his family in general, and with his daughter in particular. These days, fathers have almost universally lost their Victorian, authoritarian, paternalistic image and the relationship between father and child is often closer and more intimate than ever before. It is, however, a strange fact that some fathers become quite uncharacteristically conventional in connection with weddings. This change, which can often appear as a complete volte-face, can be puzzling, but it may help to remember that a father often has quite contradictory feelings towards his daughter when marriage is announced. On the one hand, he may well feel a sense of relief that he has eventually got her off his hands, while at the same time retaining a strong sense of protectiveness towards her. Most fathers, however well they like their future son-in-law, will have worries about how well this man will love and look after their daughter. It is perhaps not surprising, therefore, that the wedding may bring out the more traditional side of their nature.

This said, it should also be remembered that many fathers will have their own ideas about how the wedding should be planned and will actively want to join in the preparations. Others will prefer to leave it all to someone else, and may even resent the inevitable upheaval and disruption that organizing a wedding brings in its wake. A wedding is, however, essentially a family affair, and all the members of the family will, to a greater or lesser extent, get drawn into the proceedings. The extent of their involvement depends ultimately on the individual. The important thing to bear in mind is that the father of the bride should be allowed his say if he wants it, and, if he does not, should not be made to feel that his previously calm existence is tumbling about his ears.

His responsibilities on the day are twofold: practical and emotional. In the moments before leaving for the ceremony, he is often called upon to keep the bride calm (giving her a quick drink), cheerful and relaxed, even though he may be feeling a trifle jittery himself.

The following applies to a Church of England wedding where there is often confusion as to exactly what the bride's father should do during the actual ceremony. First, he should escort the bride to the place of worship (on time, preferably!) and, at the appointed hour, escort her up the aisle on his right arm. At the chancel steps, he should stand on her left. The minister may ask who is giving the bride away. This question often confuses people. In the Church of England no provision is made for a response – the answer is taken as read. However, since many men confess to feeling a trifle silly just standing there, it should be said that it is quite acceptable to murmur quietly 'I do' at the appropriate moment, although the more common practice is for the bride's father (or whoever is taking his place) to take the bride's right hand and give it to the minister, who then gives it to the groom. After this, the bride's father should stand quietly in position until the vows have been taken, at which point he returns to his seat in the front pew on the left-hand side of the church. When the time comes for the signing of the register, it is usual (although not strictly necessary, if other witnesses are to be present) for both sets of parents to go up to witness the signing. After these formalities have been completed, the bridal party leaves the church in the following order: bride and groom, small attendants, chief bridesmaid and best man, bride's mother on the left of the groom's father, and bride's father on the right of the groom's mother.

At the reception, the bride's father should above all enjoy himself, as should everyone else there. Good speakers can have a field day, but the majority of fathers can rely on sincerity and brevity when making a speech.

After the reception, when there is often a sense of anticlimax, it is usually the bride's father who is called on to keep spirits up and stave off depression.

The Bride's Attendants

There is no obligation to include bridal attendants in the wedding procession, but chosen friends and relatives and their children have traditionally assumed the responsibilities of courtly attendants to the queen of the day. Bridal attendants do not have only tradition to recommend them; they can be a great help to the bride and contribute to the smooth running of the organization of a wedding. Also, their presence, whether adult or child, adds to the interest and variety of the wedding party.

The bride can choose anyone whom she wishes to attend her but in practice most decide on their best girl friend or close relative as the chief bridesmaid. Single girls of all ages can be bridesmaids, married women are known as matrons of honour, and young boys are called page boys – convention does not admit to the presence of adult males in this role. If a number of attendants are chosen it is customary to appoint a chief bridesmaid who is expected to undertake specific responsibilities and duties.

On the morning of the wedding, the chief bridesmaid should help the bride to dress, and give her moral support. If she lives some distance away from the bride and a bed can be found for her, it may be helpful all round for her to stay the night. It all depends on how much she has to do and how early the wedding-day programme begins.

As the bridesmaids have to leave for the ceremony before the bride in order to await her arrival at the place of worship, her father, or whoever is giving her away, should be present to deal with any last-minute hazards and, perhaps, to pour a small steadying drink for the bride (and himself).

At the place of worship the chief bridesmaid awaits the arrival of the bride, keeps an eye on any small children in the bridal party and finally checks any other attendants' clothes and flowers to ensure that everything is present and correct.

When the bride arrives, the chief bridesmaid double-checks on details such as dress fastenings, head-dress, jewellery clasps. She should arrange the veil, if need be, and set the train, if there is one, in place for the procession up the aisle. She should put big and little helpers at their right stations in the procession – it is a sensible idea for adults to be chosen to bring up the rear as they can then oversee and aid, if need be, the efforts of the smallest helpers.

When the bride reaches the chancel steps or the point where the marriage ceremony is to take place, the chief bridesmaid should be ready to receive the bride's bouquet or any other decoration that may be occupying her hands. The bride's hands need to be free to accept the wedding ring. The chief bridesmaid should also remember to take the bouquet into the vestry or the place where the register is signed so that the bride has her flowers to hand for the procession down the aisle. If young children only are chosen as bridal attendants, this job can be usefully delegated to the bride's mother.

At the wedding reception the chief bridesmaid, together with any other attendants of suitable age, should undertake their share of baby- and child-minding and keep an eye on any guest who may be too old, frail or otherwise incapacitated to manage well unaided. They may also find that they will be called on to take a friendly interest in any member of the family who feels neglected, including divorced or widowed parents. All-in-all an effective chief bridesmaid deserves her thankyou present from the groom.

After the bride has changed into her going-away clothes, it is the chief bridesmaid's task to take charge of the wedding dress – unless, of course, the bride is leaving from her own home. If she is leaving from a hotel, however, provision should be made for storing the wedding clothes, particularly if the dress is hardly a slip of a thing and the bride's home is not easily available for the purpose.

Whom to choose

Most brides select as their chief bridesmaid or matron of honour the person with whom they feel happiest and most natural. If, in addition, the individual is a good organizer and gives moral support, so much the better. Sisters and girl friends in the category of 'best friends' spring naturally to mind. Small children have a time-honoured place at the white wedding. As bridal attendants, young children can look angelic; little girls delight in dressing up for the occasion and some very young helpers are capable of behaving with remarkable dignity and restraint during the proceedings. However, children under three are a risk because they find it difficult to control themselves if they feel under the weather or are intimidated by being on show in public. Nevertheless, a wedding is an occasion when sentiment rightly wins over practicality. If you would not dream of walking up the aisle without your favourite baby niece or small sister, remember to take the precaution of stationing a guardian angel in an adjacent seat. He or she should be able to take prompt remedial action in the event of tears and tantrums breaking out with the opening chords of Mendelssohn. In any event, small children should be properly briefed on their duties and if, for example, they are to carry the bride's train, a rehearsal is in order.

Being a bridesmaid or a matron of honour or page is often a much sought after honour, both by the individuals themselves and by the families they represent. The exclusion of people who expect to be asked, or who feel they have a prior right to the role because of family attachments and personal connections, is inevitably a vexed question. It should be repeated here that it is the bride's right to choose whom she has on her side on the day of her marriage. However, as in so much else to do with family relationships, especially at a wedding, tact is of the essence in turning down hopeful candidates. Take the necessary decisions and name names as soon as possible. Where problems are inherent, bitterness swiftly builds up in a vacuum of uncertainty. If you have an aversion to the idea of inviting a fatty cousin or the spotty brother of your best friend to attend your fair person, it seems unreasonable to feel that you are under a moral obligation to do so. You might try, by way of excuse, explaining that you will feel much more confident and able to face the music with the team of your choice. This is a purely subjective opinion which happily no one else is in a position to contradict or counter effectively.

How many attendants?

Numbers are usually limited by the style and scope of the occasion and also by costs. Obviously, a retinue of attendants befits the spacious architecture and long perspectives of a cathedral. Within the confines and simple appointments of a small parish church the formality of a long procession might be out of place.

There are reasons for and against choosing all small children, or all adults, or a mixture of the two. Little ones alone may look charming but could be a bit of a risk. Adults are supportive but may be less decorative than little ones. A mixture of shapes and sizes might be a bit much.

Despite the fact that most people fall on an invitation to act as a bridal attendant with appreciative joy, it is by no means unknown for the offer to be refused. The reasons given are sometimes financial and sometimes personal. At all events, do not press your suit as it doesn't make sense for the bride to have as a helper someone who has accepted the job unwillingly.

Who pays for what

The bride has the right to choose the style of the bridal attendants' clothes, and it is general practice for those who are invited to fulfil this honour to pay the bill – in the case of children, parents are expected to settle the account. However, in practice, this concession should imply a certain obligation on the part of the bride to choose a dress or clothes in which her helpers will look good. A criterion for clothes for adults might be that they would be useful later, but few people have a real need for long, formal, flowing dresses of the kind usually chosen for bridesmaids. Far better to choose a style which has a practical relevance after the wedding, such as a dress which can be adapted in some way, rather than look for designs which are intended to double up in their existing form as party dresses. Children, of course, can generally make good use of a style which can be worn at parties, and this should be borne in mind when deciding on specific dresses. If the bride wishes her bridesmaids to wear something which they consider an oddity or without any further practical use the bride should offer to pay the full cost.

The Best Man

The job of best man is an important one usually, though by no means always, filled by the groom's brother or closest friend. Whoever he may be, however, the qualities he should possess are cool-headedness, organizational ability and tact. He will probably find himself acting as the groom's messenger boy, father confessor and valet. On the day he becomes a sort of master of ceremonies – chief usher, toastmaster and paymaster. His responsibilities are as follows.

- Keeping himself informed about the arrangements; checking from time to time with the bride's family.
- Arranging the stag night, if there is to be one (preferably not on the night before the wedding), and making sure the groom gets home safely afterwards.

- Making sure that the ushers know what they should be doing on the day.
- Arranging for the buttonholes and service sheets to be at the place of worship ready to hand out to the guests when they arrive.
- Arranging for the groom's going-away clothes and honeymoon suitcase to be left at the reception the night before the wedding.
- Driving the groom to the place of worship on the day, making sure that he has the ring, and keeping the ring until the appropriate moment during the service.
- Paying fees to the minister, organist and bell-ringers on the groom's behalf on arrival at the church.
- Organizing transport and parking, with the help of the ushers, for the guests.
- Liaising with the toastmaster on the order of the speeches and on choosing suitable times for the cake-cutting ceremony and for the bride and groom to go off to change.
- Reading the telegrams, possibly omitting those best read in private.
- Replying to the groom's toast to the bridesmaids on their behalf. Unless he is a particularly good speaker, he should keep his speech short.

Ushers and Others

The ushers are chosen by the bridegroom and his best man. For a formal wedding at a place of worship there should be three ushers. One should be delegated to stand at the church door to hand out service sheets to the guests as they arrive; one should wait inside the church door to show guests to their seats – the bride's family and friends on the left-hand side of the altar, the groom's on the right; one should wait to escort the bride's mother to her seat when she arrives where this is traditional.

The other men at the wedding obviously have less to do.

The brothers of the bride and groom are often asked to be ushers, mainly because they know most of the family, but also because it is considered both courteous and pleasant to allow as many members of the family as possible to feel directly involved. Young brothers are often chosen as pageboys.

Grandfathers enjoy the special privileges of age. If particularly aged, it may be as well to organize someone to look after them at the reception and to make sure that they get a good seat in the family pews.

The Wedding Guests

There is no wedding celebration without guests. At the marriage ceremony, they lend support and reassurance. Afterwards, they help to make the party.

The invitation

A wedding invitation requires a written acknowledgement; apart from anything else the host will need a record of numbers. One invitation may cover several members of the family, and everyone named should make their intentions known to the host. Replies can be written in the third person, or in the usual form of a letter. A formal note of acceptance can read:

> Miss Ann Brown (or Mr and Mrs John Brown) thanks Mrs Peter Smith for her kind invitation to the wedding of her daughter Joan on __ at __ and has much pleasure in accepting.

Repeating the place and the date indicates that the facts are known. A formal note of refusal can read:

> Miss Ann Brown (or Mr and Mrs John Brown) thanks Mrs Peter Smith for her kind invitation to the wedding of her daughter Joan and regrets that she is unable to accept.

If a more detailed explanation is called for, it is best to put the information in a letter. The domestic news that you cannot come because you are working as a holiday help in a pub or cannot arrange a baby-sitter combines awkwardly with the lofty tone of the third person. The advantage of a formal approach is that there is no need to add further explanations beyond the grandly impersonal brevity, 'regrets she (or he) is unable to accept', which can cover a multitude of sins.

Correctly, a formal reply is dated beneath the communication on the right-hand side, and there is no need for a signature. The reply is traditionally sent in a sealed envelope, addressed to the hostess alone.

Can a guest bring along an uninvited friend? Probably not. The open arrangements that apply to many private parties do not extend to a wedding. In all cases, the guest should clear permission with the host beforehand, and not take umbrage if the request is refused.

Attendance times for the reception can pose hazards. If a guest is uncertain as to the nature of the reception he may drift in at a later point only to find everyone seated at a formal wedding breakfast, with a conspicuously empty place. Arrival times for a drinks party or a buffet party are flexible, but if a formal meal is served, punctuality is of the essence. Check with the hostess.

Many guests who are invited and cannot attend send a telegram to the bride and groom on the day, wishing the couple good luck and happiness. The message will be read out at the reception, along with those from other well-wishers. The telegram is usually sent to the bride's address or direct to the reception venue.

Presents

Most people who attend a wedding give a present. If the invitation is turned down, the obligation to repay hospitality no longer applies and it is up to the individual. It is worth mentioning at this point that no one has to give a wedding present.

The general practice is to ask the bride or her mother what she wants and to establish whether she has placed a wedding-present list at a shop. If so, this will be in the names of the bride and groom – 'the Cooper–Nutley wedding' – and is likely to include a range of presents at different price levels. The system is designed to prevent the duplication of presents, always a hazard, as each item is crossed off the list when it is bought.

Some people however take exception to being dragooned in this manner and prefer to make up their own minds in the matter. If in doubt as to what to give, a general guideline is to choose the practical and functional in preference to the decorative inessential. Sentiment will always have a place, however. An imaginative surprise may well be remembered long after the mixers and mats have been forgotten.

Presents are usually sent before the wedding to the bride, but are good news at any time and equally so for the woman who has been married before.

If the chosen article carries a guarantee, it makes sense to enclose the receipt with it as the sales record will be required should repairs or servicing be called for under the terms of the guarantee. This is an instance where the polite thing to do can be supplanted by rude commonsense – there can be no need to preserve the secret of the price of a new kettle, for example.

Cheques are always welcome. Despite the impersonality of a piece of paper, a number of small cheques can add up to a sizeable sum and enable the couple to buy a much wanted major investment which no single donor could afford.

What to wear

Just as at any other party, it all depends on the style of the wedding. At a big white wedding, women wear their prettiest clothes and, if they look good in hats, wear one. Few women feel an obligation to buy a hat specially for the occasion.

At a small family affair, everyone, with the possible exception of the bridal party, feels free to wear what they like and have to hand. Hats and gloves can be worn at all times.

The degree of formality in dress is set by what the men are wearing. If they are in morning dress – the most formal of male uniforms – the women wear their best things and their jewellery, and aim to look as if they have dressed to do justice to the occasion. If the men are in dinner jackets for a late wedding, the women wear evening clothes. If the men are in lounge suits, it is a free for all.

The old social taboo about not wearing black or white – black is associated with mourning and white is the bridal symbol – hardly applies today. Women wear what they look their best in or have in the wardrobe.

At the ceremony

Guests are expected to make their own transport arrangements throughout, unless notified. It is probable, however, that the ushers will arrange car lifts from the place of worship to the wedding reception.

Punctuality is recommended for arrival at the place of worship – ten minutes in hand is fine. Those who cut it fine run the risk of coinciding with the entrance of the bride.

When members of the congregation arrive, each one is asked at the doorway whether they are the bride's friend or the groom's friend, and are seated accordingly with a service sheet in hand. The bride's party sits on the left-hand side, and the groom's party sits on the right-hand side.

Low-key conversation and greetings are in order at this point – muted chat only because of the setting and the solemnity; greetings on account of the gathering of the clans.

At the entrance of the bride on the right arm of whoever is giving her away, the congregation stands. Members of differing denominations tend to put on their ecumenical hat and take part in as many aspects of the service as their beliefs permit. Non-believers tend to do likewise in the interests of unity.

After the register is signed, the couple make an entrance together and walk down the aisle. The congregation stands in acknowledgement and everyone smiles at the bride and groom.

The bridal party, followed by the families seated in front, are allowed to leave the place of worship first. After this, everyone files out and goes on to the reception. But the photographer will probably be waiting outside the church to take group photographs first. If guests are solicited for orders for wedding photographs at the reception, there is no need to buy unless you wish to. You can always say that you would like to look at the prints before ordering.

At the party

Procedures depend on whether traditional formalities are being observed. If so, guests can leave their coats and tidy up before standing in line to be greeted by the bridal party. The receiving line may consist of the bride and groom on their own, but is more likely to include, in the following order: the bride's mother and father, the groom's mother and father, the bride and groom, and perhaps the bridal attendants.

BARBOUR 1930

This is not a good moment for a guest to indulge in a long gossip with members of the bridal party. Simply introduce yourself, if necessary, 'I am Drusilla, Rosemary's cousin', shake hands or kiss, make friendly and complimentary remarks, and pass on swiftly into the party. Delays hold up the guests still waiting in line for a handshake and, it must be added, the first drink.

Guests circulate, introducing themselves if they feel like it as there is rarely anyone around to make introductions. Those who keep themselves to themselves may well be in for a lonely time.

At a buffet party, everyone helps themselves to food, and drink is circulated on trays, or from a bar. At a sit-down meal, guests seat themselves where they like unless there are place-names.

During the speeches, it is customary for everyone to join in all the toasts, raising a glass and tasting the contents, even if this is ginger ale.

Good-byes

Guests are not expected to leave before the departure of the bride and groom on honeymoon. Those who must leave earlier try to go quietly.

When the couples re-appear at the party in their going-away clothes, they are given a rousing send-off, photographs are taken and confetti, or rice or flower petals, are thrown at the couple for luck.

Unless the bride's mother is easily found, guests are not expected to seek her out for good-byes, as this is a traditionally low moment. It will be a low moment indeed for the father unless guests depart and put an end to the assault on the family cash reserves.

Thankyous

Strangely enough, thankyou letters and calls are not expected for wedding parties. Nevertheless, every host appreciates the guest who finds the time to express his thanks.

OGILVIE-GRANT 1929

6

FINANCING THE WEDDING

Marriages may be made in heaven, but wedding bills are paid by ordinary mortals with ordinary bank balances. Weddings can cost almost as much or as little as you want them to, but unless all you are concerned with is tying the legal knot, the sums involved can all too quickly reach alarming proportions. Persistently rising prices, coupled with soaring inflation, have made the task of giving a wedding a considerable burden on a family's resources. It is important to determine how much can be afforded and how these costs are to be apportioned, before indulging in dreams of a grand wedding with orchids, Rolls-Royces and a feast for five hundred. This chapter outlines the traditional division of financial responsibility and investigates some of the modern alternatives and cost-cutting strategies.

The Historical Background

In early times, a father had the undisputed right to dispose of his daughters to the highest bidders. Some old phrases, like the groom asking the father for 'his daughter's hand in marriage' and the father 'giving the bride away', recall these ancient rituals, in form if not in spirit. Even today, marriages arranged by the parents remain commonplace in certain societies – China, Africa, India and the Moslem world – and central to these marriages is the question of bride price (the sum paid by the groom's family to the bride's, either in cash or kind), which often has to be thrashed out with outside help. This payment is regarded as recompense to the bride's family for the loss of an asset – an extra pair of hands – in the family economy. For this reason, the custom was, and still is, confined to the poorer countries with a predominantly agricultural way of life.

The opposite system, the payment of a 'groom price', known as the dowry system, was common for centuries throughout Europe, particularly amongst the wealthy and landed classes, and is still practised in parts of Italy, Greece and France. As the women of rich families did not work, the dowry increased their attractions and gave them a wider choice of husbands. A generous dowry would lead to an advantageous marriage.

In this country, the idea of the woman being a chattel at the disposal of her family has long been an anachronism. In the new version of the marriage service in the Church of England the word 'obey' has been removed from the vows, and the bride's father, while he still escorts her to the church, is no longer formally required to 'give her away'.

Who Pays for What

Tradition, however, still plays a part in many families when it comes to divisions of financial responsibility. By convention, the bride's family is the main bearer of the financial load. They are expected to pay for press announcements; wedding clothes for the bride and her attendants; flowers for the church and the reception; transport; photographer's fees; reception costs; wedding stationery. By custom, the groom pays all fees connected with the church; bouquets for the bride and her attendants and buttonholes for himself and his best man; presents for the attendants and the best man; the honeymoon.

The traditional responsibility of the bride's family to pay for their daughter's wedding is essentially a hangover from the days of dowries. In doing so, they are performing their last financial duty towards their daughter, since after the wedding it becomes the husband's responsibility to look after her. Many fathers still happily foot the bill for their daughter's send-off, although it may be that some secretly wish that the couple would elope, thus saving them the expense. Pride, however, coupled with the desire to be seen to be doing what society expects, ensures that, in many cases, the bride's family would not even contemplate the idea of sharing the costs, regardless of their assets.

Legally, the bride's father does not have to pay for any part of the wedding. There was a case, reported in the daily press, of a father who had hardly known his daughter since her childhood. When she decided to get married, he was delighted to be asked to the wedding, but not so delighted when a few days later the bill for the reception arrived from the hotel – his daughter had informed them that he would be footing the bill. On a question of principle he refused to pay the bill, took the matter to court and won the case. The judge ruled that, by law, whoever makes the arrangements is responsible for paying the bill and that there is no automatic legal liability on a parent to pay up just because he is the father. Attitudes to the conventional pattern of financial responsibility are changing. The old rules about who pays for what are not hard and fast rules any more. The right way is whatever suits you and your family best. Recent years have brought something of a revolution in attitudes towards the financing of the wedding, and old-fashioned traditions are being discarded along with old-fashioned ideas.

Just as the decision to marry is now regarded as a decision shared between the bride and groom, and not something which is arranged by their respective families, so the decisions of how, when, where and, above all, how much, are increasingly being treated as joint responsibilities. In particular, many young couples feel that with more independence from the family, the cost of the wedding bills should be spread more thinly than tradition has hitherto dictated.

In a world in which many couples live together for a year or more before getting married and where their combined income often equals, or even exceeds, that of the bride's father, it is increasingly apparent that the old rules are becoming anachronistic.

However, as with all other matters relating to the wedding, the people involved may not always agree, and when it comes to money friction between the families can reach gargantuan proportions. Most fathers feel a strong sense of responsibility towards their daughters' weddings, and their pride on the matter can easily be bruised. Some have even been known to go so far as virtually to bankrupt themselves in order to give their daughters 'the best that money can buy'.

One of the trickiest aspects of wedding finance revolves around the fact that the British are peculiarly shy when it comes to talking about money. Many couples feel extremely guilty about the large costs that the bride's father would have to bear and feel impelled to choose a register office ceremony on grounds of economy even though this would be a disappointment both to themselves and their families. The wedding day is undoubtedly one of the most important days in the life of any couple, but in most cases it is an important one for their families too. It seems a pity that the day should be spoilt simply for want of open discussion about financial problems, among others.

Changes in the Pattern

There are many variations on the traditional pattern of who pays for what. It is quite usual these days for the bride to pay for her own wedding dress, or to contribute to its cost. Many girls go halves on the cost of the honeymoon, or the engagement ring, and almost always divide the costs of buying or renting somewhere to live even though these are traditionally the groom's responsibility. Many couples hold their own party for their friends after the wedding, so keeping the reception a small – and therefore considerably cheaper – family affair.

The problem of exactly how costs are to be apportioned highlights the fact that the traditional division of financial responsibility did at least mean that everyone knew who was paying for what, and so few disputes could arise. With the new mood of flexibility about financing the wedding, it is inevitable that difficulties will occur. Possibly the best plan is to make a list of everything that has to be paid for and decide at the outset who will fund each aspect from start to finish.

If the bride and groom are paying for the wedding entirely by themselves, one idea might be for the bride to pay for everything her parents would have paid for, and the groom could pay for the reception as well as his traditional responsibilities. If, on the other hand, the bride wants to contribute something towards the costs that her parents will have to bear, she could be responsible for paying for her dress or the flowers or the invitations and the photographs – or all or some of these. Much depends on how much she is willing, or able, to contribute. However you decide to split the costs, though, remember to make it quite clear from the very beginning where the divisions lie.

One young bride summed up the feelings of many young people these days: 'I hadn't lived at home for several years. I have my own salary, my own independence, my own flat. I felt I had no right to ask my parents to pay for my wedding. At first they felt hurt, I think, but we persuaded them eventually that this was the way we really wanted it.' Another bride-to-be points out a similar difference of opinion between the generations: 'My parents were appalled when I told them that I was paying for most of the honeymoon. They felt very strongly that it was Peter's responsibility to pay for it, and even though I explained that after the wedding all our money would be ours, not just his or mine, they still felt that it was somehow "wrong", and that Peter was "letting me down". To us, that seemed quite absurd, but now I've just accepted the fact that they feel differently. We've agreed to differ.'

Both these examples demonstrate the gap that often exists between the generations. Of all the events that may happen to a person in a lifetime, weddings are uniquely surrounded by tradition, the most tinged with conservatism. And although religion often influences the form of marriage, its roots are in the family. If getting married were something accomplished in isolation from the family, few disputes might arise. As it is, these differences have to be faced, and, somehow, resolved. There is no magic formula for arriving at a solution that will suit everyone, but it is important to remember that, in the case of its financial aspects, a wedding throws up many delicate and difficult problems that should be approached with tact, generosity and common sense.

Much of the bickering and tension that occurs between the bride and her family springs from the fact that she feels she must bow to their wishes if her parents are footing the bill. This is all very well if you happen to agree on every point from the colour of the flowers to the size of the reception, but unfortunately this is rarely the case. Some brides end up wearing a dress they dislike because Mother liked it and Mother was paying. It is undoubtedly disagreeable to pay for something one dislikes, but the wedding day is, after all, primarily the bride's day, and her wishes should be respected whether she is paying for herself, sharing costs, chipping in, or is paid for in the traditional manner.

The issue of who pays for what at today's wedding is further complicated, in some cases, when the groom's family are involved. Their traditional role is simply as guests, but it is becoming unexceptional, particularly when their financial situation is in a healthier state than that of the bride's family, for the groom's family to take on some of the financial burden – by paying for the drinks at the reception, for example. This is an excellent idea in theory, but in practice can offend or cause embarrassment to the bride's family because it might be seen as a somewhat patronizing gesture. Any such offer must be made with the utmost tact and discretion, although much depends on the relationship between the two sets of parents. Attitudes are changing, but as with all changes, and particularly those which concern events that are by their very nature traditional, these shifts of opinion take time to filter through and become, in their turn, established practice.

Cutting Costs

Rapidly rising prices – not just the major items, but the little ones too, such as postage and fares – make it difficult to compile a realistic estimate of wedding costs. A sensible precaution is to set a budget that allows either for marginal increases across the board or – and this is where it hurts – for a later decision to cut out or cut down on a major expense.

It is not always easy to reduce costs but some ways are more effective than others, and the most effective of all are those that are inconspicuous. Planning, economizing, and borrowing are the subtlest means of achieving the desired effect without making painful sacrifices. Start with the major priorities and work down the list, remembering that small savings in all areas can be just as effective a cost-cutting strategy as doing away with one element altogether.

Make a list of everything you will need under the following headings:
- Clothes (including attendants' and going-away clothes)
- Invitations
- Photography
- Transport
- Flowers
- Church fees
- Reception (including the drink and the cake)
- Miscellaneous (hairdressing, beauty, presents, etc.)

Try to obtain about three estimates for as many items as possible and this will at least give you some idea of the sums involved. Keep a file of all papers, bills and receipts. Although many of the bills will not arrive until after the wedding, make sure to pay the others as they occur so as not to leave yourself with a lump sum to find all at once.

Food

The timing of the event is all-important when it comes to your accounts. If you choose to be married just before lunch or in the late afternoon before dinner, you will have to provide a large meal for the guests. If, however, you have the wedding in the early morning or mid afternoon, you can get away with the relatively inexpensive idea of a festive breakfast or tea party. On the other hand, if your guests have come some distance you will probably feel obliged to provide something more sustaining.

Food and drink are certainly the most expensive items on your list. The most subtle way of paring down costs here is simply to offer less, avoid main mealtimes, and ask fewer people to the reception. If you are not doing the catering yourself, shop around amongst local professionals and compare at least three estimates before deciding on one of them. The lowest estimate is not always the best value for money – it depends on what is being offered. Listen to the advice of the professionals; they probably know the most successful and cheapest way of giving a reception.

Drink

Drink is one absolute essential at any kind of wedding celebration and people tend to consume rather large quantities of it. Champagne and sherry are the traditional choices, but unfortunately neither of them is cheap. There are, however, some cheaper – and perfectly acceptable – alternatives. Some sparkling white wines, for instance, need not be as expensive as champagne, but have a lively bubble to set the party alight. Still wines can be cheaper than the choices mentioned. If you are having a lunchtime reception, a good barrel of beer or cider might prove a cheap and popular solution to the problem.

Always make sure that drinks are purchased on a sale-or-return basis. It might be over-optimistic to think that your guests will leave before the last drop is drunk but at least if you do have any drink left over you will not be charged for returned bottles. If your reception is in a hotel or restaurant, it is worth asking the manager about corkage, payable on wine that you provide yourself, in order to compensate for the hotel's loss of profit. It is quite possible that, even with corkage, it may be cheaper to buy your own wine rather than choose it from the hotel's list. The ultimate economy is to offer a drink or two on the house including one for the toast, and to open a cash bar.

If you are a good cook, or someone you know is, you might consider baking your own wedding cake and having the icing done professionally, which could represent a saving of time and money. Doing the catering yourself may be hard work, but you will get exactly what you want and it will almost certainly cost a great deal less than engaging a professional caterer. A freezer, either your own or space borrowed in a friend's, is a great boon here. Choose dishes that will freeze well, and work out a programme of cooking. If you have friends who are willing, and able, to help, so much the better.

The location

The place in which you intend to hold your reception plays an important economic part too. Unless you have a great deal of space, either indoors or outside, home is seldom the best solution, although it is undoubtedly the cheapest. But a friend or relation may have a house that is big enough for holding a reception. Phrase your request tactfully so that the person can refuse without embarrassment. If the answer is yes, offer to do all the organizing yourselves and make arrangements for the place to be thoroughly cleaned and tidied up afterwards.

One solution might be to hold the reception in a local club or pub or village hall. Many of these have private rooms that can be hired relatively inexpensively for private parties. There is the added bonus of any catering facilities they may have, and you can also make arrangements to use a cash bar when your own supply of drinks comes to an end.

Borrowing

Borrowing anything from a knife to a bank-note has a traditional part in the organization of a wedding. Large pots and pans, serving dishes, cake stands and the silver cake knife, are all items that you may be able to borrow from friends for the day. It is advisable, though, to refrain from asking for precious or fragile things, which might get lost, stolen or broken.

Minor strategies

Savings can also be made in other areas. Announcements in the press, for instance, although they are not a big expense, are not strictly necessary, and every small saving counts. Invitations could be run off on a duplicating machine on bought cards.

Gold prices have risen dramatically in recent years, and it is therefore helpful to remember that a nine carat wedding ring is not only cheaper than eighteen or twenty-two carat, but also more hard-wearing, as it contains a higher proportion of metal alloy to gold.

How much you spend on dress can vary enormously from relatively inexpensive off-the-peg wedding dresses to very costly designer dresses made specially for you. The cheapest solution of all for both men and women is to hire your clothes; some outfitters stock a wide range of styles. Either making your own dress (if you are a good needlewoman) or having it made by a friend or relation as a present, can also offer substantial savings.

Essentials

Photography at the wedding is one area in which it is difficult to economize. Commissioning a professional photographer is almost an essential if you don't want to run the risk of being left without any photographs by which to remember the day. Prices, however, vary considerably, so shop around and compare standards. Look at the standard of the photographs in the window. Many photographers, for example, provide wedding photographs that have been mounted already, or arranged into an album, which is obviously a more expensive method than simply sending the prints.

Unfortunately, some tipping is unavoidable, although, strictly speaking, it is not obligatory. Tipping is simply a means of showing appreciation and thanks. It is, however, customary for the groom to tip the verger and the bell-ringers, and for the person who is paying for the reception to tip the toastmaster and whoever is in charge of the catering and cloakroom staff. If cars are hired, the drivers should also be tipped.

Hired cars, incidentally, may well be one of the most inflationary items on your list, particularly if you have set your heart on a ceremonial car. Borrowing cars from friends or relations is obviously the cheapest solution to the problem of transport. Make sure that they are fully insured, arrange for them to be cleaned and polished the day before, add a few white ribbons, and unlike Daisy in the old song, you won't have to 'look sweet upon the seat of a bicycle made for two'.

Realistic Limits

One of the problems of trying to keep finances within a reasonable boundary is that for centuries the marital union of man and woman has been accompanied by a public celebration of their private commitment with good eating and drinking, merriment and congratulations. Although none of this is strictly necessary, most couples want to mark the beginning of their married life with festivities, surrounded by their friends and family, and this costs money.

On the other hand, it is important to remember that cutting down costs need not mean cutting out pleasure. If you are working on tight financial limits, the best plan is to accept those limitations (rather than despair at the lack of funds) and work within them to achieve the best possible results. Thorough examination of all the possibilities, care and foresight in planning and, above all, as much imagination as can be mustered, will go a long way towards achieving a wedding that satisfies your dreams as well as your purse.

MARTY 1923

7

THE WEDDING DRESS

Which Dress for You?

Throughout history, the bride's robe has possessed an almost mystical significance, and to this day women profess to have a sixth sense about the way they wish to look on their wedding day.

The wedding dress is the one dress that should have no doubts attached to it. Yet this is not always easy to achieve as a simple garment has to meet so many different and sometimes conflicting requirements.

Ideally, the bride's dress should fulfil the image she has of herself on the occasion of marriage, meet the needs of her religion, arouse delight in the eye of the beloved, give satisfaction to whoever paid for it, be admired by family and friends, and reproduce well in the wedding photographs.

Tall order as this may be, it is a fact that the world is filled with women who find the very thing. Anyone embarking on the search is justified in taking heart from past experience.

Where you are going to be married is likely to have a bearing on what you will wear. There are dresses for little churches and chapels and dresses for great places of worship. A grandiose robe and imposing train would look incongruous in the intimate surroundings of a small parish church. On the other hand, such grandeur is perfectly at home in a cathedral with its imposing splendour.

A special wedding dress, whether traditional or informal in style, is by no means obligatory. Day dress is perfectly acceptable but most women would wish to look good on the occasion of their marriage.

The boundaries denoting distinctions between clothes for a religious ceremony and a civil marriage overlap at many points. Appropriateness is always a reliable yardstick by which to judge the merits of a particular design.

Religious denominations have their own customs and rites related to the dress observances of the bride who is marrying with the blessing of her faith.

High Church and Roman Catholic weddings are associated with highly traditional clothes for the bride; the Church of England appears to be tolerant of departures from convention; Quakers, Friends and the Nonconformists in general emphasize simplicity and modesty; the Orthodox Jewish faith has unchanging sartorial rituals. Your minister is the person to consult in case of doubt.

The dress should be cut out for the occasion, in every sense. You will be called upon to walk gracefully, sit, hold your head high, stand, kneel (in a High Church service), shake hands, hold hands, kiss, eat, drink and perhaps dance, all as part of the day's work. There should be no impediment to your freedom of action, and it is an idea to brave the possible giggles of casual bystanders and go through all the motions when trying on a dress in the shop.

Try to escape the trap of falling for a dress that makes too many demands as the wedding itself is likely to be demanding and will call on your reserve of confidence and energy. Don't forget that adjusting to the disciplines of a long dress, a headdress and accessories may not come instinctively to a generation more accustomed to wearing blue jeans. So keep it simple.

Among dubious benefits are a wasplike waistline (possible difficulties in breathing easily), a very long train (difficult to manoeuvre), voluminous petticoats (hot and heavy), a short zip-fastening (impractical for easy putting on and taking off).

A very important asset is a pretty backview. The dress should look good from every angle of course but remember that the back of you is the aspect seen by the congregation for the greater part of the service.

Exposure

When fashion dictates clothes which are sexy and body revealing, the question may arise of how far a wedding dress may follow the fashion. Is it acceptable to go to the altar in slit skirts or see-through fabrics, bare shouldered or bare backed? The matter no longer concerns only a few trendies as the wedding dress is increasingly influenced by current fashion.

Religious teachings are deeply rooted in traditions of chastity and faithfulness. These values, although frequently challenged in the outside world, are still expressed in many aspects of the wedding ceremony, including the customs to do with the clothes of the bride. What she wears is traditionally intended to be an outward observance of the inner meaning of the rites of marriage. It is a good idea to take into consideration the attitudes of your particular denomination as these vary considerably – some emphasizing traditional dress, others offering a freer line. It should be remembered that the bride faces the priest throughout the marriage service. If her dress is flauntingly provocative, she just might find it difficult to meet his eye.

There is no need to be too strict about following convention to the letter, or to take refuge in a dress intended to please authority, but which you do not care for yourself. It is as well to remember, that opinion on what is elegant and suitable tends to change along with fashion. At the moment of writing bare-shouldered wedding dresses have made a reappearance which might have astonished an earlier generation but would scarcely have surprised the Edwardians, who were familiar with the style.

From a purely social point of view, you should take into account the views of your partner, family, friends. Will they consider your dress deliciously seductive or simply shocking? Perhaps your best guide is your instinct. If doubts dawn as to the wisdom of your decision and you want a happy occasion all round, abstain. If none trouble you, go ahead.

Once in a Lifetime or Wear Again?

Opinion is divided on the matter of whether a wedding dress should be chosen on the basis of one-time wear, or whether this is all romantic nonsense. Surely a dress should be chosen with an eye to its continued use, goes the practical argument.

Designers, who give a great deal of thought to the subject, appear to differ as sharply as their customers. Jean Muir, who is one of the best-known dress designers in Britain, has commented, 'I don't think that nowadays there is any need for a one-occasion dress. If a design is beautiful it should be worn again and again.' But Gina Fratini, whose wedding clothes are sold throughout the country, has said, 'I am entirely in favour of preserving the most beautiful dress you have ever worn, in a box.' And Bill Gibb, who makes exotic wedding dresses to order, commented, 'I like the idea of a dream being hoarded for future generations. I can't bear the thought of a wedding dress being worn again and again and worn out.'

It is all a question of individual temperament, and perhaps of nationality too. The internationally known Paris designer, Jean-Louis Scherrer, has observed, 'English women are very sentimental. You have a tradition for preserving the wedding dress. French women are very practical. We too have our traditions. We believe in wearing a beautiful and expensive dress more than once.'

If you go along with the practical arguments that it makes sense to choose a dress which will be useful to you after the wedding steer clear of designs which proclaim bride in every line. Unless you are prepared to chop up, change or dye the dress in order to disguise its origins it is far better to choose an evening dress that can be accessorized for the wedding. Shorn of headdress and flowers, it can then revert to its original role.

Don't, however, be bowled over by the utilitarian argument which makes practicality the top priority. Consider whether or not your social life is of a kind which is likely to demand formal clothes of the sort you would wear at a wedding. If you never wear clothes like that to a party, there is not much point in choosing the dress on the basis of its future usefulness. You might prefer to use this one occasion to experience the sensation of wearing a beautiful dress without thinking about tomorrow.

Sometimes the answer to clothes which are sufficiently formal in feeling to work as a wedding dress yet flexible enough to be worn again lies in separates. A combination of a top or jacket and a long evening dress provides elegant cover for the bride on the occasion of her marriage and, without the jacket, becomes a bare-shouldered evening dress. Another idea is a dress with an overskirt which could be peeled off to reveal a straight ankle-length skirt for evening wear. One designer has come up with a five-part trousseau consisting of a blouse and long skirt for the wedding which can be matched or combined with a jacket, short skirt and shorts for going away and for the honeymoon.

Finding Your Style

A cardinal rule is that clothes should enhance the wearer's good points and minimize the bad. To be aware of your best assets does not only mean 'do I have a pretty bosom? ... yes, so I will wear a lowcut neckline.' There may be less obvious features such as the way you move, or a neat ankle, or a slender neckline. If you have a good carriage, choose a fabric which moves well such as chiffon or satin or crêpe jersey, and wear a skirt cut to just above the ankle; choose a perfectly simple round neckline.

There are no short cuts to finding the right dress for an occasion as important as your wedding. Should you glimpse a photograph in a magazine and reflect that you would like something similar for your own wedding it is important to consider whether the dress suits your figure and personality.

Sheridan Barnett, a dress designer, recommends a dress test which is not as wild as it might appear to an uninformed observer who caught you at it. He says, 'When trying on a wedding dress, wait until you can smile spontaneously at your reflection in a mirror. If there is any hesitation – just keep on hunting.' A dress designer, Bill Gibb, rightly encourages people to keep an open mind and to remember that many rules are myths. He tells this story: 'I once had a bad experience with a bride's mother who held strong opinions. She kept on telling me that her Amanda had broad shoulders so simply could not wear big sleeves.

I interrupted and pointed out that the last thing Amanda's big shoulders needed was a tight sleeve. We found a bodice with a high puffed sleeve curving into a tight, tailored wristline. Amanda never looked better.'

Unless you are a true rarity, the path of trial and error is the only way to obtain good results. Try on clothes this way and that, and be prepared to experiment. Suddenly, hopefully, everything will fall into place and that will be it.

Fitting your fashion fancy to your figure facts
Many women feel they have awkward figures and almost despair of finding a dress in which they have confidence.

Your mind will be much easier if you know that your dress has come to terms with any figure oddities. If you do not know how to begin, start with the familiar. One good plan is to opt for a style which experience has already confirmed as a success. If you have a favourite fashion look or cut or line, which you know works for you, choose that one.

Individual advice is always hard to give as personal factors invalidate generalization. Nevertheless, certain figure types do respond to certain tactics.

Broad hips. The skirt should skim easily over your hips. Try to avoid the obvious bulk-builders such as pleats, gathers and drapery. Go easy on pulling in your waist. Emphasize any part of you which is slender such as ankles, wrists, neck.

Short waist. Lower your waistline with any of the indications such as belts, sashes, seams. Tops cut to the hip point, skirts falling from hip level can help to restore the impression of a well-proportioned body. Alternatively, you can make an asset out of your shortcomings and wear a wide cummerbund or sash which disguises the position of your natural waistline and appears to lengthen the line between your bosom and waist.

Big bosom. Never dress as if you were ashamed of a big bosom. Admittedly, fashion favours the small breasted, but it may be some compensation to know that men have never really gone along with this. The Edwardians and Victorians dressed women with large bosoms beautifully – look for styles reflecting these periods. Low necklines, open necklines are naturals for you.

Short and roly-poly. The usual advice which is to make a bee-line for a plain simple style can be dull. Better to be small and interesting. A long veil with an unbroken line from top to toe creates the illusion of height. A short train helps to lengthen a back view.

Beanpole. Tall women do not usually get much sympathy from their shorter, fatter sisters. Yet excessive height, which may be combined with gawkiness, is a cause of dissatisfaction. The best approach is to break with the straight-up-and-down image and opt for a dress with a cape, an apron skirt, a tiered skirt or a cinched waist and a full skirt. Advice which is as effective for beanpoles as for the short and fat is to stand tall.

The foregoing should be read as a broad general guide only. Fashion is highly personal and the rules governing it are made to be broken by the individual.

Choosing a Fabric

The cherry-stone ditty of childhood, in which each pip represents one in a series of possibilities for the girl's wedding dress – 'Silk, satin, cotton, rags' – refers to fabrics which are as popular as ever. As for the rags, they have surely become glad rags.

The fabric is a vital factor of a dress design, as the cloth in which it is made will shape the form and function of a dress. *Silk* is soft, versatile often, falls gracefully over the contours of the body, is cool in hot weather and offers protection against sharp winds. *Satin* is sensuous; the sheen on the surface catches the light and lends seductive emphasis to the wearer's curves. It ripples successfully over thin people, but those who want to appear slimmer should opt for duchess satin, which has more substance to the weave and does not cling. *Cotton* possesses a freshly laundered whiteness and comes in a wide range of different weights and weaves, including voile, lawn, fine and heavy lace and broderie anglaise. The traditional Swiss cottons make up well and are a good choice for summer weddings.

Other fabrics to consider are crêpe, velvet, a fine wool, and taffeta, though today these may be synthetic simulations or a mixture of man-made and natural fibres. Price differentials between naturals and man-made are fast disappearing, however, as the rising cost of oil-based products affects nylon polyester as well as petrol. Nonetheless, the luxurious natural fabrics – real silk, fine wool, taffeta, velvet, silk tulle – are virtual rarities and consequently are extremely expensive.

By far the most popular fabrics for wedding dresses come from the family of nylon polyesters. Most ready-mades are in nylon polyester, as the fabric is a whiter than white, but in some forms the sheer brightness can cast a harsh light on the face.

Odd little snobberies still attach to the use of synthetics. One bride's mother whose daughter was married in a dress of polyester chiffon felt that the laboratory labelling sat uneasily in the published wedding announcement, so the bride was given away 'in a dress of chiffon'.

The best time to gain the widest selection of new fabrics is in the early spring and early autumn when the new stock comes into the shops. Some of the main department stores run a mail-order service and will supply swatches of fabric and try to match up colours. Enclose a SAE with a postal inquiry.

Remaining cool and uncrushed

Brides have a special interest in remaining cool and uncrushed and frequently ask which material is most suitable. Alas, the wonders of modern technology have not yet delivered the perfect fabric. All cloth loses some of its perfect smoothness when worn, but some materials survive the wearing process better than others. Choose fabrics which shed creases quickly and do not need continual pressing – usually fabrics with an admixture of synthetics.

The wearer herself affects the condition of a fabric. It is a thought that if you behave in a cool and orderly manner, the fabric will be right behind you.

Stratagems: avoid sitting as far as possible, keep still in the car, ease the skirt a little above the hips before taking your seat. If a long car journey is necessary a dress with a double skirt or overskirt is an answer to the inevitable creasing from sitting. The top layer can be flipped up and kept smooth. If fabrics are chosen which are renownedly susceptible to crushing, and these include many of the prettiest, such as organdie voile and lawn, buy the kind with a synthetic mix which adds resilience.

Finding Your Dress

Ready-made

The bridal departments and speciality shops are best for dresses which are immediately recognizable as wedding dresses. Many of the liveliest suppliers now stock a wide range of styles, so even if you want a dress that can be worn afterwards for parties it is worth while checking with the specialist shops. They will provide ready-made wedding dresses off-the-peg or samples on which orders can be taken. A few boutiques offer a service half-way between a custom-made dress and a ready-made by stocking sample designs which give the customer considerable leeway in adapting details, fabrics, trimmings, necklines and so on to her choice.

The advantage of going to the bridal shops extends beyond the clothes and includes, for example, private changing rooms and good mirrors, and the tacit acceptance by the management that the customer is not likely to make up her mind in a hurry and that companions and critics are expected. Accessories – such as a head-dress and petticoats needed for trying on with a dress – are usually available in order to gauge the complete effect. Also, if you are lucky, there will be somebody around who knows their business and who can advise customers on this specialized aspect of fashion.

(Continued on page 121)

A PORTFOLIO OF WEDDING DRESSES

Fashion photography adds its own glamour and believability to the dream of the perfect wedding dress. As a medium, photography is unrivalled at selecting the very detail that is so persuasive in a dress as personal as apparel for the bride.

The portfolio of fashion photography on the following pages shows the wedding dress portrayed by leading photographers in British Vogue and British Brides magazines from 1920 to the present day. The pictures are a record of the small shifts and variations of taste in bridal attire, and of changing styles of photography in the field.

The earliest shots present a demure if rather stagey bride as a studio portrait. In the thirties, the bridal figure is treated as a piece in a smart photographic composition; sitters wear languorous robes and rarely smile. Pictures of the Second World War bride of fashion borrow something from the movies in their manner and dress. The bride has loosened up, smiles, and is wearing a full-length veil and train; her clothes are a reaffirmation of tradition in the midst of rationing. After the war, the camera moves out into the street (see the bride aboard a bus). Exotic locations have become a commonplace for ready-made wedding dresses and the bridal veil is seen to go places.

The register-office bride registers as a fashion influence in the sixties and is shown in a mini dress. In the seventies, full colour enters the picture and with it a renewed appreciation of pastel and primary shades in wedding fashion and accessories. Today, everything is on the move including the bride in photography – the camera strives to catch the image of a dancing skirt, a blowing veil, the wearer's easy movements.

Despite minor alterations, elaborations and simplifications, the appearance of bridal attire is a record of constancy to tradition. To the modern eye, all these dresses made over the past seventy years or so barely seem to have dated.

In this section all the captions accompanying the photographs are taken from the original text.

Opposite: 'Youth, grace, romance – they all belong to this bride in her wedding-veil of orange-blossoms and tulle, and her tiny cap which fits her head with just a bit more tulle to veil her eyes, and over her shoulders, long mists of tulle in panels with more gathered in the back to form the veil. The wedding flowers are tied in a bouquet her great-grandmother might have carried, with row after row of small round roses, tiny chrysanthemums, first white, then yellow, and in the centre of all, three bride's roses, white and prim, then all about, soft maiden-hair fern and lace and lengths of narrow ribbons.'

1925

Opposite: GOWN FROM LUCILE
'*A robe de style – a picturesque gown with memories of more romantic modes adding charm to its billowing folds – is a lovely fashion for a wedding dress. Here, white lace with golden threads falls in a deep bertha, and the same gold-embroidered lace makes the slim oval insets on the skirt and the edging at the hem. The fitted bodice and the full skirt are of white satin scattered with raised satin flowers, over a lining of flesh coloured satin. The train is of satin, and the cap-shaped veil of old lace and tulle banded with orange-blossoms. The bouquet the bride carries is of white orchids and lilies-of-the-valley.'*

THE NUN-LIKE BRIDE
'*Veil of Duchesse lace, Brussels net, and rose point lace; bouquet of white hyacinths.'*

CECIL BEATON 1929

Mrs John William Mackay

*Opposite: 'Jean Patou designed
this wedding gown "Hyménée"
of classic beauty and
simplicity. It has a long,
moulded bodice and a belt,
crossing in front and fastened
in the back, to which is
attached the court train.'*

CECIL BEATON 1929

'There is nobody like Norman Hartnell for making the most of a picturesque occasion, and in this lovely wedding dress he combines a medieval fitted feeling with much sophistication of fabric and decoration. Cobwebby white lace makes the dress itself, which is encrusted all over with faintly glimmering crystals. The long train of white net falls away from the front of the dress, showing the lace, and clouds of tulle scarcely veil the little Juliet cap of lace and crystal. The arum lilies are made of white satin.'

HOYNINGEN-HUENÉ 1931

'A town wedding. Mrs
Peter Quennell in Enos'
classical Romaine gown
with cellophane flowers.'

HORST 1936

Opposite: THIRTY-FIVE
YARDS OF TULLE
'If yours is to be a Grand-
Manner wedding, yours too
might be this magnificent
dress of white silk and rayon
lace and thirty-five yards of
silk tulle. The head-dress, tulle
and a real calla-lily on a
white lace cap. If you wish,
tuck a veil beneath the cap
or wear a chou like this,
and no veil.'

'War brides prefer white:
and here is a wedding dress
romantic enough to be any
heart's delight. This
beglamoured bride wears a
silvery-white lamé gown with
heart-shaped neck.
Camellias crown her veil of
Brussels lace.'

NORMAN PARKINSON 1944

BRIDE ON A BUDGET
'The wedding dress is in fine white pique, important, dazzling, fresh as a newly scrubbed choirboy. The immense skirt has unpressed pleats, big stand-away pockets, edged, like the halter collar and cuffs, with broderie anglaise. Price £15 6s. 4d.'

HONEYMAN 1951

TONY ARMSTRONG JONES 1957

Epitome of a Happy Wedding
'The bride in a gleam of white satin tosses her bouquet to the luckiest. Her dress, with its simple short sleeves and yards of train, is by John Cavanagh; the floating, floor-length veil of silk tulle is held by a bowed white satin band, from Simone Mirman.'

VERDICT FOR SUMMER: LIGHT AND AIRY
'Cardin's bride wears a froth of point d'esprit spiralling into a half-moon train. A circular veil enfolds her.'

A Low Waistline Decreed
'Balmain uses a simple shape in tulle, cascading with myriads of pearls.'

PETER RAND 1968

STUNNING CIVIL CEREMONY
*'Enchanting white dress with
lots of party frills, chosen for
a register-office wedding; in
ninon, dropping to a little-girl
low waist, sashed with white
satin ribbon, fastened by a
sugar pink rose.'*

*Opposite: 'Slender as a
column: sleeveless jersey dress
by Ronald Joyce with a
billowing cape.'*

DICK ZIMMERMAN 1971

DICK ZIMMERMAN 1971

TEA GOWN REVIVAL
'(Left) swooping plunge – at
the back too – in cream crêpe
by Ossie Clark; (right) froth
of frills on a cream silk chiffon
dress by Alice Pollock.'

Opposite: Alan Randall, 1978
Overleaf left:
Christos Raftopoulos, 1980
Overleaf right:
Stefano Massimo, 1980

(Continued from page 103)

Alterations are usually part of the service, but check on the time that it takes. It is rarely rewarding to agree to major changes to a ready-made dress; an adjustment to a hemline, or a tweak here or a touch of easing there is fine. In the event of radical change, however, the original design may disappear in the process and you won't know what you are going to get in its place.

The best way to judge a bridal department is to look at the state of the dresses. Are they new and fresh? Is there plenty of choice so you can make comparisons? In addition to home-produced dresses are there some interesting imports from abroad?

It happens, and often in shops where the prices are keenest, that the management employs staff who are pushy and dedicated to the hard sell. If you feel vulnerable to this type of high-pressure selling, yet wish to take advantage of the price differential, always travel with a hard-headed friend. Anyway, two heads are less likely to be pushed into anything.

It is not wise to put a deposit on a dress unless you seriously intend to buy. The law allows retailers to charge for reserving merchandise which is withdrawn from offer and it is unlikely that a deposit will be returned in these circumstances. The fact that you have had a genuine change of heart about the dress has nothing to do with it.

The age-old dilemma of wondering how to try on an item bought in one shop with its companion or accessory which is to be bought elsewhere admits of no easy solution. How to judge if a hat or head-dress will go well with the dress unless they can be seen in conjunction? Why not brave the curious stares and take along whatever is needed to form a sensible decision?

Other sources of ready-made dresses to be worn at the wedding are dress shops selling party clothes and the evening-dress departments of large stores. Luckily, shades of white and cream and all the related pale colours are always in fashion. If buying an inexpensive dress on grounds of economy, make sure that this will not require extras such as slips or a body-stocking which will invalidate its bargain value.

Designer rooms in large stores, which present clothes designed by well-known makers, may provide a dress which is right for the wedding. If you like the clothes of a particular dress designer it is worth writing to the head office to ask for stockists in your area.

Hiring

Hiring a dress can save money, time and trouble. The starting price for hire is likely to represent a considerable saving on the alternative of buying, or of having a dress made. Then again, hiring can simplify organizational problems. It may be possible to find all the necessary clothes for the wedding party under one roof as dress-hire firms supply men's clothes and bridal attendants' clothes as well as accessories. Hiring has obvious points in favour for anyone without space to accommodate wedding clothes either before or after the event.

Some big hire firms offer a custom-made service in which the customer orders a new dress to be made to her own specifications. The customer is the first to wear it and afterwards the dress is returned for further hire. Charges here are not cheap, but will be much less expensive than buying a dress of comparable quality.

The case against hiring is that it offends against the romantic notion of having a dress that is yours alone, a possession which can be kept as a memento. There are certain practical reservations too, to be weighed in the balance. Some dress-hire firms do not possess unblemished reputations for cleanliness, or efficiency, and the range of styles, though sound enough on traditional dresses, is rarely noted for individuality.

There are other sources of hire outside the firms specializing in this business. Some well-known dress designers or theatrical costumiers are prepared to consider requests to lend out on suitable terms. If you see a dress which you covet there is nothing against writing to ask if the owner or designer would be prepared to arrange to lend it to you for the day. If dresses of value are borrowed, circumspect borrowers will arrange to take out insurance cover against damage or theft.

Custom made

A few, usually London-based, dress designers make beautiful evening clothes which can be worn for a wedding and some of them are prepared to accept commissions to make designs to order. Customers arrange to see the new season's collection at the house salon, and place an order for one of the existing designs or commission a specially made wedding dress. First-time clients should write asking for approximate prices. An idea of the designer's current work can often be seen in the fashion pages of leading magazines or newspapers reporting on the new spring or autumn collections.

The dressmaker dress

Ordering a dress from a professional dressmaker is rarely an economy move but it has advantages for anyone who wants a dress she will not see on anyone else. If you have a design of your own creation a dressmaker is usually willing to try to make it up, if feasible. Also, the idea has all the merits of personal service when the client can arrange things to her own liking.

Tracking down a reliable dressmaker is like discovering gold as they are rapidly disappearing in a world of mass-production. But the apocalypse has not yet happened, and dressmaking services do exist all over the country for those determined to find them.

The best sources of addresses are in the classified advertisements in specialist magazines, fashion publications and the personal columns of the national press and local press. Sometimes a needlework school or craft shop can give a lead.

It is highly risky to go to an unknown and untried maker for a commission as important as a wedding dress. If the name is new to you, always ask for references and take them up and look at some existing work. The best personal recommendation comes from a client who is pleased with the results of her own commission. In any event, take a friend with a good eye to one of the fittings.

If things do not go to your liking there is little that can be done after the fabric is cut. Such matters as whether the style suits the wearer are subjective and rarely open to financial redress.

Some makers have established a reputation for wedding clothes and will supply a range of basic patterns which can be adapted to individual needs.

Customers usually supply their own material, but not invariably, and this is a point to take up at the first meeting.

The home-made dress

Economy is not always the main reason for making a wedding dress at home. Many fond parents or friends do so for motives of sentiment and the challenge offers a splendid opportunity to demonstrate dressmaking or dress design skills. It can be cheaper than buying ready-made, but many choose this course because they want a custom-made dress and it is less expensive than ordering from a professional dressmaker.

Making a dress at home requires special caution. A priority is keeping the fabric clean, and this is not always easy in a busy crowded household. Experienced dressmakers pass on the following recommendations.

1929

Try to work in a room with a carpet as it is difficult to keep a long dress off the floor. The movement of fabric on a polished surface produces static electricity and acts like a duster. Put your trust in a big sheet or covering. Spread it over the surface where the cutting is to be done – a bed is a good idea but don't cut the coverings beneath. Use the sheet as a protective wrap for the dress while it is being worked on, and as storage when the job is completed. Check the sewing machine for cleanliness and any excess oil on the working parts. Before cutting the fabric, make sure that you already have every bit of material, trimmings and details – a vital element may prove untraceable in the shops and rethinking could be needed.

Keep the pressing iron clean; if stained it can be re-polished with an iron cleaning preparation. Play safe by placing a soft cloth over the dress before ironing it. A steam iron is suitable for most fabrics but ensure that the thermostat is functioning properly before dashing away with the smoothing iron.

Finding a dress pattern

Looking for interesting variations on the ordinary run of wedding-dress patterns can be a disheartening experience. The bridal sections in the set books are fine on traditional designs but tend to offer a limited choice, and rarely of an imaginative nature.

The answer is to cast your net wider and to consider evening-dress designs or even some day-dress patterns; these are generally more inspiring and can be adapted to suit.

Another approach for anyone with a sense of design is to combine different parts of different patterns – a sleeveline from one with a neckline from another, for example. Makers recommend taking a full sketch of the dress you want, when shopping and hunting down each component in the printed patterns.

If by chance you see a photograph or an illustration of a dress which you admire, a pattern-cutting firm will provide a pattern of the design. However, it is important to assess whether a dress that looks wonderful on a fashion model, or in a drawing, is right for your personality and figure.

A basic qualification for a wedding dress is that the design should be easy to get in to and out of. For one thing, the order of the day is dress after hair, so a dress that is made to be stepped into is less of a risk than one which is slipped over the head. However, even if the latter is chosen, a long aperture is desirable whatever the precise form of the fastening.

Yours alone

Even in this day of ready-made regalia, the notion of wearing a dress which is uniquely yours has not been supplanted. Professional dressmakers and designers are an answer but there is one other source of inspiration. Young fashion school students or textile designers often make their own wedding clothes, design for their friends or produce dresses, sketches and fabrics which inject a lot of originality into conventional thinking. Students or recent graduates are often pleased to accept commissions from individual customers if they want an original design.

The best place to see students' work is at the summer degree shows or fashion shows held at the end of term. It is usually possible to gain admission. Check with your local education authority as to time and place.

Remember that students' work tends to score on creativity but may not be as practical as you might wish. Always allow plenty of time for work to be executed, obtain detailed estimates, put any agreement in writing, and don't expect a young designer's best work to come cheap.

Customers who are interested in hand-made crafts such as appliqué, crochet, embroidery, painted designs, beadwork, macramé, knitting, quilting, tapestry, weaving, lace work, hand printing and dyeing – all of which have an honoured place in wedding costume – will probably be able to find a young exponent of the craft at art school or one who is a recent graduate.

Rescuing granny's cast-off

At one time, the idea of wearing an 'old-fashioned' dress had remarkably little to commend it especially to anyone wanting to look their best. What would once have been dismissed as a 'dated' dress certainly has a place at the wedding today, and the current interest in wearing original old clothes brings a whole new range of possibilities into focus. The kind of nostalgic garments that are valued today are in a style that lends itself to the occasion but are probably not those originally made with the bride in mind: 'best' things, evening clothes and occasional finery.

By far the most popular sources are the productive Victorian and Edwardian periods, as clothes for women at that time were long, decorative, demure and feminine. Many modern brides find themselves in sympathy with these fashions, at least for a day.

The custom of wearing a valued old dress has a long provenance: a traditional way of symbolizing family continuity is for the family or relations to lend a dress or antique veil to the new bride. Others will beg, borrow or buy a beautiful old garment. The watchword in this specialist field is to know your subject. Knowledge of the period or type of old dress in which you are interested is of greater value than money.

Old clothes come in many states and conditions from collectors' pieces to irredeemable rags. The general run of second-hand garments which might be considered for the wedding are often badly flawed or soiled by time and wear. If you buy unwisely and attempt to clean your period piece at home it may come to pieces in your hand. However, if it is worth putting up with a few repairs for the sake of the charm of the fabric, or the detailing, or the beguiling style, there are sources of help on restoration. Costume museums and needlework schools are sometimes prepared to give advice on repairs and renovation. If the dealer or supplier is reputable they may pass on a useful tip or two.

Some periods of fashion provide naturals for wedding clothes and among them are the ladylike occasion dresses of the twenties and thirties, dance and ball gowns of the forties and fifties, and all formal wedding dresses of the period. No doubt the immediate past, the sixties and the seventies, will soon become ripe for plunder as they too slip away. There must be many parents and grandparents who wish they had held on to their own wedding things for a future generation that sets such a high value on yesterday's throwaways. Perhaps the reader will learn from such profligacy and will harbour her own clothes for tomorrow's bride.

If a complete old dress is impractical there are other possibilities in the notion of combining the old with the new. Among the many permutations are the following: combining a top which is an original with a new skirt; using old trimmings in good condition such as ribbons, laces, frills, flounces and inset embroidery as a means of enlivening a dress made in new material; using rare old fabric such as lace or tulle or chiffon as an overlay with a new underskirt; wearing an original white petticoat as a wedding dress skirt with a new blouse.

The strong style of a period dress gives you a firm lead on the selection of accessories, though restraint has to be exercised – an excess of devotion to a historical style can become fancy dress.

Most big cities have their dealers and suppliers but the days are over when bargains can be found on the beaten track. Sources of goods and/or information on second-hand clothes, apart from dealers, include antique shops, market stalls, sales, jumble sales, Oxfam shops, craft shops, art schools, schools of fashion and fashion magazines.

Special Circumstances

Winter weddings

Not enough thought has been given to the fashion dilemmas of marrying in winter. Wedding dresses by definition seem to be made in flimsy fabrics which offer no protection against bleak winds and draughts.

You could look for a dress in fine wool or wool mix, but this may have to be specially made. Silk is relatively warm. Some dresses are trimmed with fur or made with maribou edged hoods and these at least keep the head warm and provide an appealing idea for a head-dress. You could travel in the car wrapped in a deep shawl, or wear a long cloak or a baby shawl which lies lightly on a dress. Gina Fratini, the designer, produced a winter wedding design composed of a white dress worn with a long velvet cloak, and a small lacy bonnet for a head-dress. The wearer could sweep up the aisle in a cloak, take it off during the signing of the register and reappear before the congregation in the dress alone. Alternatively, she could remain cloaked during the whole ceremony, removing it to reveal her dress at the reception. A guard against cold is to keep the head, wrists and feet warm; think about gloves, evening boots and a furry hat. Take a rug in the car for your feet, include a handkerchief and paper tissues in the car, check that the driver whether relation or a chauffeur has a big umbrella to hand; *in extremis,* a nip of brandy.

Remember that it may be difficult to find white or cream-toned shoes in the shops in autumn or winter. A winter wedding is one instance where it could make sense to buy shoes ahead of the dress. If not exactly the right shade, plain white shoes can be sprayed with colour at home. The use of bright colour as an element in your dress, vividly coloured flowers and berries in a bouquet, and clear colour for make-up can warm up the appearance of things wonderfully.

Dancing at the nuptials

If the wedding is to be celebrated with a dance, the dress for it should combine dignity and dash. It is doubly important to be able to move around with ease if bopping, whirling or waltzing are part of the proceedings.

A dress with a train is fine providing that this is of the right length. When picked up by a tab at the end of the train the fabric should form a graceful loop from the floor to the hand of the dancer. If the train is too short for the job it will become hitched round the dancer's knees. If allowed to trail it may become entangled in everyone's feet.

Some brides prefer to remove their head-dress for the dance, or choose a style which can be securely anchored. Some hairstyles are easier than others to wear when dancing. To be comfortably shod is more than ever a priority.

Having a baby

As pre-marital pregnancy is an unchanging fact of life, it may solve at least one minor problem if the bride's dress is in order.

As far as size and style is concerned the factor to be considered is how far advanced the pregnancy will be by the date of the wedding. Women vary considerably in their physical response to pregnancy. Some blow up into barrage balloons in a few weeks; others can wear their usual clothes until quite late in pregnancy.

If the dress is to be worn during the early stages the only allowance that need be made is perhaps to order a size larger than usual, and to avoid fabrics such as jersey satin or silk which cling to every curve. If the dress is to be ordered some time ahead of the wedding, allow for a larger bodice as the breasts become larger as well as the pregnant line.

In later stages, it is wisest to resist the impulse to take refuge in a voluminous tent which probably won't fool anybody. Instead, choose a dress which does not attempt to disguise but which is cut out to suit the proportions of prospective motherhood. Good lines are dresses cut to fall from the shoulder, dresses with a yoke and no waist, and dresses with raised waistlines.

Comfort is important. The dress, whatever its style, should have an easy fit, free of any feeling of tightness as pregnancy can be accompanied by queasy feelings. Whether or not a cover-up is attempted depends on the bride's own attitudes towards her pregnancy. If discretion is essential this seems a moment when the mysteries of a full-length veil could be put to good use.

Clothes for a register office marriage

Despite the fact that there are no sartorial conventions on dress for a civil marriage, most people want to look their best for the event. In practice, the style of dress, for the bride especially, tends to depend on the arrangements that follow the marriage. Women who look well in hats wear one. Flowers are worn and carried. The witnesses dress as they please, but tend to wear what they would for any special daytime occasion.

Sometimes the bride chooses a long white wedding dress but some discretion has to be shown here. If white as a fashion is to be worn, and there is no reason why it should not be, the effect should be appropriate for a secular occasion.

The groom usually wears a lounge suit and a buttonhole, and he can key his clothes to the style of dress worn by the bride. If she is wearing white, and there is to be a formal wedding reception, he may prefer to complement her and wear morning dress. It is by no means unusual for men to prefer wearing morning dress for their marriage. In this case, the bride should wear whatever looks right with a partner who is formally attired.

Clothes for a Service of Blessing

Choosing clothes for a Service of Blessing depends on how far the occasion is to conform to some of the traditions associated with a marriage service. Some people, for a number of reasons, wish to create an atmosphere and sense of occasion that has a wedding character. How far a Service of Blessing may be treated as a proxy wedding ceremony in terms of clothes and effects is a matter for you and the officiating minister to decide. It should be added that although there are some liberal-minded clergymen in the field, the church authorities tend to view such extra trimmings and observances with some disfavour. The official word is for the arrangements to be low key and discreet in keeping with the service itself.

Decisions on dress for the wife will probably be influenced by her views on whether she does or does not wish to strike a traditional bridal note. Her judgement may be determined by whether she is single or is marrying again.

If she wants to be a bride, and the minister is agreeable, many of the options that are open to the traditional bride are open to her. Otherwise she wears whatever she looks her best in, be it short or long, white or in colour, day-dress or evening-dress. The question of the degree to which a woman who is marrying again should follow the formal regalia of a white-wedding bride is for her to judge. There are many compromises and shades of fashion design which will enable her to fulfil a bridal role without adopting the dress signals of the bride of tradition.

In all cases, the wife for whom the blessing is being held should wear some form of head-dress or hat or a token flower or ornament in the hair. Flowers can be carried and/or worn.

The man usually keys the style of his dress to the level of formality of the bride's dress. It is usual to wear a lounge suit, conventional neckwear and a buttonhole. A point worth making is that sometimes, and especially when the husband was the single person, or his wife was single, the man wishes to follow tradition and celebrate marriage in morning dress. He may wish to do this irrespective of his wife's former marital status. If he does decide to wear a morning suit, his bride should wear whatever complements a partner who is formally attired.

When bridesmaids are in the party, they dress according to the bride's style, wearing long dresses if she is so attired or day clothes if that is her choice.

A safe guideline for guests attending a Service of Blessing is to dress as for a church wedding.

When a Service of Blessing is immediately preceded by a civil marriage, the religious ceremony should be judged as the priority consideration in the choice of clothes.

No Inspiration?

It can happen that you have absolutely no idea where to begin, which is all the more frustrating because your contemporaries seem to know just where they are going.

Become a dress watcher – study fashion whenever you see it: in movies new and old, on TV, at the theatre, in shop windows. Clearly much of what you see will be irrelevant to your particular needs. But if you do not know what you like, one of the ways of acquiring an opinion is to gather more information.

It is always a good idea to look for the style of dress which is known to look good on you in everyday life. Go to the civic art galleries and study portraits of women wearing interesting costume – is there a line, a colour, a mood that sets you thinking? Browse through books dealing with historical costume, modern fashion, old bridal manuals. Keep a sharp eye out for appropriate ideas in the fashion pages of magazines and newspapers. Don't be put off by the horrendous expense of so many of the most attractive designs – reading periodicals is also a way of picking up original ideas which can be adapted. Bridal magazines are an obvious source; remember that there are American, French and Italian brides' publications, which are available at specialized outlets.

All kinds of things may spark off ideas: a colour, a fabric, a flower, a piece of jewellery, an old photograph. Family associations or traditions or personal interests may provide a train of thought. The location of the wedding or the reception may inspire the style of your dress.

Actual examples of unusual romantic links with the past are: choosing a fabric colour to harmonize with flowers picked from the family garden; using roses as a theme for colour and flowers; selecting a dress based on Elizabethan or Tudor costume, such as might have been worn by Juliet in Shakespeare's play; decorating a dress in small sea-shells and embroidered Celtic symbols as a memento of a holiday where the wearer first met her partner.

Should you chance on an illustration which shows exactly what you want, a firm can translate a photograph or sketch into a pattern for dressmaking.

Best Shopping Time

When to shop obviously depends on how much time there is in hand. Clearly, the right time to buy is when you see just what you want.

If arrangements permit, it is best to have decided on your dress about two months ahead of the wedding. This gives sufficient leeway for dress alterations to be carried out, any special orders to be put through and second thoughts to be acted upon.

If the dress is to be made, two or three months' notice may be required by the dressmaker. If the customer is supplying the material, this decision can be taken well in advance.

As a rule it is rarely sound practice to acquire the finished dress far ahead of the wedding. Plans may change, and a practical point is that your body weight may alter. Tradition has it that the bride loses weight but the myth should be viewed sceptically. The dress bought months ahead of time may no longer fit as well as on the day when it was bought. An extra curve or a spot of shrinkage in your measurements may spoil the line of the dress, and this is particularly relevant in the case of many classic styles with a fitted bodice and neat waistline.

The sales

When planning the timing of shopping expeditions remember the difference made by the sales. Bargains can be picked up. Many bridal boutiques and departments offer dresses with a substantial mark-down in price. Sometimes the dresses are shop soiled and their value is in proportion to the ease with which they can be cleaned. A disadvantage is that the new styles are unlikely to be available, and shops at sale time are renownedly low on all kinds of clothes and accessories which are readily obtainable in normal conditions. Then again if you happen to be looking for specifically seasonal clothes towards the close of that season, these may be pretty thin on the ground as shops work far ahead of nature's calendar.

Shopping in a hurry

Sometimes through circumstances, or perhaps because the individual prefers it, everything has got to be got together in no time at all. The most effective approach to shopping in a hurry is to decide on the main targets – those acquisitions on which your heart is set – and take the rest as it comes. Speed of action can concentrate the mind wonderfully.

Storing a Wedding Dress

The tradition is to preserve the wedding dress with care and to bring it out in later years for the delectation of your children. Some people like to make a christening robe out of the fabric.

If a dress is to be kept with care – and the following applies also to storing a dress for some time in advance of the wedding – the procedures are as follows. Wrap it in dark tissue paper to prevent fading and store it in a cardboard box in a dry cupboard. Always mothproof if the dress is to remain untouched for some time. Avoid putting the dress in a polythene bag as, if any damp should intrude, the rot will set in. Also, it is a good idea to pack the sleeves or any suitable trimmings and furbelows with tissue paper in order to keep everything in good shape.

Accessories

The head-dress

Perhaps the trend of going without a hat outside has given the custom of wearing a head-dress at the wedding a special fascination. Whatever the reasons, there is a renewed interest in hair decoration and head dressing.

Do you have to wear a head-dress? The answer depends on your religious denomination and there are differing points of emphasis. Most Roman Catholic and Jewish brides for example are expected to wear some form of covering on the head. The Anglican churches are inclined to leave the matter to the woman in question. If in doubt, the best person to give advice is the officiating minister.

In general whether there are formal pressures on her or not to conform to the custom of wearing a head-dress, most brides like to continue the tradition as a gesture to religious convention blessed by fashion.

On the question of wearing a veil, women are often in two minds. Many women begin by being totally opposed to the idea of wearing a veil, particularly one which covers the face. They feel that the symbol is out of keeping with today's emphasis on intimacy and openness between equal partners in marriage. However, many admit that when they tried on the mysteries and draperies of a veil, the sheer prettiness overcame their scruples. Some adopted a compromise idea – to wear a veil but off the face.

If you are to wear a veil over the face, the tradition is to arrive veiled at the place of worship, to remove the veil from the face at a chosen moment, either before or during the ceremony or in the vestry, and to reappear before the congregation as a married woman, radiantly unveiled.

One tip: the wearer beneath a full veil is virtually in a hothouse and she may flush because of increased body temperature. Wear the veil off the face in the car when travelling to the place of worship or hold it well out in order to keep the air circulating inside. It can be re-arranged before entering the door.

Veils are invariably transparent and come in all shapes and sizes. There are veils which extend to the tip of a long train, fall to the floor, to the ankle, to the waist, to the shoulder or chin or mouth or eye. There are veils of silk, chiffon, lace, nylon, organza, net. Veils can be ready made or made to order, or you can make one yourself. Some of the most beautiful veils are of antique lace and it is a long-standing and still observed custom for families to lend veils handed down from one generation to the next.

Head-dresses can be bought ready-made in bridal departments. Always try on a head-dress with your dress before taking the decision to buy, unless you are in no doubt about it. Study it from every angle, especially, as in the case of your dress, from the back. A hat or a head-dress should look well from every vantage point.

Many of the methods which women have used through the centuries to decorate their hair can be revived for a wedding. You could wear a garland of whole fresh flowers, or parts and petals of flowers as hair decoration (see page 152). There are dried flowers, fantasy flowers in imaginary colours, leaves, tufts of feathers in natural colours or dyed, ribbons which are plaited, tied and woven through tresses of hair, added hair pieces as a basis for decoration, hair pins, combs, tiaras, Alice bands. Look for details in fashion and beauty articles in magazines and newspapers and advertisements. Your hairdresser will be able to advise – ask him or her to produce an idea which has an affinity with your dress as well as fitting your face.

Stages in the making of a floor-length veil

1a

1b

2

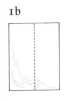

3

4

MARION APPLETON

Hats too are available in white and pale colours all the year round from bridal departments, and from general hat counters in spring and summer. Some of the most popular styles are Juliet caps, bonnets, boaters and straw hats trimmed with ribbon or flowers.

Feel confident that your hat or head-dress is secure and won't slip around on your head. Small combs can be sewn into the lining of hats and caps or a hat pin may work. The best way to fasten a veil is to weave a series of fine hairpins into the veil and through the hair, following the line of the head-dress. When this is set in place it will cover the fastenings. If a veil is safely attached it will not put the security of the head-dress at risk.

Making a veil
A wedding veil is not too difficult to make at home, and has the extra advantage of easy access for try-ons with the dress.

When choosing a style of veil, it is necessary to decide on the way it is to be worn. If the veil is to be worn over the face, the head-dress can either be placed on top of the veil, or the veil can be flipped over the head-dress. Your decision here may well influence the style of head-dress, which must be related to the style of the veil. This applies to all combinations of veils and head-dresses.

First decide on the length that is best for you, bearing in mind the way it will look with the wedding dress. There are at least three lengths to choose from, to the floor, to the elbow, to the shoulder.

A floor-length veil

The prettiest full, floor-length veils are generally made with four layers of net, two touching the ground, and two to elbow length.

The veil is made in 72 in (183 cm) wide net. When measuring fabric, measure from the crown of the head to the floor, or to the end of the train of the dress. Allow for an extra half yard (half metre) of net. Double this measure, and you will have the yardage for the under veil (1a).

Measure from the crown of the head to the elbow, and double this measure for the shorter, top veil (1b). Inexperienced dressmakers will find it convenient to have the two lengths cut to measure, rather than to use their own scissors.

The making stages are indicated in the diagrams. Fold both pieces of net in half across the width of the fabric (2). Pin these together along the folds and gather with loose running stitches $\frac{1}{4}$ in (0.5 cm) from the fold (3). Attach the gathered veil to the head-dress securely (4). If the head-dress is secured with a hair comb, which it may well be if the design is fine or small or delicate, attach the veil to the comb. The top layer of the veil can, if wished, be tossed forward over the head-dress and worn over the face.

Shoulder-length and elbow-level veils

These usually consist of two layers of net. When measuring the fabric, measure from the crown of the head to the elbow or shoulder, depending on the length of the veil. Double the measure and you will have the length of material required. Fold in half across the width and run gathering stitches $\frac{1}{4}$ in (0.5 cm) in from the folded edge. (See the diagram for the full-length veil.) Attach the fabric securely to the head-dress or hair comb. One layer of net can be placed over the head-dress to serve as a face veil. For a fuller veil add an extra length of folded net, making four layers of net instead of two.

On your feet

In all dresses other than floor length, shoes are an important part of the picture. As a general rule it is best to reserve choosing shoes until the dress is in hand, as heels need to be keyed to hemlines, and colour and style of shoe and skirt related.

This is an occasion when a pair of comfortable shoes is even more desirable than usual. The bride is expected to be on her feet for the better part of the day, is called upon to walk with grace and will need all the support she can get.

Always wear new shoes around the house first in order to ease any stiffness; scrape the slippery soles and heels so as to guard against skidding; put the shoes on and check that any fastenings are in working order.

You can wear boots, bootees, flatties, dance pumps, slippers, court shoes, fine sandals. Brightly coloured shoes can look good with white. Gold or silver shoes work well for all kinds of dresses for the wedding and afterwards. If a half-tone or unusual shade is wanted, do not overlook the advantages of colouring a plain white pair at home. If a cream tone is required this can be obtained by dyeing it at home.

Some church ceremonies require the bride to kneel. Unless she wears a dress with a train which covers the shoe, her sole will be bared. Everything here should be in good order with the price tags removed.

What to carry

A bouquet, a posy, a basket of flowers, a fan or specially bound prayer book are among the traditional accompaniments carried by generations of brides. When choosing, it is wise, as usual, to consider what the day's arrangements hold for you. A priority is to choose a token which contributes to the visual impact of your appearance. Your hands will need, very probably, to be free to receive a ring. There is likely to be handshaking, hand holding, eating, drinking, toasting and, perhaps, dancing during which you may or may not wish to carry your posy – all such points need consideration.

1923

It is best to be highly selective. If a prayer book is to be carried, a bouquet could be an embarrassment of riches. Some people like the idea of perambulating with a parasol, a pretty idea for summer weddings. It can be opened up at the reception and for the wedding photographs. However, if it is to touch hard ground during the service, remember to mask the tip with tape which will muffle the resounding tap.

Bouquets are usually retained for the receiving line. One bride reported that she found her cluster of roses especially helpful as a means of gently warding off bearers of over-enthusiastic greetings or anyone with bad breath.

Silver bells, silver horseshoes and pictures of black cats – all traditional good-luck symbols – can be carried on a ribbon over the wrist. Some critics find these a debased tradition but those in favour ignore such strictures and go on merrily swinging their silver luck.

Underwear

Underwear to be worn with a wedding dress deserves to be chosen with care as the correct decision can shape up the figure beneath, improve the effect of the dress on top and contribute to the wearer's general feeling of security.

If you have a good figure and the dress is complete as it stands, then the less worn underneath it that is compatible with decency, the better.

When underwear is chosen all the finer points of fit and measurement and effect should be carefully checked. If a bra is to be worn it should help to produce a shape which follows the form of the bodice. A bra can make a bosom appear rounder, flatter, more together or further apart, in addition to lending support and uplift. Some ready-made bridal dresses are made with darts which seem to call for pointed breasts – a point to watch.

If a neckline is low-cut or reveals the shoulders ensure that the bra does not make an unscheduled appearance as you move around. Additional security can be provided by sewing safety catches into the shoulder seams of a dress – this will hold wandering straps in place.

If the dress is diaphanous and unlined it is best to choose a bra or body stocking in a skin tone which will merge with nature's hue. The alternative of underwear in solid white worn beneath a see-through white dress will be conspicuously visible. If a slip is to be worn to add opacity to a transparent skirt, check that the lengths and hemlines tally.

Try on all clothes that are intended to be worn together in a rehearsal well ahead of time – even to tights or stockings.

The Trousseau

It is safe to say that the word 'trousseau' is no longer constantly on the lips of girls about to marry. At one time a fine trousseau – a supply of new clothes and linen brought by the bride as part of her dowry – was a major investment on the part of the bride's family.

If the trousseau has not entirely disappeared along with the dowry, it has contracted to a few new possessions for the wedding and after. Buying underwear for the wedding day, a going-away outfit and perhaps some honeymoon clothes is about the sum of it.

As ever, much depends on the attitudes and finances of the individual. There is a tendency to use the event as a good excuse to lay in a few things which may come in handy and for which money may not be found in the future. Some women who enjoy pretty underwear – a traditional item of trousseaux – invest in some glamorous additions. So may someone marrying a man likely to appreciate the gesture. The majority however go cheerfully, if negligently, into marriage barely equipped with a handful of briefs.

The romantic custom of acquiring a new nightdress for the first night of married life is still popular, regardless of the probability of its actual use, and applies alike to couples who are new to each other and those who have been on intimate terms for years.

Going-away Clothes

Going-away clothes have no great reputation for practicality but tend to enable the bride to make a well-dressed exit from the reception. The custom of the bride changing into special day clothes for her initiation into married life has survived the knocks of reality. Often, even when the bride is departing fast in the direction of a spot of home decorating, or leaving on a camping holiday, there is little indication in her dress of her departure destination.

However one aspect of the custom is as valid now as in the past. Going-away clothes present an opportunity to invest in some day clothes that will stand the wearer in good stead for some time to come. Easily the best buy is an outfit that can be worn with a flourish for the wedding wave-off, with a hat or a fur, or flowers or jewellery, and which can revert to a non-wedding role on another day. On hats: a whole generation is rediscovering their appeal but there is little surviving etiquette on wearing one for this occasion.

A further consideration is to select clothes that are comfortable and suitable for the honeymoon form of travel or to choose something that is likely to give good service at your destination.

The Trousseau

IRIBE 1920

8

WEDDING CLOTHES

The Bride's Attendants

When you are planning who will wear what, remember that you are considering the pageantry of a group. The bride and her attendants are linked in the eyes of the beholder, and all the clothes, flowers, colours and ornamentation should harmonize. This is a challenge as bridal attendants are customarily linked by ties of friendship and family but rarely by height, colouring, age, sex or tastes.

Your starting point should be yourself. Once a decision has been taken on the wedding dress, it will provide a basis upon which to make judgements about the accompanying effects.

Looking for clothes that look good together is a question of experimentation, trying out this combination with that and having an inner conviction about the end result. There are few rules, but some devices can help to create the impression of an organized composition. The ideal is that each element should be interesting for itself, and in assembly the whole picture is one in which the sum is greater than the parts. Colour, pattern and style are three keys to coordinating arrangements.

Colour

Don't be afraid of its power at the wedding as colour can add tremendous enhancement, originality and, in winter, the feeling of warmth. Sources of spot colour could be: dress details in the shape of sashes, cummerbunds, edgings, trimmings, braids, buttons, visible linings, petticoats, pinafores, jewellery, shoes, flowers, buttonholes and bouquets.

Sometimes one key colour can be used to good effect. The wedding dress might be in the palest shade of the principal colour, the attendants' clothes in a brighter or stronger variation of the same colour and all the additional adornments in combinations and permutations of the theme.

Do not try to combine too many unrelated shades in one arrangement – a riot of colour may work well in a herbaceous border but clothes are something else.

Do not attempt to match colours in different mediums – a dress pink, a shoe pink, a ribbon pink, for example; the chances are that you will have as many different pinks as items. It may be easier to aim for tones that blend and mix and harmonize in preference to hoping for a happy match.

One practical and entertaining way of drawing up a colour scheme is to use artists' materials such as crayons and paints and inks together with tear-outs and scraps of the actual colours that you want. Keep all the references together on a pad of paper or a notebook and use it as a master plan when shopping, so that you can match the colours accurately.

Pattern and style

When the style of the wedding dress has been decided on, clothes for the supporting cast can be considered. The guiding principle in choosing is to look for styles that work well with the bride's dress, enhance the wearer and look good in the wedding group. Fabrics offer a fine source of ideas for linking the ensemble by pattern.

There are so many interesting possibilities for helpers' clothes that it would be impossible to contain them in a list here. However, certain styles are long-standing favourites at weddings, and a mention of them may provide a starting point for further ideas.

Mostly, these designs are drawn from the fashions of the past which can be brought up to date. Perhaps part of the continuing secret of their success is that the styles have a universal appeal that suits the long, the short and the tall. On the list: Victoriana, Edwardiana, a modification of the Elizabethan dress of Shakespeare's Juliet, the crinolines beloved by the southern belles of America, ladylike 'occasion' clothes from the 1920s, 1930s and 1940s, folk costume, high-waisted flowing Grecian clothes. Many of these provide ideas for small children too, but they have some categories of their own: the dresses and blouses and pantaloons worn by young sitters for Gainsborough and Reynolds in the eighteenth century, the rustic unpretentious dress depicted by Kate Greenaway in her drawings of children in the late nineteenth century; and for boys, military dress, Scottish kilts and shirts and sporrans, sailor suits, velvet trousers and a silk shirt, or breeches with a peasant-style top.

Use the historical associations of period dress as an inspiration but not as a blueprint. You have to guard against exaggerated fidelity, which could turn the wedding party into characters from a costume drama.

Separates are a good idea for bridesmaids' clothes – as they are for the bride herself – on grounds of flexibility and future usefulness. These sets of clothes can be teamed together to achieve an appropriate air of formality for the wedding and combined with other clothes for less formal wear afterwards.

It is best to establish in advance of the day exactly what everyone will wear, down to the smallest detail. Hair-styles, underclothes, petticoats, make-up effects, jewellery, accessories, shoes, stockings, socks and flowers both singly and collectively contribute to the final effect. If everyone is left to follow their own devices, some jarring inconsistencies may occur.

Young Attendants

Ideas for young attendants that go well together where there are several to be dressed, or where there are pages and bridesmaids, include the following: little boys wearing shirts in the fabric of the bridesmaids' dresses; cummerbunds made in the same colour or fabric as sashes; boys' trousers or breeches made to tie in with the colour of the girls' clothes; pages' buttonholes repeating the buds or blooms in the bride's or bridesmaids' bouquets.

Some dress ideas seem to possess a timeless appeal: an all-white or cream scheme in which the flowers, dress, shoes are in shades of white; combinations of white and cream; wide sashes tied around the waistline of ankle-length dresses; pantaloons peeping beneath a skirt; pinafores and blouses; pretty apron skirts; dresses in Liberty prints; velvet dresses with lace collars; all-in-one buster suits for little boys in pale colours; pink or white ballet pumps for girls.

Clothes for the youngest members of the bridal party must be fidgetproof and have secure fastenings. Small children should feel happy in their clothes, especially when they are expected to behave with special decorum. Many parents look on the occasion as an excuse to acquire some agreeable party things for their offspring, and those who are good at dressmaking will probably prefer to make the dress at home. These clothes are invariably expensive and have only a brief life as their wearers will soon grow out of them. Ballet shoes are fairly cheap, but need elastic added across the instep to keep them on.

The rules about children's head wear in a place of worship are the same as for adults. If caps or berets or hats are planned for the boys, these should be removed in a Christian place of worship and worn in an Orthodox Jewish ceremony. It is customary for girls to wear flowers or other decoration in the hair out of respect for tradition.

Bridesmaids' presents

The bridegroom is responsible for choosing and paying for the thankyou presents for the bridal attendants. It is pleasing if the present is a memento of the occasion and has some special association with the wedding. In this category might come jewellery chosen to complement the bridesmaids' dresses on the day of the wedding, an arrangement of dried flowers echoing the selection in the bridesmaids' bouquets, a photograph frame to hold the wedding pictures.

General suggestions: jewellery with the wearer's birthstone, a bracelet or necklet with a charm or symbol, a travelling alarm-clock, a good-quality fountain pen, a box to hold jewellery, an evening handbag or purse, a particularly well-produced art book, an early edition of a book by an author in whom the recipient has a known interest, a framed print.

Small children tend to come in for tokens and savings certificates. Excellent as these are, children are only human, and do appreciate something in the hand on the day. The paperwork, if chosen, could be accompanied by a small plaything. Ideas for presents for young attendants could include: a new board game, a mug with the new owner's initials or name on it, a birthday book, a small photograph album, a small piece of jewellery, a simple camera with some film, any designs by the well-known children's illustrators such as Beatrix Potter or Kate Greenaway, a classic illustrated children's book, a recording either classical or pop, a torch. Cash, though always acceptable, is rarely given on this occasion.

The Men in the Wedding Party

The clothes worn by the bridegroom are determined by religious rites, the social style of the occasion, the bride's family's wishes and the bride's own dress. If the bride's family want morning dress to be worn by the bridegroom at a big white wedding at a place of worship, it is usual to follow their wishes unless objections are raised early on in the proceedings.

If the bridegroom wears morning dress, the other men in the bridal party are expected to follow suit, including the ushers, the bridegroom's father, the best man and the bride's father.

At a small- or medium-sized family wedding the bride and the groom talk over whether it is to be the formality and tradition of morning dress or the practicality and ease of a lounge suit.

At a Jewish wedding, the bridegroom wears a dinner jacket and black tie. At an Orthodox ceremony, his head will be covered by a *yarmulkah* – a skull-cap – according to an ancient rite of Judaism. However, the tradition is dying out at a reformed service.

At a register-office marriage, the dress of the bridegroom is influenced by the type of party that follows. If a formal reception is planned and the bride is wearing white, it is by no means unusual for the man to wear morning dress. The general custom, however, is for a lounge suit to be worn, with a buttonhole and neckwear according to taste.

A wedding is a splendid chance to wear any finery or regalia to which the bridegroom is entitled. The Scots rush into kilts; soldiers, sailors and airmen take to dress uniform. Anglican clergy usually lay aside the surplice and marry in secular dress, with or without a clerical collar according to conviction.

Morning dress consists of dark striped trousers without turn-ups, a waistcoat, a cut-away jacket with tails and a white shirt worn with a tie, stock or cravat. The all-grey morning dress is a favourite at very formal weddings.

Morning clothes can be custom-made at a tailor's where the tradition is to introduce some little refinement or point of difference that adds a personal touch to the formula. It could be in the cloth, the cut of the lapel, the emphasis in the style of waistcoat. To a man's tailor a new morning suit is an inspiration.

The majority, however, who have little need for morning clothes in the usual course of events, will hire everything that is required. The main dress-hire firms have branches in many parts of the country and can supply both clothes and accessories such as a topper, tie or gloves.

The selection of styles for hire – which also includes dinner jackets – has improved in recent years, and so has the sizing system. However, it is important to establish that the right size is available for hire on the day for which it is required as a misfit can lead to embarrassingly comic consequences.

Hired clothes must be returned on time, an obligation which the best man usually carries out on behalf of the groom.

Toppers are usually in grey at the wedding, and are worn out of doors but carried indoors. The groom's topper is taken by the best man on his arrival in church and parked somewhere safe. As the amount of time when a topper is likely to be worn is inevitably rather brief, there is a move afoot to dispense with this accessory, but some people hold that it is all part of the tradition of the day, that Englishmen look good in toppers and that their presence adds uplift to the wedding photographs. If the bridegroom has a topper, the other men in the bridal party follow the form.

Marriage is regarded by many bridegrooms as a good excuse for a new suit and a chance to buy clothes that are likely to be of further service.

Any man who is particularly interested in fashion should take advantage of the opportunities presented by his own wedding. Among some recent sartorial innovations for men at the wedding are the following: the idea of relating some detail or accessory or colour worn by the bridegroom to the bride's effects; a buttonhole that repeats a flower in the bride's bouquet; the bride and groom both wearing white or cream; the groom wearing a tie in a print which echoes a design chosen by the bride.

A frock coat is an interesting alternative to a morning coat and as it is made without tails is more flattering to a wearer who is not notably long in the leg. A lapel brooch in place of a buttonhole would revive an honoured manly custom of wearing jewellery at the wedding.

Going away

When morning dress is worn the groom changes into a lounge suit for his departure on honeymoon. When a lounge suit is his choice for the ceremony no change is necessary and he goes off with his bride as he is.

The Guests

Women

The fact that a group of wedding guests is almost always immediately recognizable as such suggests that their clothes are the signal. The accepted approach is for women to be dressed in a manner that exudes an air of festive formality – the key to the style was set years ago by the English social season and remains unchanged in essence. By everyday standards, it is dressed up, but now there is a lot of latitude in style.

The conventional solution is a hat and attractive day clothes. The vexed question of whether a guest who never wears a hat should buy one specially for the occasion is usually settled in the negative, unless she happens to be a member of the bridal party.

There is an old taboo on wearing black for the occasion because of its funereal associations. Perhaps this still applies to all-black, but an element of black, such as a black straw hat with flowers, seems admissible on grounds of elegance.

Men

If it is known that the men in the bridal party are wearing morning dress and toppers, men guests can follow suit if they wish. However, there are few weddings where morning dress is considered essential for rank and file guests. The usual custom is to wear a lounge suit for a church or register-office wedding, and hats and neckwear are according to taste. At Jewish weddings, which are usually held in the evenings, the men wear dinner jackets and black tie.

When the groom wears a lounge suit, it is customary for the other men in the party to do likewise and to avoid the disparity of appearing splendiferously attired in morning dress.

As an unwritten rule is that dress is not mentioned on wedding invitations, the question occasionally arises as to the best way of indicating the bride's wish that men should wear morning dress. The code can be altered and a line included stating 'morning dress' on the invitation, or everyone can be told by word of mouth or note. A separate handwritten note can be included in the wedding invitation to the effect that as the groom is wearing morning dress, you would appreciate it if the principal men in the party followed suit.

In the usual course of muddled events, there are likely to be inquiries from men as to what to wear. The best answer is to tell them what the groom is wearing and to give a lead as to what is expected of guests.

It should be remembered however that few men actually own a morning suit, and this will have to be hired from a men's outfitters, at some expense to the guest.

Unless the wedding is specially formal, most men wear a lounge suit and a collar and tie. Weddings that take place in the evening and are followed by a formal dinner party may require guests to wear evening dress and black tie.

Boys tend to wear their Sunday best suits for a daytime wedding. Little boys usually wear party clothes. A general rule is that a religious ceremony calls for a certain amount of respect in the clothes of the congregation.

At a civil marriage

Guidelines on dress for guests are more open than at a marriage at a place of worship but the level of formality is keyed to the style of the entertainment following the marriage. If a formal wedding reception is held, the clothes are as for a reception following marriage at a place of worship.

MARTY 1920

9

FLOWERS, MUSIC, PHOTOGRAPHS, KEEPSAKES

Flowers

It is difficult to imagine a wedding without flowers, so closely entwined are their traditions, customs and meanings with every stage of the occasion. Flowers are fresh and lovely in their own right, and offer those who arrange them well a splendid opportunity to make a show of it. It is part of the charm of flowers that they do not have to be expensive florists' blooms. Imaginatively arranged to make a good effect, a handful of well-chosen stems will make a difference to the place where they are put out of all proportion to the cost and effort of arranging them.

Flowers are traditionally worn or carried by the bridal party, and almost everywhere the bride goes flowers await her, at the place of worship and at the reception. There are several different types of flower arrangements that play a part at the wedding and each one deserves thought. There are flowers as personal adornment – such as the bride's bouquet and head-dress or the buttonholes for the men in the party – there are flowers as backgrounds in the place of worship, and at the reception flowers are part of the decoration.

Who pays for what

There is considerably more flexibility these days about the old divisions of costs. Traditionally, the bride's family paid for the flowers in the church and at the reception, and the groom's side paid for the bride's and bridesmaids' bouquets, corsages for both mothers, and buttonholes for both fathers, the best man and ushers. However, it sometimes makes more sense to have one bill from the florist and one cheque in payment.

Choosing a florist

The majority order the flowers from a florist as few people feel sufficiently confident about undertaking the task of doing the flowers themselves – a time-consuming and skilled job and one that has to be carried out immediately beforehand when there are so many other details to be attended to.

As a general rule it is preferable to use a local florist as this will cut down on transport/delivery costs, and also because local suppliers have a vested interest in doing a good job in their locality. You can often judge the calibre of a florist by the condition of the flowers in the shop. If the stock looks cool and fresh and orderly, it is more than likely that the florist will reproduce those qualities in their wedding services.

Try to give the florist as much information as possible about your preferences, prejudices and ideas on colour. They will probably want to know details about the style and shade of the wedding dress and bridesmaids' clothes – fabric samples are a help. They will also want your ideas on the flowers to decorate the church and reception. If the order is a big one, the florist will probably want to make a preliminary visit to the places where flowers are to be arranged well before the day.

Most florists that undertake weddings have a book illustrated with examples of bouquets and posies which will probably be the designs they are skilled in making. Most suppliers will carry out customers' orders but it is sensible to listen to their advice (with the proviso that no one wants to be bulldozed into accepting an idea that is not to their liking). Always arrange for alternatives in case of bad weather or unavailability. All arrangements should be confirmed in writing, including a clear understanding on how the flowers are to be delivered on the wedding day.

A good florist will expect to check the state of the flowers at the church and the reception if they have been arranged on the day preceding the wedding, in order to establish that all is well, top up the water and replace any wilting blooms.

A far from unusual predicament is that the bride expects to receive what she has ordered and the florists send what they can. If the colour of the roses, for example, turns out to be closer to yellow than the specified cream, and yellow fights with the chosen fashion, what can be done? If there is sufficient time in hand, a good florist will try to rectify the situation, if they are responsible for an error. However, it may be that no cream flowers are available and another choice will have to be made. The uncertainty that inevitably surrounds such a seasonal subject as flowers makes it all the more important to give the florist clear guidelines on alternatives that are acceptable and those that are not.

Flower care

Fresh flowers must be handled with great care; they may bruise, wilt, or droop – rather like some humans – if treated badly. Once a stem has been cut, its life expectation is likely to be short. So treat your flowers gently, keep florists' flowers in the box in which they are delivered and always inquire as to the best way of keeping them fresh. Flowers should be kept in a cool place but not in the refrigerator, as all extremes of temperature should be avoided. Spray with fine moisture if they begin to droop. In general the set-piece arrangements in the church or at the reception are assembled the day before the wedding. Make sure that someone is responsible for checking them on the day of the wedding.

It is wrong to throw them out afterwards as there are many places that would like them – hospitals, old people's homes, even neighbours. So find them a good home. At a place of worship, leave the flowers for Sunday Service, then distribute.

The Choice of Flowers

The exact choice of flowers will probably depend on the season of the wedding, which will determine availability. Within the choice, the preference for a particular flower's scent may be a consideration. You will never satisfy everyone on such a deeply personal issue as perfume, so better please yourself. Glasshouse-grown flowers tend to be scentless and are unlikely to conflict with applied perfume. If the chosen flowers are heavily scented, go easy on the perfume and anyway check that bottle and bloom go well together.

Flowers should be chosen according to season. In spring, snowdrops, daffodils, narcissus, primroses, camellias, violets, primulas, tulips, lilac, pussy willow, crocuses, bluebells. In summer the range of possibilities is at its widest, and it is perhaps for this reason as much as any other that June is such a popular month for weddings. Roses, a great favourite, are at their best, and a great many garden flowers which were once considered too commonplace for a bride's bouquet are now used to great effect by florists. Some examples are: daisies, cornflowers, columbines, forget-me-nots, sweet peas, lavender, delphiniums, peonies, gypsophila, pinks and honeysuckle. From the hedgerow there are countless species, including cow-parsley (or to give it its prettiest name, Queen Anne's lace), which adds fresh white fragility to the bunch. In autumn all the harvest festival ingredients are available: deep, rich, russet tones from autumnal leaves and flowers, ripened ears of wheat and barley, poppy buds (poppy petals droop), vine leaves, Michaelmas daisies, fruits and berries on the branch.

The colour of flowers

There are far too many different species of flowers to group effectively according to colour but a rough and ready guide to some fairly widely available types is the following:

Lavender to purple hues: lilac, violet, Michaelmas daisy, sweet pea, iris, orchid, pansy, freesia, clematis, foxglove, delphinium, African violet, lavender, anemone, crocus

Blue hues: cornflower, lupin, delphinium, forget-me-not, hyacinth, bluebell, hydrangea, morning glory

Ivory to white hues: rose, carnation, gypsophila, camellia, magnolia, gladiolus, tulip, daisy, hyacinth, syringa, lily-of-the-valley, gardenia, jasmine, lily, lilac, orchid, chrysanthemum, snowdrop, narcissus, geranium, freesia, stephanotis, stock

Yellow to cream hues: rose, honeysuckle, marigold, gladiolus, tulip, mimosa, cowslip, primrose, primula, daisy, dandelion, orchid, buttercup, chrysanthemum, dahlia, crocus, freesia, broom, jonquil

Pink to mauve hues: rose, carnation, sweet pea, hyacinth, aster, peony, pinks, delphinium, hydrangea, apple blossom, wild rose, clover, geranium, hollyhock, freesia

Red to coral hues: poppy, tiger lily, dahlia, poinsettia, rose, tulip, sweet pea, holly berry, phlox, begonia, zinnia, gladiolus

In winter, effective use can be made of holly, preferably with red berries, mistletoe, ivy, and Christmas roses (helleborus). Other fresh flowers to consider are those which have established themselves as wedding favourites, probably partly due to their extensive season of availability – roses, carnations, freesias, anemones, orchids, gladioli.

The language of flowers

As flowers and herbs carry a wealth of folk meanings and superstitions, these can be a basis for choice. Books dealing with the subject and copies of old herbals are a store of fascinating information on the hidden language of courtship, which can only be touched on here. A first list would include: red roses and rosebuds for 'love', red tulips for 'a declaration of love', scarlet poppies for 'great extravagance', red poppies for 'consolation', white chrysanthemums for 'truth', buttercups for 'memories of childhood' or 'riches', white lilies for 'purity', hyacinth for 'sport, game or play', parsley for 'festivity', mint for 'virtue', violet for 'faithfulness', honeysuckle for 'fidelity', cornflower for 'hope', hyacinth for 'constancy', orange blossom for 'fertility' and 'happiness', lilac for 'first love', carnation for 'pure love' or 'deep love', sage for 'riches' or 'health', rosemary for 'remembrance'.

Flowers at the wedding have a long history in which symbolism and tradition are inextricably intertwined. Hyacinth was a favourite flower for bridal wreaths in ancient Greece and Rome and is still a favourite today; myrtle, with its white, sweet-smelling flowers and lustrous dark leaves preceded orange blossom in the bridal bouquet. It should be remembered here that while orange blossom is thought of as the traditional wedding flower, it is exceedingly difficult to obtain in this country and is fragile and difficult to work with. If wearing or carrying orange blossom is a priority, the owner of an orangery will have to be contacted who is prepared to part with their blossom, and a price must be agreed – it is in flower between April and June. Sometimes, for special orders, the blossom is flown in from warmer climes, but experience suggests that the flowers frequently arrive damaged in transit.

Syringa, or mock orange, is often used in place of the bridal flower, but it is in season only during June and July. It, too, has white flowers and is strongly scented; the scent is very similar to that of the true orange blossom.

Marigold, green broom and rosemary were all favourite wedding plants in Tudor England and deserve to be considered today.

Although few women believe in the superstitions, an understanding of the symbolism of flowers and herbs at the wedding is an intriguing study and puts a fresh perspective on choice. Also a knowledge of the historical why's and wherefore's adds meaning to what can be a routine transaction at the flower shop on the corner.

Historically, flowers at the wedding symbolized fertility. The significantly named 'baby's breath' (gypsophila) with its clouds of miniature white flowers is a strong favourite today because of its decorative qualities; in the past, French brides were said to believe that mignonette – meaning 'little darling' – in the bouquet would hold a husband's affections. The orange tree is a traditional element in love charms and good-luck emblems; Saracen brides wore its flowers as a sign of fecundity and the crusaders are said to have brought the custom to the west.

The custom of the bride throwing her bouquet to the bridesmaids remains as popular as ever. The longstanding tradition is that whoever catches it will be the next to be married.

The bridesmaids at the wedding often carry a bouquet or a posy of flowers. Sometimes, a long garland of fresh flowers is carried as a link between many bridesmaids and this can look particularly good when held by young children. But not if their hands are occupied with managing the bride's train, of course.

As with every part of the whole, the bridesmaids' flowers should be chosen to complement all the other components in the picture – the fashion of their clothes, the colours, what the bride is wearing and her flowers.

AVERY 1921

Flowers for the Bridal Party

The mothers of the bride and bridegroom customarily wear a corsage of flowers but this is purely a question of personal preference. If a corsage is to be worn, the choice of flower should be in a colour likely to harmonize with the clothes of the wearer. Sometimes, all the women guests are presented with buttonholes or flower sprays at the place of worship.

The groom, the bride's father, the bridegroom's father, the best man and the ushers all wear flower buttonholes in their left lapel. Red or white carnations are popular. A more original choice for the groom is a flower that matches the bride's bouquet; or he could wear a sprig of heather for luck, a blue cornflower, or a rosebud.

It is the job of the best man to button up the buttonhole arrangements for the men in the party.

The Bride's Flowers

The bouquet

A bouquet of flowers is traditionally carried by the bride and her attendants, including the young pages, if this is wished. A bouquet of flowers can take a surprising variety of forms – there are the structured, carefully composed arrangements at which British florists excel; small posies, nosegays, a basket filled with fresh flowers, an armful of flowers, or simply a single important stem.

When choosing personal flowers appropriateness is as ever the best yardstick, combined with personal preference for colour, type and perfume. A simple country wedding with an unaffected style of dress calls for a similar theme in the flowers. Formality in dress and soaring ecclesiastical architecture provides an opportunity for more ambitious effects.

Flowers for the hair

Of all the ways in which flowers can be worn as adornment, a head-dress made in fresh petals is one of the most beguiling. Increasingly, very formal veils are giving way to the simpler style of wearing flowers in the hair, which is appropriate for both a religious and a civil wedding. In many more instances, however, fresh flowers are worn in combination with a veil.

Flowers are one of the easiest and most versatile ways of endowing a shining head of hair with a bridal air. Whether your hair is long, short or at an in-between length, there are many possibilities; one flower in perfect shape tucked into the hair at the side; a scattering of tiny flower heads set on florists' wire and pinned in at random; combs, slides, and Alice bands covered in flowers and

Opposite: David Bailey, 1973
Overleaf left: Clive Arrowsmith, 1973
Overleaf right: Mirella Ricciardi, 1980

leaves attached with fine florists' wire, bound in satin ribbon and set to hold the hair in place; a semicircle of flowers worn at the back of the head, to which a trailing veil is attached; a skull-cap made of a base covered in flower heads or leaves; a Juliet cap decorated with flowers; a crown of flowers worn on the brow.

Shoulder-length hair can be parted and rolled back and coiled with ribbons and flowers; long hair can be piled up softly on top and surrounded with small rosebuds and forget-me-nots; short hair can be worn loosely curled with roses on either side of the head, perhaps linked with a head-band or ribbon.

The primary consideration is what suits you and your hair-style. If you need fresh inspiration, the best source is likely to be your hairdresser. Take a selection of basic combs and slides and ribbons and borrow – if possible – a few flowers either real or artificial and ask the stylist to experiment with different ideas in front of a large mirror. When you find the answer, take the idea to the florist and discuss whether it will be practical to incorporate fresh flowers in the suggested style. The major florists are usually prepared to suggest creative ideas for using fresh flowers as head-dress.

Remember that flowers will only last for a few hours without moisture; they will have to be delivered on the wedding day and put on at the last moment, so it is tempting fate for anyone to set their heart on some elaborate floral extravaganza.

Remember, too, that flowers may look beguiling in fashion photographs, but in real life blowy weather can play havoc with the arrangements. One way to secure flowers of a suitable size is to push a fine hairpin through the seed cup or centre of the flower and bend one prong or both back to catch a lock of hair which will hold it in place. Try out the idea beforehand and order extra flowers in case of accident.

Flowers in the Background

The flower arrangements at the church, chapel or cathedral will depend on the views of the minister concerned, who else may be getting married on that day and the procedures for providing flowers in the normal course of events.

The first move is to find out whether anyone else is getting married on the same date and whether it is possible to share the flowers and the costs.

It is courteous to establish whether the minister has strong views about the placing of flowers in the church and to clarify such questions as the availability of the altar, for example, for flowers.

In country parts, church flowers are usually beautifully arranged by people who have the good gardens in the neighbourhood. It could be worthwhile to inquire whether they would be prepared to do something special for your own wedding (if the answer is in the affirmative, it would be a reciprocal gesture to send them a wedding invitation).

The church appointments that are customarily highlighted with flower arrangements are: either side of the chancel steps, the entrance to the church, the high interior window sills down the length of the building, the ends of the pews, the pulpit, the lectern and, sometimes, the altar. It is pleasing to have a small vase of flowers on the table in the vestry where the register is signed.

See also page 33 in 'The Register Office Marriage'.

Flowers at the Reception

When the reception is being held in a hotel or restaurant the flowers are often part of the package deal, which is helpful financially, but which may mean you relinquish your rights to have a say about the choice of flowers or the way these are arranged. Check on the position of the customer here, bearing in mind that the flowers will probably have to be shared with other receptions on the same day. Ask the manager to check with the florist that the colour scheme will harmonize with your own, or that at least there will be no jarring notes.

Many establishments have no objection to an outsider coming in the day before to bring and arrange the flowers. In addition to decorating the reception area with flowers, it is a diverting idea to place a glorious arrangement at the entrance, particularly if there is to be a receiving line, as this provides waiting guests with refreshment for the eye.

Flowers on the dining tables are best kept low and simple so they do not obscure the view across the table. A posy of small-faced flowers can be placed in a miniature vase on top of the wedding cake, trailed round the cake or arranged as a festoon round the base. The flowers on the wedding cake can be related to your wedding theme, or bouquet.

If the reception is held in a marquee, the support poles can be wound round in flowers. The surface is covered in mesh wire and covered in a profusion of petals and leaves. Suspended baskets of flowers work well in these circumstances.

When the party is held in a private household and space is at a premium, flower arrangements should be placed high up – flower pedestals can be hired – in order to leave the maximum amount of room for guests to circulate and to free table surfaces for food and drink.

A new departure in this country, which follows American practice, is to eschew familiar garden effects and to go tropical. Rented palm trees, tropical and exotic green-leaved house plants can decorate the reception rooms as they do offices, banks and public places. Sometimes they can be hired or borrowed.

Cutting the Blooming Cost

Florists' bills can be alarmingly big, and without careful planning it is a simple matter to pay a small fortune for a handful of blooms. The best way to achieve value for money is to consider some alternatives to conventional choices, to have fewer flowers and to concentrate on the points, people and places where every flower counts.

Flowers are there to be admired, so place them where they are likely to achieve the maximum exposure to public gaze. When people are sitting and looking around in the church, waiting in a receiving line, gazing at the bridal procession – this is where the money should be spent. On the other hand, at the reception, for example, there is much to look at and plenty of diversion, so you could economize here.

Use plenty of soft foliage to make a few flowers go further – soft grey leaves, for example, go well with rose-pink flowers; if you live in the country make use of its resources – but a disadvantage of hedgerow flowers is that these lack lasting power and should be picked on the night before use and stood in deep fresh cool water in order to counter their propensity to droop when cut. Harvesters of the hedgerows should note that in summer chickweed and ferns, and in winter old man's beard, are weeds that make good backgrounds for country flowers. Friends' and neighbours' gardens may also prove an inexpensive source of flowers, branches and blossoms, and many florists do not object to using these as long as they can pick the supply themselves.

The bride's and bridesmaids' bouquets could be made at home to simple designs. One idea is a loose posy shape with the stems bound tightly in ribbon.

AVERY 1921

Fake or Dried Flowers

Artificial flowers are coming into their own for several reasons. First, the imitations are now so close to the real thing that, at a glance, fragrance excepted, it is genuinely difficult to distinguish the true from the fake. Secondly, fake flowers are not subject to seasonal limitations. They can be retained for years on end and make a pleasing memento. Fakes are frequently made into head-dresses and bouquets, and can be arranged in a most effective manner with fresh flowers and foliage. Some made-up flower shapes are imaginary and do not pretend to simulate nature, but represent all kinds of unusual possibilities for wedding decoration.

Dried flowers, though extremely expensive if bought commercially, provide a range of colours and ideas, and offer solutions to flower-starved winter brides. Again, these can be combined with fake flowers and fresh ones for special effects. Flowers made from feathers are soft and unusual and come in interesting colours as well as swansdown white.

All these substitutes for growing flowers are a blessing for anyone with an allergy to the fresh kind.

Music at the Wedding

The image of the ringing wedding bell is the emblem of weddings but the music for the ceremony often receives scant attention. The fashion, the food, the flowers are all dwelt on with devoted attention to every detail; the music, however, tends to follow stereotyped lines. Though the set-pieces in the Anglican church tradition are hallowed by time and familiarity, it is surely regrettable that so many expressive and satisfying possibilities should be left unexplored.

The value of well-chosen music for creating atmosphere and mood should not be underestimated. The sound and the beat changes the tempo from solemnity to celebration – the theme of the day. Music pervades the religious ceremony in nearly all denominations and the selection of the music is a reflection of your personality.

There is an enormous repertory of music which enhances and enriches the wedding service. There are hymns, anthems, psalms, marches, processionals, choral music, organ music, solo singing, instrumental music – for example, for trumpet, bagpipes or flute.

Your two best allies in finding a satisfactory choice of wedding music are the minister of the place of worship where the wedding is to take place and the regular organist. They have considered your problems many, many times in all likelihood, and may be able to put you on the right track.

Two important factors will govern your choice of music in addition to the repertoire of the organist. The religious denomination in which you are to be married will have its own musical traditions and taboos and the minister will probably have his own views on what is, and what is not, considered to be a suitable piece of music to be played at a wedding at which he is officiating.

It is generally up to the individual minister to decide and he may permit the playing of secular music in church. The Roman Catholic church, however, is likely to take a harder line if you have an unconventional choice in mind. It is a consolation to Catholics that the church's musical tradition is very rich and brides can take their choice from the wealth of music written for the Mass. Although instrumental music has been an essential part of Jewish weddings for many centuries, the beliefs of Orthodox Judaism have denied other music a place at the service. However at Reformed Jewish marriages, other music is sometimes played.

Finding the performers

Go and listen to the organist playing at the place of worship where you are to be married. It is unlikely that you will discover an unsung maestro in small parish churches but local talent tends to be reliable. It is always better to enlist the cooperation of the regular organist. He may be prepared to play a favourite piece of yours, even if he has to practise an unfamiliar composition.

If you wish to employ an organist of your choice, the decision should be made in consultation with the minister. Also, if doubts persist about the regular organist's capabilities, the minister may know of a suitable replacement. He will certainly be able to give advice on the question of arranging for a choir and bell-ringers.

You may count among your friends musicians and singers who would like to perform or play for you. If this is the case, your preferences should be put politely to the organist and the minister.

If there is no resident choir and you wish for choral singing it may be possible to enlist a local amateur group or a school choir in the neighbourhood. A choir adds richness of tone and enables choral music to be added to the repertoire; choristers will fill the gap when Uncle Joe's sonorous voice fails to reach the top notes. A boys' choir, dressed in white surplices, is a beguiling sight, laced with the promise of elevating singing.

Choosing the Music

The organist and choir will perform best the music they know and like, so have full discussions in order to establish the possibilities.

At most Anglican weddings, for example, there are five basic phases at which music dominates the mood: before the entrance of the bride; the processional to the altar; the singing of the hymns; during the signing of the register; and, finally, during the recessional, when the married couple come down the aisle.

The bride with musical knowledge will need no advice on choosing music for a wedding. Innovators should perhaps be warned against the desire to be different at all costs, and to remember that a sense of the appropriate is, on this occasion, at least as important as a sense of the dramatic.

Given reasonable judgement on your part, it is worthwhile pursuing your ends in the face of opposition from reluctant organists, indifferent ministers or choirmasters, or a mother who wants you to have what she had on her own day. Nor should the inevitable response to a proposal for change in grander church circles ('the Rector would never allow it' . . .) be permitted to put you off without pursuing the idea further.

Before the ceremony
The music played before the entrance of the bride should help to create a sense of occasion. Some of the guests will be moving about, chatting and finding their seats, but others will be glad to sit and listen to the music chosen by you. For this reason it is a good idea to put the titles of the musical arrangements in the printed Order of Service which is handed out by the ushers as the congregation enters.

Never underestimate your friends and relations; they will almost certainly appreciate your efforts, particularly if you have taken trouble with your choice.

You could arrange for an unorthodox choice of music at this stage but many of the congregation will be listening with half an ear. If you wish to choose a piece which will please the majority of music lovers, you would be safe with compositions by Bach or by the Victorian S.S. Wesley, who has become almost as established a ceremonial composer as Handel or Purcell. Three familiar favourites at this point are: Nimrod from Elgar's Enigma Variations; Sheep may safely graze, by Bach; and passages from Handel's Water Music.

The processional
The music at the entrance of the bride is usually soft and solemn, but it should also be triumphal in message and the opposite of gloomy. Often a hymn is sung. Your choice of music at this point is limited by two practical details. The first concerns the length of the aisle. You should try to time how long it will take you to walk its length, as you do not want to find yourself standing foolishly at the chancel steps waiting for the music to end nor to have to scamper across the floor in an uneasy silence. A hymn is a good solution, since it can be stopped at

any verse, or repeated as necessary. The second point to bear in mind is tempo. You do not want to have to gallop up the aisle in unseemly haste nor to have to walk painfully slowly in order to keep in time with the music. So try to choose music which the organist will be able to play in a tempo that you will find comfortable.

The processional music, if not a hymn, could be one of the old favourites: the 'Wedding March' from 'Lohengrin' by Wagner or the 'Wedding March' from the incidental music to *A Midsummer Night's Dream* by Mendelssohn. Both of these have, however, suffered somewhat from over-exposure, and the Wagner March not only has some school-boy words attached to it – 'Here comes the bride, short, fat and wide' – but is also, as the musicologist Philip Hope-Wallace has pointed out, a fairly inauspicious choice in that if ever a wedding night ended in disaster it was Elsa's to Lohengrin. Other possibilities might be: the 'Wedding March' from Mozart's 'Marriage of Figaro'; 'Trumpet Tunes' by Purcell; the 'Trumpet Voluntary' by Jeremiah Clark; 'The Arrival of the Queen of Sheba' by Handel; or Bach's 'Sinfonia' from 'Wedding Cantata'.

The hymns

You will probably have time for three hymns. Since this is the moment when all the congregation joins in, it is as well to choose both words and music that they will enjoy. Everyone likes a good, rousing sing, so those quiet, contemplative numbers that may have moved you in the past could fail to unite a wedding congregation. Almost every churchgoer will have their own particular favourites, but there are several aspects that should be considered in making your choice. First, make sure that you read *all* the verses of the hymns you are considering. Some of the words of the most popular hymns are inappropriate for a wedding. This need not mean that you have to rule out those hymns. Either ask the minister to tell the congregation to omit the offending verses, or, if you are having the words printed on the service sheet, simply instruct the printer to leave them out. The second point to remember is that there are often alternative tunes to certain hymns, so make sure that your organist knows which one you want. The most familiar is usually best, as there is nothing worse than trying to sing a favourite hymn to a tune you don't know. Thirdly, make sure that your organist plays the hymn in a key that is acceptable to most people; the hymns in many hymn books may be pitched unnaturally high or low for untrained voices.

The most popular hymns are the 'praise' and 'love' hymns: 'Praise, my soul, the King of Heaven' (Queen Elizabeth II's entry music at her wedding at Westminster Abbey); 'Praise to the Lord, the Almighty, the king of creation'; 'Come down, O Love divine'; 'O perfect Love'; 'Love Divine, all loves excelling'.

Other favourites include: 'Lead us, Heavenly Father, lead us'; 'Dear Lord and Father of mankind; 'The King of love my Shepherd is'; 'O worship the King'; and Blake's 'Jerusalem'.

Many people find the rhythm of psalm singing difficult, and tend, as a result, to garble the words. If there is a choir, they will give a firm lead, but if not, it might be wiser to confine your choice to the familiar settings. Two much-loved psalms on this occasion are psalms 121 ('I will lift up mine eyes') and 23 ('The Lord is my Shepherd') to the tune of 'Crimond'.

Music for the pause

The music played or sung during the signing of the register is essentially a means of bridging a gap in the proceedings of the service. Music lovers might commission a solo singer, or an instrumentalist or, if funds permitted, a string quartet. (Music colleges, universities with music courses, the music press and the Musicians' Union are sources of information on available musicians.) Or musical friends might be willing to perform here.

At the pause in the events, during the singing, remember that people will be chatting, albeit in a subdued way, admiring the flowers and probably perusing the bride's mother's hat, so a decision will have to be taken as to whether you wish them to be aware of your music, or whether a familiar piece by Bach or Handel which acts as a musical background, might not be more fitting.

The recessional

After the signing of the register, the music for the procession down the aisle should be jubilant and joyous. Many of the pieces that are often played at the entry of the bride are, however, also suitable for the exit of the bride and groom and the bridal party. A good effect can be achieved with a piece that starts quietly and grows to a triumphant climax. Some favourites are: Widor's Toccata in F, Karg-Elert's 'Now thank we all our God'; Handel's Firework Music; Pachelbel's Toccata in C; Bach's Fantasia; and Mathias's Processional.

A Carillon of Bells

Peals of bells are as much a part of the wedding day as the cake and the long white dress. If the church you are to be married in has bell-ringers the organist can arrange for them to be there on the day. Otherwise it may be possible to engage their services from a neighbouring parish. Again, the minister or the organist can advise. It is worth trying to have bell-ringers, as they broadcast the good news with a joyful peal of bells ringing out across the scene in a manner for which there is no substitute.

Recorded Music

Some people like to play taped music at their wedding. This can be done providing the permission of the minister is obtained but it requires an expert who will be able to judge the acoustics and the effect in the church. The tape will afterwards be a treasured memento.

Fees and Tips

The organist will usually want a fee for his duties, particularly if the programme has included difficult or unusual pieces. Occasionally, his fee is combined into a 'package' with those of the minister and the bell-ringers. These should be paid by the best man on the groom's behalf either at the beginning or end of the service.

Music at the Reception

The departure of the bride and groom for the reception need not, however, spell the end of the musical entertainment for the day. Many a reception has been immeasurably enlivened by the addition of music, either live or taped. Whether you plan to have dancing or not, music at the reception always adds a diversion and a celebratory note. The choice should reflect your secular musical tastes and could range from a string quartet to a jazz band or a mobile discotheque. Much depends on the style of the reception, but do remember that if your party is to be a family affair, you should try to vary the music in the programme. If you are holding your reception in a hotel or restaurant, the manager may be able to organize the musical entertainment for you.

If you are organizing your reception yourself, ask around amongst your friends and family for ideas. The Musicians' Union or The Royal College of Music might be able to help, and if you want pop or rock music, there are plenty of advertisements in newspapers and in the Yellow Pages for mobile discotheques. Another idea, and one which could work out substantially cheaper, is to play a taped selection of favourite music on a good tape-recorder. A juke box can be hired with your selection of records.

Photographs

Photography has improved spectacularly, both technically and as an art form, in recent years. It seems strange, therefore, that wedding photography should be the one area which has lagged behind. It is often the case that one of the most important days in people's lives is recorded in a stiff, stultified way – or with photographs that are badly composed or out of focus.

It is really worth spending the time and trouble to find a photographer who will be able to provide you with a memorable record of a special day that, after months of preparation, passes in a flash. The photographer may be one of the smaller cogs in the wedding wheel, the results are of lasting value.

There is a world of difference between an imaginative professional wedding photographer and someone who does a routine job of work. You may have a friend or relation who will offer to take the pictures at your wedding, but, however keen they may be, you will be taking a risk in entrusting them with the sole task of recording the day. A professional photographer is undoubtedly a more reliable choice. Of course, that doesn't mean that your friends should be discouraged from bringing their cameras to the wedding. As long as they don't have final responsibility it won't matter if they get carried away by the festivities and forget all about taking the photographs.

Your professional photographer need not be a specialist in wedding pictures, but it will help if he or she has done this work before. Ask around in your neighbourhood – it is better to find a photographer who lives in the locality and will not have to drive a long distance as this will obviously increase costs. Visit several different photographers and ask to see some examples of their work. Find out what their charges are. Remember that the most expensive will not necessarily be the best, nor the cheapest the best value for money. Photographers' fees have risen steeply in recent years, mostly due to the increased price of film production and processing, but because of the immense pleasure brought by photographs it is wiser to try to make economies elsewhere.

When searching for your photographer, bear in mind that he or she should be quick and efficient, and, if possible, cheerful and conscientious. Above all, it is important that you should like him. Remember, too, that he will be mixing with your guests. If you and your guests warm to the photographer, it is more likely that he will be able to get good pictures.

If you are impressed by the work of the photographer you have chosen, it is more than likely that he or she will be able to take photographs of a similar standard on the day. On the other hand, it is unlikely that a photographer whose work you do not really like will be able to produce work significantly different, however impressive the sales talk.

Once you have decided on your photographer, discuss with him exactly what sort of record you would like of the day. A formal group shot may be a pleasant memento of everyone together, but do remember that it takes some time to set up and it is difficult to ensure that everyone is looking their best at the same moment. Formal groups often look posed and unnatural, but they are usually popular with older members of the family, so it's worth considering. A good photographer should be able to relax everyone so that they look happy and

R de LAVERERIE 1936

natural, but you should try to avoid fixed grins and toothy smiles. Ask your bridesmaid or your mother to bring along a mirror and a comb so that you can have a quick tidy up while the photographer is setting up his equipment.

The happiest record of a wedding is often captured by informal shots taken with a hand-held camera throughout the day, known in the trade as photo-reportage. Depending on the light conditions, the photographer may or may not need to use flash, but most people look better in natural light, so encourage him to photograph without artificial light where possible.

The photographer may make a selection of prints and send them to you after the wedding, but if you prefer to select your own, do ask for the contact sheets to be sent to you first. These are miniature prints of the photographs in black and white, which are relatively cheap and easy to print.

Tell the photographer how many people will be at the wedding, give him a list of important family and friends that you would particularly like photographed, and tip him off if there are any awkward family situations of which he should be aware. Whether you choose colour or black and white film is essentially a matter of personal taste. The photographer may have his own preferences, in which case you may have some persuading to do if there is disagreement. The considerable technical improvements in colour film, and its accuracy of reproduction, have made colour the most popular choice for wedding photography. It is felt that colour adds detail where detail is significant, colour provides the richer account, and that as life is seen in colour, so should be the wedding.

Colour is much more expensive to reproduce at present than black and white. Mounted transparencies are an option but these require a slide viewer for display. The merits of black and white film should not be overlooked. Some of the greatest portraits are taken in black and white by well known photo-graphers, and black and white is the medium for reportage.

One approach in wedding photography is to arrange for colour to be used for the group shots, and to photograph the action and the faces in black and white.

You could ask the photographer to come to where the marriage is to take place and to the reception venue before the wedding so that he will have a clear idea of the possibilities in advance. If you do decide that you want some formal group shots, remember that it may be unwise to rely on having them taken out of doors without having taken the precaution of settling on alternative locations; if it is cold and blustery, everyone will appear frozen and miserable. Remember that your guests cannot leave for the reception before the bride and groom, and will probably be looking forward to their champagne, so try not to keep them waiting too long. There may well be more time to sit for photographs at the reception before all the guests have arrived. One stratagem is for the bride and groom to wait until the reception is well under way, and then slip off quietly to another room with the photographer. Most hotels will be able to make the arrangements.

Photographs of the best man, the ushers and the bridesmaids can be taken before the wedding itself. Although a competent photographer should not need coaxing to capture the highlights of your wedding, he does need to know your personal plans and wishes. You might like the idea, for instance, of having photographs taken of the bride, her parents, the groom and his best man, before the ceremony. Other possibilities before the wedding include: the bride putting the final touches to her appearance, setting off with her father and arriving at the church; the guests arriving at the church. Earlier on, the photographer could take some pictures of the flowers, the cake, and perhaps the interior of the church decorated for the wedding. Sitters sometimes worry about the fact that their physical peculiarities are going to be perpetuated in the photographs, and wonder how best to handle the problem in front of the camera. Sometimes the photographer can help here, and in some cases, regrettably, not.

Two by no means unusual causes of concern are the following. When the bride wears glasses she may be bothered that the light will catch her lenses and be refracted, to the detriment of her appearance in the photograph. It is as well to tell the photographer that you will be wearing glasses but this is such a widespread practice that he or she will have come across the problem many times before.

When the groom is shorter than the bride there may be some concern that this disparity of height will become the focus of the formal studies. One solution in this instance is for the bride to be shown seated, and the groom to be shown standing by her side, which restores idealized comparative proportions to the pair in the picture.

As a general rule however, the most evocative photographs on this occasion show the sitters as their natural selves, albeit in a good light.

If you want to have photographs taken inside the place of worship ensure that the minister does not object, as some feel that the use of flash is an unnecessary intrusion on the privacy of the ceremony. If permission is given, a discreet photographer would be able to take pictures of the bride and her father going up the aisle, the couple at the altar and signing the register, and the bridal group coming out of the church. With today's advanced technology in films and their processing, it is also possible to take pictures with little natural light and without flash by using fast film. Ask your photographer whether he thinks this would be possible in your case.

The reception offers many chances for pictures which catch spontaneous action and unselfconscious expressions. The famous photographer Norman Parkinson (who took the wedding pictures of Princess Anne) once said, 'the best photographs of the bride are those that combine happiness, humour and the maximum of naturalness'.

Some moments that you may want to make sure that the photographer covers are the cake-cutting ceremony, the toasts and speech-making, the couple leaving in their going-away clothes, the bride throwing her bouquet. Apart from these highlights, he will catch other good moments himself simply by circulating amongst the guests during the reception.

Make sure that your photographer has all the facilities he needs on the day – electric plugs for flash and any other special requirements or props – and that he knows what will be happening and who are the main participants.

Instant print photography is simple, but it is limited in its scope. These photographs should therefore not be regarded as a substitute for conventional photographs, but rather as a source of alternative shots obtainable without fuss or difficulty by an amateur.

Keepsakes

A souvenir is meant to be a personal reminder, and may be almost anything; sentiment can turn the most humdrum scrap of trivia into a precious memento.

Wedding photographs are easily the favourite form of record; cynics have gone so far as to suggest that much of the paraphernalia of the wedding is done for the sake of the photographic record.

Prints can be framed, blown up to poster size, or arranged in an album to form a pictorial record of the event from the dressing of the bride to the final going-away wave. The instant colour camera, though an expensive form of photography at present, can be carried by the amateur and used to snap all the odd, rueful, funny, strange, humorous situations during the whole planning of the wedding as well as recording the day itself.

From the wedding ceremony itself there is of course the wedding dress to preserve, or the veil if of special interest. The flowers chosen for the bride's bouquet can be dried and pressed and possibly framed. If you do plan to press flowers it is important that these should be perfectly fresh so it is likely that duplicate flowers will have to be used. The flowers from the bouquet could also be made into a pot-pourri of petals, which will scent a room or, placed in bags, will sweeten linen cupboards and wardrobes.

If the bride carries a prayer book during the ceremony this can be signed on the flyleaf by all the guests present. The menu card or place cards can be signed as a keepsake. Other possibilities include keeping the cork from the first bottle of champagne opened at the party, or the first bottle shared by the bride and groom; inscribing the pen held during the signing of the register with the date; framing an embroidered handkerchief carried by the bride in her purse or choosing the purse itself as a souvenir. An elaborate ambitious project which might commend itself to an embroiderer is to invite the guests to sign their names at random on a plain linen or cotton tablecloth and to pick out the calligraphy in embroidery. A simpler notion is to embroider a sampler with the name of the bride and groom and the date of the wedding.

If you want to have something specially made the possibilities are plentiful and interesting. Many imaginative craftsmen are prepared to undertake such commissions. A traditional example is engraved glass, a potentially beautiful souvenir. The glass must be of good quality to make the engraving worthwhile. Engraved drinking glasses, goblets, wine glasses, or a bowl or a flower vase are all suitable subjects for treatment. An engraver is commissioned and you work out the details of the design with him. The engraving could consist of your names and the date of the wedding, or a monogram in which the initials of the bride and groom are decoratively entwined. Ceramics are full of possibilities for commemorative pieces too. Craftsmen potters will undertake small commissions of this kind and produce cups, bowls, pots and decorative pieces, bearing a reference to the couple and the day. Many craft shops will arrange for existing work to be inscribed with names and dates. However, a commissioned work is a one-off and is unlikely to be cheap.

A less expensive plan is to compile a 'keep-book' in which all manner of printed mementos, scraps of experience, and snapshots can be incorporated as a record of the wedding. The sort of items which might deserve a place are the wedding invitation and any specially printed stationery, samples of fabric from the dresses, the published photograph or sketch that triggered off your selection of wedding dress, handwritten cards accompanying wedding presents, and so on. Ready-made albums are available but you can make your own, adding as much detail as you care to include. It is worth remembering that if photographs and cards and samples of the wedding stationery are to be kept, they will look better and last longer on good-quality paper.

Another approach is to buy something specially rewarding for the house which you keep for its own sake rather than for its practical function. This might be a print, a picture, a lamp, or a well-produced book, or whatever gives you pleasure.

Those lucky enough to have a garden might plant a sapling tree, a rose bush or some herbs in memory of the wedding. A house plant is a strong contender but there is the dreaded prospect of it withering on you, with all the attendant unfortunate implications. Best for the green fingered.

An exchange of presents of jewellery between the bride and groom is a traditional way of giving and receiving a personal keepsake. For men the possibilities can include: a watch, cufflinks, wedding ring or a necklet and pendant if he would wear one. For women: the ideal is likely to be a piece that she will wear frequently as it seems a waste for the gift to be kept most of the time unworn in a box. However, if someone in the family wishes to make a generous gesture, the occasion of marriage is a traditional moment for giving the bride an investment-level piece of precious jewellery which could be designed expressly for evening wear.

An increasingly popular idea in wedding mementoes is to have the day recorded on film, sometimes even with an accompanying sound track. In the church itself, it will again be necessary to get permission for this, but at the reception a movie camera can provide a record of your wedding in a way that still photographs could never capture.

And if you are going to film your wedding, it is as well to record all the sounds that go with it – the service itself, the wedding bells, the toasts, speeches and the reading of the telegrams. A tape-recording of the church music, the bride and groom making the responses, can bring back all the excitement and emotion of the day in a powerful and unusual way. Remember to have a rehearsal beforehand to check the acoustics – whoever is organizing the recording will have to stand well forward in the church to catch the sound. You may feel you dare not entrust this to an amateur, in which case employ a specialist – he could even turn the recording into a disc for you. A less complicated alternative is to invest in professional recordings of the pieces chosen for the ceremony. The speeches at the reception can easily be recorded on tape, and so can the music played at the reception. If a disco dance is part of the proceedings the taped music makes an excellent souvenir.

The ultimate in wedding souvenirs must be a video recording of the day. It is a good idea if you own a video cassette recorder, or are likely to, or know someone who might lend one. It is, however, possible to hire the equipment.

1929

10

THE RECEPTION

The reception after the marriage can be what you make it. Although the marriage ceremony is bound by rites, laws and ritual, the celebrations afterwards are for fun and fraternization. There are customs, but no rules.

All manner of parties are held today in the name of a wedding reception although common to all the most successful occasions lies a great deal of thought and organization. As far as the set-piece procedures are concerned, these can be followed to the letter, as some can be adopted and others discarded, or the event can be treated as a good party without the wedding formula.

A reception can be held at any time, anywhere appropriate and for as many or as few people as is wished. Hospitality can vary from a glass of something and a nibble through to a sit-down feast with fine wines.

The traditional justification for holding the party is to enable the two families to meet on friendly ground, for thanks to be expressed, for presents and support to be given to the newly-weds and for the first few hours of married life to be full of congratulations, sociability and champagne.

Despite the challenges involved in entertaining a somewhat disparate group of people who are likely to be linked only by an interest in the welfare of the bride and groom, the rewards can be considerable. People who might never have run across each other in the usual course of life can take pleasure in each other's company, generation gaps can be surprisingly overcome, old rivalries tempered, and long lost friends and relations restored to the circle.

When considering the options, a mercenary factor has long accompanied and coloured such deliberations. The material benefits that are likely to accrue from holding a big party may well tot up to a far bigger sum than the catering costs. Many newly-weds do very well for themselves from the presents and proceeds that flow from a big party, though the charm of this investment may well be lost on the father who pays the bill and has no need of a new toaster.

Although in practice most people who accept an invitation to the wedding do feel they should contribute an offering, this owes more to the spirit of generosity than to etiquette. There is no obligation on a guest to send anything.

Who is Invited

Everyone who is invited to the wedding ceremony is also asked to the party afterwards. But not necessarily the other way round. Sometimes only a few people can attend the actual marriage ceremony – when the marriage is held in a small place of worship with limited seating, for example, or at a register office marriage where there are no facilities for numbers of guests.

As many people as you wish can be invited to the party alone, although there is nothing against the idea of confining the reception to family only, plus a few close friends. Sometimes, two parties are held, in which case the guest lists can be separate. When the formal wedding reception comprises a small family party, occasionally a bigger party is held later on for friends of the bride and groom. However, guest lists always have to be arranged with tact, making allowances for the feelings of excluded members who hold they have a right to be asked to all the fun that is going.

The officiating minister is invited to the wedding reception and so is anyone who has made a special contribution to making the occasion a success.

The Traditional Reception – Step-by-step Procedures

The traditional wedding reception follows a minuet-like order which has the advantage of familiarity to both hosts and guests. Before dispensing with traditions, it is a good idea to consider why they have survived, as in many cases they serve an unchanging practical function.

The line-up

The point of a receiving line is to enable the bridal party to greet all the guests and to make introductions to new members of the family. The line-up is usually composed of the following people, in this order; the bride's mother and father, the bridegroom's mother and father, the bride and groom, the bridal attendants. On the side of this custom is that its observance enables the bridal party to say hello to everyone and nobody is overlooked. Also, at a party where many people are not known to one another, a line-up signposts who is who.

Against the idea is that the procedure lacks spontaneity. The handshaking and kissing holds up the flow of the party as people wait in a queue with their eyes wistfully fastened on a far-off tray of drinks. Among widely practised expedients is to shorten the line by allowing the bridal attendants to join the crowd, or for the bride and groom to receive guests on their own.

After guests have been greeted the next step is for the couple to circulate among the guests, trying not to overlook anyone who might feel an outsider, or to spend too much time with Uncle Joe who has stumped up a healthy cheque.

The cake-cutting

The cake-cutting ceremony takes place immediately before the toasts and speeches. The bride and groom together cut the first slice of the wedding cake, which in wedding folklore is a symbol of fruitfulness and fertility. The most practical advice – particularly if the cake has a firm icing – is to bravely thrust the point of the knife, held at an upright angle, through the sugar, and to make successive sawing movements. An attempt to use the blade like a lever and to press it down may meet with a crumbly resistance. The cake is then cut up during the speechmaking and handed round after the last joke.

One way of expediting procedures is to have a spare tier on hand that is cut up in advance ready for serving. If cake is to be sent to friends, it should be cut to fit into the boxes. Some couples like to keep a tier for a future christening, others reserve it for Christmas. Sometimes sherry is served with the wedding cake: this was a Victorian custom.

The toasts

After the cake is cut and whatever type of food is being offered has been served, and after glasses have been replenished, the toasts are proposed. The bride's father or the best man or a close friend of the family proposes a toast to the health of the couple with the words 'to the bride and groom' or, more informally, 'to Anne and Robert'. Glasses are raised and the contents sipped or swigged. The speech that follows can be brief and usually recalls incidents, anecdotes relating to the relationship between the bride and her family or the bride and groom. Bawdy references are best kept to a minimum, and if a blush is to be provoked, the best excuse is a really funny joke.

The bridegroom replies and thanks the bride's parents for the wedding, using their first names if this comes naturally, and also including his own parents in the thankyous. Everyone should be thanked for coming to the wedding, and this is an opportunity for a warm expression of gratitude for gifts received or about to be received. The bride's parents are always included in the thankyous irrespective of their financial contribution to the occasion, on the basis that without them, it could never have happened in the first place. (There seems to be no reason, now that women have found their voices in public, why the bride should not add her own vote of thanks to the family and the guests, but at present this would be a departure from tradition.) The groom's speech is rounded off by thanking the bridal attendants, whose health he proposes in a toast to the bridesmaids. The best man replies on behalf of the attendants. As a general rule, there are no more speeches after this, but if there is a good speaker in the house and he or she has not yet spoken, now is the moment. All the speeches are best kept reasonably short. (See also pages 187–8.)

After the last speech, the best man reads out any congratulatory telegrams that have been sent by absent friends and relations. As this is a strictly family audience, it is a good idea to omit any shockers.

Going away

Someone should be detailed to make sure that if the married pair have a train or plane to catch, they change into their 'going-away' clothes in good time.

If tradition is to be maintained the bride and groom change separately. The bride can continue the old custom of being attended by her bridesmaids who help her to dress. When the groom changes, the best man is expected to chivvy him along, lending a clear head, moral support, and a willing arm with the luggage.

The suitcase containing the bride's going-away clothes and honeymoon clothes should be brought to the reception place in advance. A small point is that if this suitcase is stowed away in the boot of the car before she takes her leave she may need some spare make-up in the changing room. It has happened that the bride has supplies of make-up at home, make-up packed in the suitcase, but not even a lipstick to hand when she changes.

It is best to get a move on with changing. While you are deliberating on the shade of lipstick or hunting for a pair of tights, the guests may be having an extra glass or two; and some may be anxious to leave, but cannot depart until you do.

Parents usually say good-bye at this point and the couple rejoin the party for a send-off. This can take many forms. One tradition is for the wedding couple to run through an archway of hands as in the game, Oranges and Lemons. Often, the bride throws her bouquet – an old custom – for it to be caught by someone as a memento. Rice, confetti, or real or paper petals are thrown at the departing pair. If this last idea prevails, supplies are handed round in advance. However, confetti throwing is becoming less popular due to the litter it causes. Rice is easier to shake out of clothes than confetti.

When the couple depart by car, it is highly likely that some spark will have emblazoned the pronouncement 'just married' on the rear window, or tied on a trailing tin can. While this may be a cause of embarrassment to the couple concerned, it provides a lift at the moment when the party is virtually over, and cynics can always ponder on the predictability of human nature.

Party Options

Wedding receptions today are held in pubs, halls, reception rooms, hotels, restaurants and at home. The type of party is likely to be influenced by the timing of the marriage ceremony, the expectations of the guests, whether friends and relations have travelled a distance and will be in need of a decent meal, the facilities where the party is to be held, and of course by the budget.

Any party can be given a special theme (beyond being a successful occasion), which is expressed in the arrangements, decor and design, flowers, music and entertainment.

A sit-down lunch or dinner

A sit-down meal provides the chance for a top table with traditional seating arrangements; seated guests tend to feel well done by, and the generous hospitality repays everyone for their support. If wished the bride and groom can lead the way to the top table. The general rule is to time the wedding breakfast sometime in the afternoon and for the guests to be waited on.

A buffet party

The advantage of choosing a buffet party is its lack of formality. It also enables the party to enjoy food and drink without incurring major service costs. There are many variations, however, in the balance between total self-sufficiency and as near to a waited-on meal as makes no difference. Guests can do all of the work, some of it or practically none.

The usual procedure is for guests to help themselves from a table and to return for seconds or the following course. The party is cleared up by the hosts or the caterers. Sometimes guests help themselves to the main course, and are waited on for the wedding cake, dessert, and coffee. Help-yourself service can be combined with the comfort of sitting down to eat when tables and chairs are provided.

When a buffet meal is served at a standing reception the food should be easy to manage – no drippy sauces or delicacies that disintegrate. A practical test is whether the ingredients are easy to eat with a fork only. One imaginative hostess solved the problem by serving small juicy hamburgers eaten with a helping of fluffy creamed potato, which helped to secure the meat on the fork.

A drinks party

This can be held at any time of the day or night and the major costs are the drink and service. The food can be eaten with the fingers – either hot and/or cold, savoury and/or sweet. Hot sausages, mince pies, small patties, bridge rolls, crisps, nuts, dips and vol-au-vents are staple choices. If the party takes place in the afternoon, tea-party food offers possibilities with a choice of teas to drink, cakes, sandwiches, biscuits and treats of a strawberries-and-cream sort; sparkling wine and champagne for the toasts.

A party breakfast

If the ceremony takes place early in the day a celebratory breakfast would be sustaining and give special meaning to the term that covers all the food on this occasion – the wedding breakfast. Edwardian breakfast food might fill the bill – scrambled eggs, kidney and bacon, poached haddock and egg, kedgeree, egg and bacon – with Buck's Fizz to drink (made of orange juice and sparkling wine or champagne). An alternative is an American Sunday brunch menu – bagels, cream cheese, smoked salmon, spring onions, lashings of coffee and vodka and tomato-juice cocktails.

Dancing at the nuptials

As a celebration, a dance offers an unrivalled opportunity for protracted merry-making, and is of special appeal to everyone who might otherwise be feeling a bit flat after the early departure of the bride and groom.

A dance can be a grand occasion or a get-together in a local hall; it can be held at a restaurant with a dance floor, at home (if there is space) or in a garden or a marquee. Dances are held at hotels, motels, pubs, hired rooms and halls.

In the Church of England, marriages may not be solemnized after 6 pm. If the congregation is to wear evening dress, it is courteous to have a word with the minister in advance in order to establish that the idea has his blessing. Register offices, too, close at 6pm. At a synagogue, late afternoon and evening weddings are traditional, and are customarily followed by a dinner-dance. The timing of the ceremony may mean that there is an inconveniently long interval between the marriage and the party, and if guests are invited to both it may be necessary to make arrangements on behalf of people with nowhere to go.

Big hotels will shoulder all the work, for a price, and undertake to book bands, and arrange the food and drink and flowers. There are package deals available. In London the five-star hotels will lay on whatever is ordered and have been known to fulfil the bride's fantasies by transforming a ballroom into a grotto or a garden.

It may be possible to hire a restaurant with a dance floor for the evening or, if the party is fairly small in number, a table could be booked and special arrangements made on an evening when the public are admitted as well.

Local halls are a popular choice. This will call for a disco or a band – information can be found in the music press. If live music is played, the group will need to take a break from time to time and the interlude can be filled with music on pre-recorded tapes or records. A juke box is a jollification with your own selection of records.

When choosing a location remember that too much space is a positive dampener on a dance which depends on atmosphere as well as the willingness of guests to move away from the walls and to get going on the floor. A long-standing tradition at dances is for the newly married couple to take the floor for the first dance.

Broke girl's dance

A wedding is a time when the knowledge that you want a thing may encourage other people to give it to you. One enterprising host provides an example of what can be done with some support, some money and a soaring wish. She booked a local hall. She commandeered the goodwill and time of several friends and relations who agreed to contribute the food, flowers and help in place of conventional wedding presents. She cooked numerous turkeys before work (she worked full-time), and cut them up for the freezer in the evening. She borrowed cutlery, serving dishes and so on. On the day the turkey was served hot in a spicy sauce, and friends brought salad dishes, cheese, fruit and alternative main dishes; her father and the groom split the wine bill; the only professional employed was a disc jockey.

Live entertainment

Providing live entertainment at the party introduces a diversion, and is a way of helping to make the occasion specially memorable. All the entertainers, artists and performers whose talents traditionally enliven social gatherings have a place at the wedding reception.

Singers, dancers, soloists, instrumentalists, pianists, musicians and classical and pop performers of many kinds, together with entertainers with a good act, can each and every one be booked to appear at private parties.

A favourite at outdoor weddings during the summer months is a troupe of Morris dancers to add a village green festivity to the proceedings. Pipers and drummers are traditional ceremonial at Scottish receptions. The English and the Welsh revere brass bands. A chamber music ensemble playing pieces from their repertoire fills the space with the sound of music, and seals up the holes of awkward silence that may occur at the beginning of the party when the guests file in and the two sides of the family are strangers to each other.

If a dance is to be held, the host is spoilt for choice as far as dance music is concerned, paralleled by the number of groups playing in the different musical styles. A diverting luxury is a contrast of music, for example, to alternate a big band sound with reggae or rock and roll.

Watchword: be wary of offers to entertain by friends – the result may well be considerably more fun for them than for the captive audience, which may long to break free. Accomplished non-professionals are, of course, honoured exceptions to the general rule.

The Caterers

Choosing a caterer

Plenty of time to compare estimates and services is important as places known to do a good job tend to get booked up for months in advance. Always obtain at least three estimates before making a final decision and always confirm everything in writing. Try to get a personal recommendation or, in the absence of one, gain some experience of the caterer's level of service. If holding the reception in a restaurant, a hotel or a pub, try to order a meal there. One guideline is to take note of the level of punctiliousness and care in the handling of your inquiries. If the firm seems efficient at this point, it is a hopeful indication that they will look after you efficiently on the day of the party.

The exact number of guests expected should be confirmed with the caterer a week before the date of the reception. As charges are usually on a per head basis, the number of guests confirmed will be charged for, whether they turn up or not. If additional guests arrive, and there is a sit-down service, expect extra charges to be incurred.

It is important to be clear in your own mind as to your requirements. The problem here is that you may have to take decisions before you are fully aware of what you want. A caterer will need to know the answer to four questions: the date and timing of the wedding reception, the numbers of guests involved, the type of hospitality to be provided – with or without a meal – and the limits on an approximate price per head.

How much drink?

As drink is so expensive, and as the general rule is that wedding party guests will drink every drop that is provided and still be waiting for more, some compromise has to be worked out between being a generous host and the cost of the hospitality. Meanness is ill advised and runs counter to the whole spirit of the occasion, which is not a necessity but a voluntary celebration intended to give pleasure.

How much wine per head is a constant source of debate, with serious drinkers belittling the usual reply of half a bottle per head and abstainers perceiving Bacchanalian dissipation in the same measure. An average of half a bottle of wine per head should be sufficient at a drinks party, but guests will drink more if a meal is served. Soft drinks should be provided for non-drinkers and young children. A cup of coffee or tea is always welcome.

A long bar where guests can refill their glasses is an undoubted joy to serious drinkers, but is likely to lead to a greater consumption of liquor than if drinks are circulated on a tray. This method enables the caterer to control the supply of drink according to an earlier briefing by the host.

If a cash bar is to be operated it is important that the guests know where they stand. The usual practice is for the hosts to offer a welcome drink and a drink for the toasts, and additional supplies to be paid for by the guests. A cooperative barman is essential and he will expect to be included in a round of drink and to be tipped as well.

A check list
Check out the following points:
- Does the bill include the hire of rooms? If not, what are the charges?
- Will there be additional charges should the party continue beyond the usual two or two and a half hours allotted to a wedding reception?
- Is there sufficient time built into the schedule between the planned end of your party and the next one on the caterer's order books?
- Can the customer supply flowers and, if so, who may arrange these and when? Are flower containers available for the purpose?
- Is a microphone available should one be needed?
- Are cloakroom and lavatory facilities sufficient for the number of guests expected?
- If a cloakroom attendant is required is there an extra charge?
- Will a changing room or rooms be required for the bride and groom and is there an extra charge?
- Are high-chairs to hand for the very young?
- Are there facilities for wheelchairs should disabled guests be expected?

The caterer will set up the rooms for the type of party ordered and clear up afterwards but this may not apply when the party is held in a local hall.

There are endless possible extras, which may or may not carry additional costs depending on whether you have accepted a 'package deal' or are paying for individual items as ordered. Some people want a red carpet outside the entrance. Others wish to display at the party their presents with cards bearing the names of the donors. A toastmaster can be a help at a big wedding, keeping proceedings rolling along on time, and is of special value when the host is reluctant to undertake heavy hosting duties. In each and every case, establish costs and arrangements in writing.

Catering costs have a strange way of mounting despite every attempt to nail them down in a final figure. Establish at the beginning details on two likely sources of cost increases – service charges and tipping. Is there a cover charge in addition to a service charge? Will the staff expect to be tipped on top of the set 'service' charge? The caterer will probably murmur that it is up to the individual customer. The answer to the question of whether the service charge goes to the business or the staff may have a bearing on your decision here. If there is no service charge, tips will be expected (10–15 per cent is usual).

Choosing the food

Wedding receptions as a general rule are not noted for good food and drink and there are many lost opportunities. In these days of fast food, junk food and standard dishes, people really do appreciate any sign that trouble has been taken over the menu and wines. An original dish, an imaginative idea, or an interesting choice of wine can enliven hospitality which can readily become stereotyped if some thought is not given to it.

The food does not need to be elaborate or very expensive but should be good of its kind. If ham and chips are on the menu, the ham should be tasty, the chips crisp and plentiful.

One of the problems inherent in catering for a wedding reception is that the party is likely to include vegetarians, meat-and-two-veg addicts, the old and the very young, the pickers and the dieters. As no meal is likely to give equal pleasure to everyone, there is a case for pleasing yourself in offering guests what you would like the occasion to be remembered by.

Fresh food in season is always the best value. One main dish – whether hot or cold – may have more impact and interest than lots of accompaniments. However, an alternative, however simple, such as a fish salad, cooked rice or other vegetable, should be provided for those who dislike the main offering. Remember that barbecue food, picnic food, classic English dishes, regional dishes and simple, home-made food are general favourites.

Caterers are likely to have a standard menu at fixed prices but it is worth inquiring about the cost of a special order – perhaps economies can be made elsewhere in the budget which would enable one of the firm's specialities to be served.

As the final item is likely to be the wedding cake – let this taste as good as it looks. Anyone who has enjoyed a matured, rich, fruity, spicy cake with its traditional covering of almond paste and sugary icing knows that this is a fitting culmination to a feast. Perhaps a friend would make one as a wedding present. If need be, this can be iced by a professional.

An Unusual Location for the Party

The popular choice for a location for a wedding reception is the neighbourhood's favourite place for the event. However, if you want an unusual location for the party you will have to look further than the Yellow Pages. Possible contacts for premises are any group, guild or club with which you or your fiancé are associated, or with which either family has connections.

If the party is going on from the place where the marriage takes place, the distance to the party venue should not exceed about twenty minutes by car.

Banqueting and conference rooms might offer a possibility. Inquire at the local Town Hall, as local authorities act as custodians of spacious old houses, and it may be possible to hire the reception areas.

Restaurants offer all manner of food specialities and can be colourful and entertaining. If numbers justify it, some proprietors are prepared to close the doors to the public for the afternoon or evening. Some may have private rooms that can be hired. However space is usually limited and surprisingly few restaurants can accommodate many more than forty people at a sitting.

If the party is to be held in a pub, unless there is a bar which can be closed to the public, the reception will have to be held during afternoon closing-times between 2.30 or 3 pm and 5.30 or 6 pm. A public house with a garden might offer more flexible timing.

If moving off the beaten track, it will probably be necessary to arrange for your chosen premises to be licensed to serve alcohol. A temporary licence to consume alcohol can be granted by the Magistrates' Court. The local police station will advise on how to make the application. Good parties have been held aboard a boat, at a zoo, in a theatre, on a pier, in a barn, around a swimming pool and beside the sea, so be resourceful.

Jollying up the village hall

A village hall always represents good value, but sometimes the atmosphere is redolent of a girl guides' meeting, or the baby clinic. If the place is to take on a festive mood the space will probably need colour, flowers, lighting, music and a decorative table. As catering facilities are traditionally elementary, it is best to keep arrangements simple, and not to overlook the convenience of disposable plates, table coverings and napkins. Printed wedding stationery, initialled table napkins and menus, books of matches and pretty place-cards can play a part in enlivening the table setting. A lot can be achieved by tricks of lighting – candles, spot-lights, coloured lamp bulbs.

Clearing away is as important as setting up the hall for the party in this communal amenity. Everyone concerned should be aware of their re-sponsibilities and who is disposing of the rubbish.

A party at home

A wedding is at heart a family institution, and where better to celebrate it than at home. There is a sense of privacy and ease about a party held in private surroundings which eludes festivities held in the impersonality of hired reception rooms.

Women who have the resources and the space at home, and parents with the inclination, avow that there is no substitute for being in familiar surroundings on the day of marriage, and leaving as a married woman through the front door of childhood and dependence.

But many practical points should be taken into consideration before a firm decision can be taken to hold the party at home. Does the available space tally with the numbers on the guest list? Could the list be pruned in order to keep the priority of a home-based reception? The space question is crucial and is not exclusively a matter of standing or sitting room, but of the availability of many ancillary and support services. Lavatory, bathroom and cloakroom facilities, the size of the kitchen, are all questions to be assessed. Car or coach parking facilities may deserve consideration, too.

Wedding presents

Wedding presents can be displayed at home whether or not the party is held there. This is a long-established custom that enables neighbours, friends and relations to inspect the spread of presents (which should be insured).

In a marquee

The allied prospect of holding a party in the garden in a marquee is steeped in summer romanticism but here too the logistics must be realistically assessed. Is the garden of a size to accommodate a marquee of the required size? (One for sixty people measures 60 × 60 ft, 18 × 18 m.) Unless the parents are prepared for the lawn to be trampled underfoot, special floor-boards will have to be laid, incurring additional costs. However, should a marquee fit in with plans, many catering firms will work from vans. This brings in extra kitchen services and reduces the pressure on the cooking area indoors.

Borrowing a house

Generous relatives or friends will sometimes lend their house for a wedding party. The address is given on the wedding invitations and in all formal announcements in the usual way without reference to the name of the owners. One of the most important practical provisos, if friendly relations are to be maintained, is for reliable arrangements to be made for clearing up after the party. Most lenders will expect the house to be returned in good order – assuming that this is the state in which it was lent – and for the borrowers to accept full liability for breakages, damage, and wear and tear.

The Self-catering Party

Having the party at home is one thing, keeping the catering in the family is another. Anyone who plans to organize a full-scale wedding reception at home without professional help needs a meticulous order of work, undiminished energy, an optimistic cast of mind and dependable helping hands. If a sit-down meal is to be served with hot food, the ratio of helpers to guests – using a caterer's figures – is one pair of hands to ten guests.

The success of the operation will depend on delegation, borrowing, hiring and attention to detail.

Depending on numbers, all except the most lavishly equipped householders will need to supplement existing equipment from ashtrays to chairs to saucepans. For people living within delivery distances, almost all the goods that are needed for a party can be hired. Hire firms will supply small tables, trestle tables, chairs, china, cutlery, glasses, plates, linen, table accessories, ashtrays, flower pedestals, waste-paper baskets, a cake stand and silver knife for the cake cutting, an urn for boiling water for tea and coffee, and druggets to cover the flooring. The last is not a faddy point as the cost of hiring druggets to protect the carpets is a fraction of the expense of having carpets cleaned professionally if spillages should occur.

If a dance is planned, a portable parquet floor can be laid for an evening.

Planning ahead

Almost the first move is to arrange for a promise of a loan of deep-freeze space for a month before and for refrigerator space for three days before the wedding. Borrowing human skills is as relevant as soliciting equipment when the host is working alone; we may live in a selfish world but most people are prepared to help out at a wedding. So if a friend or neighbour is prepared to assist by baking the cake, icing it, supplying or arranging flowers, helping to cook some of the dishes and so on, accept the offers: and don't hesitate to suggest the idea yourself. People will enjoy participating.

The order of work

Tables can be laid the night before, the flowers arranged and the drink delivered. On the day the following posts may need to be manned: *the household* – someone other than the mother of the bride should be delegated to deal with last-minute contingencies, calls, the doorbell, telegrams; *the kitchen* – by whoever will oversee last-minute stages of food preparation and dishing up, and who will be responsible for checking that all the dishes thoughtfully prepared in advance do in fact make their scheduled appearance on the table (a source of understandable aggravation is to discover, at the end of the day, some delicious sauce untasted in a forgotten basin); *the buffet table* – even when guests help themselves it keeps proceedings rolling merrily along if there is assistance on hand to help with the service.

How much drink?

Arrangements will have to be made for storing and chilling the white wine or champagne. On the day the bottles can be bedded down in the bathroom in a bath filled with ice, but the post will have to be manned if access is to be safely maintained, and the inevitable jokesters warded off from locking themselves in with a Bacchanalian supply of the blissful white grape.

It is always best to order drink on a sale or return basis; allow an average of a bottle of wine per head when a meal is served, and about half a bottle per head at a drinks party. Some compromise will have to be struck between profligate generosity and parsimonious limitation. If people are permitted to help themselves they will consume a far greater quantity than if the host controls the circulation of drink and filled glasses are handed round on a tray. The bar will need a bar-person. Never any difficulty in finding volunteers for this one but you will need a dependable collaborator.

Planning the menu

No serious cooking should be done on the day itself, save in the unlikely event that someone is prepared to exempt themselves from attendance at the marriage ceremony in order to remain in the kitchen.

Most of the dishes will have to be cooked in advance and stored in a deep freeze which will to some extent determine the choice of recipes. Another limiting factor is the kitchen, the equipment, the size of the oven and the size of pans. When assessing whether to serve a hot course or not – in theory a hospitable idea especially when guests have travelled some distance – it should be borne in mind that reheating one course is a major palaver in a small kitchen. If you go ahead and serve a heated dish, this may call for a hired oven, boiling plate or hot trays. When planning amounts of food, remember that if a choice of dishes is offered for one course, people tend to help themselves to some of each in preference to making a meal of one. Also, guests usually eat more of the hot dish than of the cold, whether the occasion takes place in winter or summer. A general guideline to timing is to be aware that no matter how minutely the day is planned every kitchen activity takes almost twice as long as is expected.

Choosing the dishes

Elizabeth Jane Howard, the novelist, writing about the wedding breakfast has commented that 'enough is by no means as good as a feast'. This is the right approach and is not a matter of extravagance but of the care and consideration that goes into all entertaining.

The food at a wedding party at home can be an opportunity for a good cook to indulge in culinary labours of love. The gesture is likely to be appreciated by the many who wish the occasion to be associated with excellence in every way.

This is not the place in which to explore detailed recipes but a few general observations may apply: if simplicity and value for money is a priority, serving one principal dish with its proper accompaniments may be a brighter answer than attempting a range of composite dishes. A whole salmon and its sauce, or a handsome cut of beef, lamb or gammon are always popular.

The advantage of entertaining at home is that everything can be arranged as the host wishes – so if a new recipe or favourite family food is wanted, it can go on the menu. If experiments are to be made, it is wise to try them out on the family beforehand so both cook and consumer know what to expect.

The drinks party

A drinks party makes fewer demands on the host than serving a meal. Drinks and a bite to eat and a wedding cake can be managed with only a few helping hands unless large numbers are involved.

The advantages of a drinks party are the freedom from complicated organization, the relative low costs and the flexibility – a few additional people, latecomers and extras, can be easily accommodated. The timing is easy too – the event can take place at any hour of the day or night.

The disadvantages are almost wholly experienced by the guests. The very young, the elderly, anyone who has had to travel a distance may find a drinks-only party somewhat unrewarding. Also, as so much to do with the wedding centres on convention, account may have to be taken of the fact that in some communities a wedding party is not considered a wedding party without a decent meal. However, in the metropolitan centres and among many groups a drinks party is the conventional way of celebrating a wedding.

Small eatables, finger foods of a nibble-and-bite type, are usually served; drinks are circulated on a tray. Miniature hot sausages, savoury dips, crisps, bridge rolls, nuts, sandwiches, little patties are the staples of cocktail-party food. A compromise between offering a proper meal and just a snack is to provide some treat in addition to the usual cocktail-party provisions. A cheese fondue, French pâtés, a cheese board with a wide selection of English and imported varieties are the kind of thing which is suitable. In summer, ice-cream with strawberries or raspberries and cream is appealing.

Seating Arrangements at the Top Table

There is a traditional seating plan at the top table for the bridal party at a sit-down meal. The placing is designed to accommodate all the usual members of the wedding party in which both sets of parents are present and correct. However, changes in the old order may have to be made in order to accommodate new partnerships, or re-marriage, divorce and separation, as well as taking into account family frosts and friction.

The seating plans below show the traditional top table seating plan together with some suggestions for meeting some unexceptional exceptions to the rule. The bride sits on the left-hand side of the bridegroom. Usually the officiating minister is included in the top-table guest list.

The bride's parents as hosts

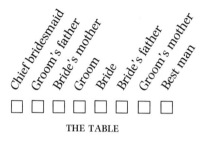

Chief bridesmaid · Groom's father · Bride's mother · Groom · Bride · Bride's father · Groom's mother · Best man

THE TABLE

This seating arrangement also applies if the bride's mother and stepfather are the hosts. If the bride's mother and father are hosts and she has remarried and her husband is present he can be seated next to the chief bridesmaid.

The bride's mother as host

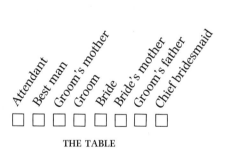

Attendant · Best man · Groom's mother · Groom · Bride · Bride's mother · Groom's father · Chief bridesmaid

THE TABLE

The bride's parents as hosts and bride's stepmother present

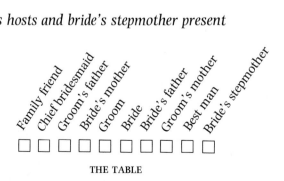

Family friend · Chief bridesmaid · Groom's father · Bride's mother · Groom · Bride · Bride's father · Groom's mother · Best man · Bride's stepmother

THE TABLE

The bride's parents as hosts and bride's stepfather present

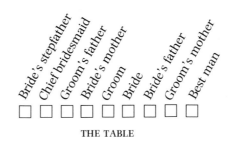

The bride's parents as hosts, and both her step-parents present

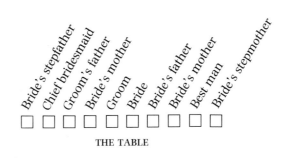

The bride's parents as hosts, with groom's parents and stepmother present

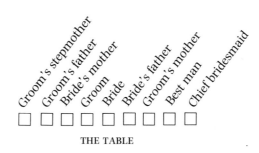

The bride's parents as hosts, and groom's parents and stepfather present

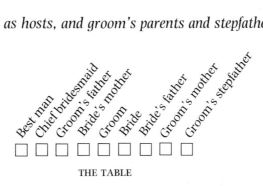

The bride's parents as hosts, groom's parents and step-parents of both present

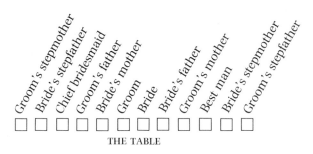

Bride and groom as hosts without parents

The bride and groom sit side by side, the bride on the left of the groom; the usual parental places can be filled by whoever gives the bride away, or by the best man, bridesmaids or close family friends. At table, the sexes are usually separated but nothing untoward need occur if this custom is ignored.

Double wedding with brides' parents as hosts

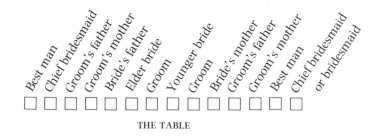

The Usual Problem of Unusual Family Circumstances

A wedding can bring out the worst in family relationships especially where there is bitterness in the aftermath of a divorce or break-up of the family. The appearance of new partners in public may well provoke resentment and uncover old wounds. There are no easy answers, and the obviously tolerant approach – to forgive and forget for a day – is no doubt much easier said than done. However, in some small way, the minor currency of etiquette, which regulates the small change of human behaviour, can be called on as a pacifier.

In the seating arrangements it is best to separate the divorced parents, if possible, and keep the present partners together, bearing in mind that the natural parents of the bride sit either side of the happy pair (see pages 184–6).

Divorced or remarried parents can stand together in the receiving line, but if this causes embarrassment the bride and groom can greet guests on their own, and parents and step-parents can mingle in the crowd.

If the bride's father insists on the presence of his second wife and this is offensive to the bride's mother, the step-parent can be present in the role of a distinguished guest. In this case she is one of the congregation and the crowd but does not fulfil a parental role in the formalities. One way of easing the potential abrasiveness of the situation when the bride's mother is without a partner is to take great care to ensure that she is accompanied at all times by friends or family. The rare tactful relation should be rallied to the cause. If there is an available man friend of the mother, send him an invitation at once.

Many offspring know their stepfather or stepmother better than their biological father or mother and a great deal of affection may exist between the two. In such a case if the bride's father is willing, the stepfather takes over the father's role at the wedding.

When the bride's father is giving his daughter away and the bride's stepfather is present as well, one way of distributing the honours is to ask the stepfather to make one of the speeches.

It can happen that feelings are beyond mending even for the few hours of the occasion. Apart from appealing to parents to take the larger view, to recognize that this is the bride's day and her wishes should be respected, there is no other course of action but to keep arrangements as informal as possible. A buffet party or a drinks party can cast a merciful anonymity over warring factions.

Making a Speech

There is an established routine about the order of speech-making at a wedding and traditions about who says what (see page 171). Many speeches would be twice the speech if they were half the length. As a guide, a foolscap sheet of paper typed in double spacing holds about 430 words and takes about two and a half minutes to deliver at a reasonable pace. Think hard before going over on to that third sheet.

Speak naturally. Use simple words. Do not fall into the trap of supposing that the formality of the event demands the language of pomposity. If the prospect creates serious feelings of anxiety, it is always possible for the speaker to announce that he (or she) does not wish to hold up the festivities with a long and tedious speech, state the purpose of the speech – thankyou, a toast and so on – and leave it at that.

The making of a good speech on this occasion depends on having something to say that the audience wishes to hear. Entertaining anecdotes, inside knowledge of the relationship between the two families or the background to the courtship of the marrying pair are the making of good listening on this occasion. However, a sincere comment or two will be highly acceptable and the undemanding nature of the wedding audience may well convince a hesitant speaker that he has missed his vocation. Clearly, an experienced speaker who is associated with the couple will have a particular pleasure in putting his talents to effective use.

Don't rush it. Talk about one third slower than you normally would. It is a sound idea to learn the lines if the address is to last for more than a sentence or two. By all means make a note or two on a card with the main points. But reading a speech means the talker's head is down and he misses eye-to-eye contact and loses his audience. Remember that the end of a short speech is as important as the beginning. Phrases such as 'that's about all I have to say' are decidedly an anticlimax – unless they signal a release from further clichés. So before you start decide on how you are going to finish.

Speeches are not essential at weddings. Some people prefer to omit them, particularly at a reception following a civil wedding or a second marriage.

The Wedding Cake

The rich cake has been part of the wedding breakfast since the days of ancient Rome. Its origins, like so many on the wedding day, are rooted in traditions of fecundity and fertility. The rich fruit cake, tiered, iced and decorated, reached its apotheosis in Victorian times, when chefs and cooks deployed incredible flights of fancy to create examples of the art of cake decoration.

The ritual of the bride cutting the first slice has its origins in a wish to ensure a fruitful marriage. The modern bride may be thankful that the old custom of physically breaking the cake over the head of the newly wedded woman has been superseded. The guests would scramble for fragments of the cake, which were said to bring good luck; this belief is retained in the peaceful custom of sending pieces of cake in cake boxes to absent friends.

A break with tradition
As people invent their own forms of celebration to suit themselves, the style of the wedding cake is no longer confined to the traditional white-iced rich fruit cake. Sometimes a big, iced chocolate cake is served as an alternative to a formal white wedding cake. Silver and chocolate and white and chocolate have a natural decorative affinity. A cake design can express all manner of personal ideas and interests – a suggestion is given on page 194.

The home-made wedding cake
Few people would dispute the fact that if one had the time and skill and inclination to produce a home-made wedding cake it would be a very much

more satisfactory effort than the run-of-the-mill bought kind. The following detailed recipe is for a two-tiered cake for a small to medium-sized reception. The bottom tier will be plenty for the reception and packing in boxes to send away to absent friends. The top tier can be kept in the traditional manner, for the christening cake or for Christmas. The flavour and keeping properties of the cake described here are excellent, and as it should be made at least three months before the wedding, there is no worry about it being a bother during the last hectic days before the occasion.

BARBOUR   1930

The Cordon Bleu wedding cake (two tier)
This recipe by Muriel Downes of the Cordon Bleu School of Cookery is, in its class, simple and can be iced by an enthusiastic amateur, but as expectations are high in wedding cake icing it would be wiser to rely on a practised hand.

The cake needs to be baked in 12 in (30 cm) and 7 in (18 cm) round cake tins. Choose drum-type cake boards 14 in (36 cm) and 8 in (20 cm) respectively. Pillars, cake-boards, and icing pipes can be obtained from most high-class bakers and large stores, and you will need to find albumen-based powder for the royal icing, and white almond paste in packs for the marzipan if you do not wish to make this yourself.

If you would prefer a square wedding cake and do not want to go to the expense of buying cake tins specially, the mixture can be baked in cardboard boxes, well lined with greaseproof paper. The depth of this particular cake is $3\frac{1}{2}$ in (9 cm). With the aid of a long, clean ruler, it is easy to get the top of a round cake smooth and level, but the sides are never so simple and for this reason a white satin ribbon should be used to decorate them. This should measure $1\frac{1}{2}$ in (4 cm) wide and give a highlight to the otherwise matt surface. You could stand a liqueur glass of fresh flowers on top of the cake, echoing a colour from your dress, your bouquet, or the reception room itself.

The Cordon Bleu wedding cake – the recipe

A two-tier wedding cake for a small to medium-sized reception. It should be made at least three months before the reception date.

INGREDIENTS

4 lb (1·8 kg) sultanas

2 lb (0·9 kg) currants

1½ lb (0·7 kg) seedless raisins

12 oz (340 g) glacé cherries

6 oz (170 g) finely chopped
   candied peel

2½ lb (1·1 kg) plain flour

1 level teaspoon salt

1 level teaspoon ground
   cinnamon

1 oz (30 g) cocoa

1 pinch ground nutmeg

grated rind and the juice of
   1 lemon and 1 orange

2 lb (0·9 kg) butter

2 lb (0·9 kg) caster sugar

4 oz (115 g) ground almonds

1 tablespoon black treacle

18 eggs

½ pint (0·3 l) brandy

First prepare the cake tins, lining well with greaseproof paper. The cake is rich and so will not stick to the tin. Tie a band of thick brown paper round the outside of the large tin.

Clean and prepare the fruit. Moisten with about half the brandy, cover and leave to soak overnight. Cream the butter until soft, beat in the grated orange and lemon rinds with the sugar. Beat well until the mixture is light and fluffy, then stir in the cocoa, spices and black treacle. Now add the eggs one at a time, beating thoroughly with your hand, or in an electric mixer. Sift the flour and salt and fold in with the ground almonds. Add the rest of the brandy and the lemon and orange juice and lastly the fruit. Turn into cake tins, smooth off the top with a palette knife dipped in water. This moisture helps to prevent the cake top from becoming too hard with the long baking. Have the oven set at mark 3 (325°F, 170°C) and allow five hours baking for the larger cake and just under three hours for the smaller one. The cakes may be covered with a double thickness of brown paper when they are brown and it is wise to reduce the heat to mark 2 (300°F, 150°C) after two to three hours.

When cooked it is advisable to leave the cakes in the tins for about an hour or so before turning them on to a cake rack. Do not remove the greaseproof paper but, when they are quite cold, wrap in several more thicknesses of greaseproof paper and store in an airtight tin. Like all very rich cakes, they are best when made three months before you plan to eat them. If you wish, during the storing times, the cakes may be unwrapped, pierced several times with a knitting needle and well sprinkled with brandy. This can be done two or three times, but only pierce the cake for the first sprinkling. Rewrap and store when this is done, preferably in a cool place.

Almond paste

INGREDIENTS *(This recipe makes about 2 lb or 0·9 kg)*

1 lb (0·45 kg) ground almonds	juice of ½ lemon
10 oz (285 g) caster sugar	1 tablespoon sherry
6 oz (170 g) icing sugar	½ teaspoon vanilla essence
1 large egg	2 tablespoons orange flower water
1 egg yolk	

Place the dry ingredients in a bowl and mix together; whisk the egg and extra yolk with the remaining ingredients and add this to the mixture of almonds and sugar. Pound lightly to release the almond oil and knead the mixture with the hand until smooth. Almond paste should be put on about a week before the icing. A wedding cake should have at least two coats of royal icing before it is decorated. This ensures a good white colour.

The 7 in (18 cm) cake should be covered in the following way. Brush the cake thinly with hot apricot glaze. Place the almond paste on top of the cake, roll it so that it covers the top and falls down the side. Dust your hands with icing sugar and smooth paste on to the side of the cake. Turn it upside down, press to flatten the paste on top and roll a bottle around the side to give a clean edge. For the 12 in (30 cm) cake, brush the top only with hot apricot glaze. Roll out half the marzipan to about the size of the cake top. Use caster sugar to prevent it sticking to the pastry board. Lift the cake, place it upside down on the almond paste and then cut and mould the marzipan flush to the edge. Turn the cake over. Knead the remaining marzipan into a long sausage, roll out with the rolling-pin to the depth of the cake. Trim the edges and brush the paste with apricot glaze. Press this strip round the cake and make a neat join. Finish by rolling it with a jam jar. For the two cakes make up about 7 lb (3·2 kg) of almond paste. You will need about 5½ lb (2·5 kg) for the larger cake and the remainder for the smaller cake.

Apricot glaze

Turn 1 lb (0.45 kg) of apricot jam into a saucepan and add 4 tablespoons of water and the juice of ½ lemon. Bring slowly to the boil and simmer for 5 minutes, or until the mixture is thick. It is then ready to use.

Royal icing

INGREDIENTS

2 lb (0·9 kg) icing sugar	2 tablespoons lemon juice or
4 egg whites	orange flower water
1 teaspoon glycerine	

Pass the icing sugar through a fine nylon sieve; whisk the egg whites to a froth and add icing sugar a tablespoon at a time, beating thoroughly between each addition. Stir in lemon juice or orange flower water and the glycerine. Continue beating until icing will stand in peaks. The bowl should be covered with a damp cloth when using icing. Give the cake two flat coatings of royal icing before starting the decoration. The first coat need only be quite thin. The next day, coat again and allow to dry before decorating. You will require about 5 lb (2·3 kg) of royal icing for the large cake and 2 lb (0.9 kg) for the small one. The amount of icing depends on the number and thickness of coatings.

Decoration

For icing the cakes, use the following pipes:

No 1 plain pipe

No 2 plain pipe

No 6 star

If you are not very experienced and wish to undertake the icing, it is wise to practise before piping these cakes. Make up $\frac{1}{2}$ lb (0·2 kg) batch of royal icing and practise on the bottom of a cake tin. This is improved if a little of the icing is spread over the tin so that you have a good base on which to pipe.

To serve as a guide line for the scalloping on the cake tops, cut a circle of greaseproof paper, 5 in (12·5 cm) in diameter for the top tier and 10 in (25 cm) in diameter for the bottom. Fold the circle in half three times to make a shape rather like an ice-cream cone. Cut a shallow semicircle from edge to edge at the rounded end of the cone and open out. You will then have a guide for piping the scallops. Place each guide on top of the cake.

At the side of each cake, pipe a fine guide line 1 in (2.5 cm) from the top and another 1 in (2·5 cm) from the base of each cake. You will then be able to fit a ribbon between the two lines.

Before starting to pipe on the cake, mark the edge at regular intervals with diagonal lines made with a No 2 pipe. This is easily done if you continue the arc taking the point of the scallop over the edge of the cake down to the guide lines at the side. Fill in the gaps $\frac{1}{8}$ in (3 mm) apart, working from left to right. Repeat the lattice working from right to left with a No 1 plain pipe, making sure that the lines are exactly on top of the first lattice. Now fit the ribbon between the two lattices at the side of the cake with the aid of a little icing along the top edge of the ribbon. Pipe the bottom lattice from the horizontal line to the cake board, taking care that the lines correspond with the top lattice. Finish all the lattice edges by piping a fine shell border with a No 6 star pipe, which should overlap the ribbon at the side. It is probably easier to make a separate bow to trim the ribbons around the cake, so that if you should make a mistake, you will not have to cope with creases. Pretty flowers to use for the decoration on top of the cake are miniature roses, stephanotis and hyacinth bells.

MARION APPLETON

The initials cake – a break with tradition

This idea for a home-made wedding cake takes the shape of the forename initials of the marrying pair. The design of this cake and the following instructions for making it are by Sue Mann.

MARION APPLETON

Buy each of your initials in a large, simple style (Letraset from office stationers). Place the letter under tracing paper, trace and outline with a square the depth of the letter. Divide this square with nine horizontal and nine vertical equidistant rules.

Lay a sheet of 9 in (23 cm) square graph paper under a larger sheet of greaseproof. Enlarge your letter, treating the squares of the graph paper in the same way as the small squares you have drawn over your original letter.

Following the shape of the letter square by square, you will finish with a 9 in (23 cm) tall letter drawn on the greaseproof paper. This will be exactly the same as the original letter you chose. Use this letter as the template or guide for shaping your cake and marzipan topping.

And so to the cake itself. Use a recipe for a rich, close textured fruit cake, which will best hold its shape when cut. (See wedding cake recipe on page 191.) Each cake can be made in a 10 in (25 cm) square.

Place the template of the letter shape on the cake, and with a sharp, long-bladed knife, carefully cut your cake into the initial shape. Watchpoint: it is essential that you keep the knife as vertical as possible to keep the cake square at the corners.

Your cake is now ready to be iced. The first step is to prepare it for the marzipan layer. Marzipan does not adhere to a fruit cake without help. The traditional base is an apricot glaze (see page 192). Each initial requires about two or three tablespoonfuls of jam. Using a pastry brush, apply a thin layer all over the cake, paying particular attention to the sides. Allow to set.

Roll out your marzipan using icing sugar to prevent the paste from sticking to the rolling surface of pin. Half an inch is a good thickness, although you can vary this. Take your greaseproof template of the initial, and cut out your marzipan topping around it. The sides can be made out of strips the depth of the cake.

The next stage is to cover your cake with the marzipan. Since it is cut in a thick layer, be careful when you handle it not to let it stretch. Lay it gently on to the cake, and gently press the sides into place. Level off the top with a rolling pin, and smooth the joints with your fingertips, making sure that the top and the sides stick together firmly to make a seal. Place the cake on a substantial base. Ice the cake with two thin coats of royal icing (see pages 192–3) and also supply a thin layer of icing on the surrounding base.

The last stage is the decoration of the cake. The cake can be decorated with small green leaves and pink rose buds made in coloured marzipan, which can be arranged on the initials so as to define and enhance their shape. First the leaves: draw a leaf shape of the appropriate size on a piece of card. Colour enough marzipan for all the leaves by kneading in a few drops of food colouring until the streakiness disappears. Roll out the marzipan until it is very thin, and use the template to cut out each individual leaf. Fix the shapes on to the cake with a little stiff royal icing. Make small rose buds out of deep pink marzipan. Start with a tiny conical shape. This is the base of the bud. To make each paper-thin petal, take a small ball of marzipan between finger and thumb, and tap it into a broad petal shape. Fold this around the base, and make more petals to complete the flower.

1920

11
PRESENTS

A Wedding-present List

How to get what you want, in the nicest possible way, are the often conflicting objectives. Only a few bold souls have a ready answer to the question, what would you like for a wedding present? The position of the bride is that she knows perfectly well what she would like but hesitates to roll off the make, brand, colour, and size, in case this sounds grasping. Also, the suggestion might cost more than the inquirer had in mind; or, worse, be much less interesting.

Wedding guests generally send a present – but there will be people who do not attend the party who may wish to send a gift, people who do attend but cannot afford to spend much money on you, and possibly people who may not even be acquainted with either you or your partner.

A very wide range of options for presents is therefore a priority. The first move is to work out a list of potential gifts. The list given here is a comprehensive record of presents, mostly practical and mostly intended for the home. The list on pages 199–201 is in no way intended to be read as a guide to the needs of the complete household or to imply that all are essential. They are simply items from which you can pick and choose for your own list.

Should you be unsure about what you really would like – an understandable uncertainty – a sound lead on the principle of selection was laid down by William Morris. He wrote, 'having nothing in your home which you do not know to be useful or believe to be beautiful'.

An established way of dealing with the matter is to place a list of chosen present ideas with one of the big stores and perhaps to leave separate lists with specialist shops as well – a craft shop or kitchenware specialist, for example.

It should be said that not everyone accepts the practice of being directed to a specified list. Some people and some communities prefer to make up their own minds on what to send. Also, if a friend or relation is known to have the sort of taste you admire it is probably better to leave the decisions to them.

Apart from these reservations a wedding-present list at a store has a great deal to recommend it. The system avoids the irritating likelihood of duplication of presents and an embarrassment of toasters, which can be the consequence when everyone does their own thing. People who want to give a present are told which store has the list. Present givers ask for the list, check through the options and investigate the goods; when the order is given, the specified object is crossed off the list by the management. Stores are usually prepared to pack and mail the gift, enclosing the donor's card.

If a major investment such as a dinner service is on the list, you can suggest that people give you the service in components, or bit by bit or plate by plate. This works very well where a group of friends or colleagues would like to present a substantial gift collectively.

When the wedding presents are being organized by yourself or a parent, the best plan is to make some copies of a list of your own, perhaps following the format shown on pages 199–201, with your own items. Keep one master copy yourself, give one to your family and circulate others around friends and relations. Make a careful note of who has agreed to give what so as to avoid duplication. Frequently the bride's mother has the job of telling everybody what is wanted and acting as a clearing house when the presents arrive.

Should the inevitable occur and duplicate presents arrive, there is the question of whether it is advisable to say what has happened or to lie low and give the unwanted object to Oxfam or a friend. First, consider whether the offending offering is in fact as surplus as it seems. To possess two irons or kettles, or a spare of any day-to-day equipment, is no bad thing when repairs take so long and may be expensive. But if you have no future use for a present, there is a strong case for asking for it to be exchanged. Put the request, if there are doubts as to which of the givers to ask, to the person who is likely to be the most sympathetic to your request, and if this does not apply in either case, choose the person to whom the business of exchanging the goods will cause the least inconvenience or go straight to the shop and ask them to exchange it.

Second marriages

There seems no good reason to discourage wedding presents. It is highly likely that these will come your way, especially if you hold a wedding reception. A list will signal your wishes, and will probably be expected.

Thankyous

In the usual pre-wedding rush it is all too easy to forget who contributed the pepper pot and who sent the cracked flower vase. It is best to get organized and make a written note of the sender and what they have sent as the parcels arrive, before the card accompanying the presents gets mislaid. If you can, send thankyou letters as soon as the presents arrive. Fortunately most givers are sympathetic to the demands made on the bride and do not get shirty if they have to wait some time for an acknowledgement. Printed or ready-phrased cards of thanks are a chilly and impersonal way of expressing gratitude and no-one will thank you for one. A handwritten letter or card is required.

The Presents

Glass, china and linen have maintained their popularity as traditional wedding presents. Also, depending on the materials in which the goods are made, they should have a long and useful life. However, anything can be added to the list of presents – things funny, odd, valuable, cheap, new, antique, practical or personal. It is a matter of what you fancy for yourselves. Highly practical presents, such as DIY equipment, have a place on your list, as well as the traditional objects of beauty or utility.

If glass or china is on the list, and this is likely to be bought from a particular store, a safeguard is to establish that the service includes reliable packing. The experience of Elizabeth Jane Howard, the novelist, is salutary: 'They all sent glass and it was invariably broken, not only beyond repair, but beyond identification. "Thank you so much for all that lovely glass" I wrote ...'

Presents of money, investments or savings bonds are frequently given. These are usually given to the partner the donor knows best. If the presents are displayed at the wedding reception, it is not customary to set out the cheques, but some people like to discreetly display the top half of the cheque with the recipient's name, allowing the curious eyes of wedding guests to speculate on the exact amount written in the spaces out of sight.

Storing the Presents

Perhaps you have nowhere to store the presents but a bulging cupboard in the temporary accommodation or at a parent's home. It is by no means unusual for presents to have to be stored for some time before they can be absorbed into married life. The strategy is as follows: open every parcel; ensure that fragile objects are individually wrapped in a protective covering such as newspaper; blankets, a duvet, rugs, coverings should be mothproofed; inflammable or combustible things should not be stored in a cupboard in enclosed space; check that extra insurance cover is taken out if necessary unless any existing policy covers the value.

Guide to a Wedding-present List

For the Table	MAKE	DESIGN	COLOUR		MAKE	DESIGN	COLOUR
Breakfast service				Vases			
China dinner service				Canteen of silver			
Everyday dinner service				Place settings			
Coffee set				Cake knives and forks			
Coffee pot				Carving set			
Teapot				Coffee spoons			
Butter dish				Fish knives and forks			
Dessert plates				Fish servers			
Egg cups				Grapefruit spoons			
Mugs				Ladles			
Jam pot and spoon				Serving spoons and forks			
Soup tureen				Steak knives			
Serving dishes				Teaspoons			
Tumblers				Candlesticks			
Wine glasses				Cheese board and knife			
Sherry glasses				Cream jug			
Liqueur glasses				Entrée dishes			
Port glasses				Gravy boat			
Brandy glasses				Place mats			
Champagne glasses				Salt and pepper mills			
Cocktail glasses				Salt, pepper and mustard set			
Goblets				Sauce boat			
Wine carafe				Sugar bowls			
Decanters				Sugar sifter			
Cocktail shaker				Table centre piece			
Water jug set				Tea strainer			
Fruit bowl				Toast rack			

Kitchen Equipment	MAKE	DESIGN	COLOUR		MAKE	DESIGN	COLOUR
Baking tins				Cooker hood			
Barbecue equipment				Cookery books			
Bread bin				Corkscrew			
Bread board and knife				Deep freeze			
Brooms, brushes				Dish washer			
Carving dish				Double boiler			
Casserole dish				Dustbin			
Coffee grinder				Dustpan and brush			
Coffee maker				Egg whisk			
Cooker				Electric kettle			

Kitchen Equipment	MAKE	DESIGN	COLOUR		MAKE	DESIGN	COLOUR
Floor polisher				Pastry board			
Fondue set				Plate drainer			
Food processor				Pressing iron			
Frying pan				Pressure cooker			
Garlic press				Refrigerator			
Grapefruit knife				Rolling pin			
Hostess trolley				Rotisserie, spit			
Hotplate				Salad bowl or bowls			
Ice-cream maker				Salad servers			
Ironing board				Saucepans			
Jam-making equipment				Sieve			
Juice extractor				Sink set			
Kettle				Skillet			
Kitchen cabinet				Soufflé dishes			
Kitchen knives				Slow-cooking pot			
Kitchen table/chairs				Spice rack			
Kitchen scales				Store cupboard provisions			
Kitchen scissors				Storage tins, jars			
Knife sharpener				Tea-maker			
Liquidizer				Toasted sandwich maker			
Measuring cups				Toaster			
Mincer				Trays			
Mixer and attachments				Vacuum flask			
Mixing bowls				Vacuum ice bucket			
Non-stick pans				Vegetable rack			
Nutcrackers				Waffle maker			
Omelette pan				Wine rack			
Oven-to-table ware				Yogurt maker			

Linen	MAKE	DESIGN	COLOUR		MAKE	DESIGN	COLOUR
Bath mats				Oven cloth or mitts			
Bath sets				Pillow slips			
Bath towels				Pillows			
Bedspread				Quilt cover			
Blankets				Sheets			
Dinner mats				Tablecloths			
Duvet				Table napkins			
Eiderdown				Tea towels			
Hand towels				Traycloths			

General Equipment	MAKE	DESIGN	COLOUR		MAKE	DESIGN	COLOUR
Alarm clock				Medicine chest			
Ashtrays				Mirrors			
Bathroom set				Needlework basket			
Bathroom scales				Photograph album			
Bed				Photograph frame			
Bicycle				Pictures, paintings			
Bookcase				Prints, photographs			
Books				Radio			
Camera				Radio cassette			
Camera equipment				Records, tapes			
Carpet sweeper				Rugs			
Ceramics				Scissors			
Chair				Sewing machine			
Clock				Side table			
Clothes				Slide viewer			
Clothes drier				Sofa			
Coffee table				Spin or tumble drier			
Curtains, fabrics				Stationery			
Cushions				Step ladder			
Dining-room table and chairs				Stereo equipment			
Electric blanket				Storage unit			
Electric clock				Subscriptions			
Electric fire				Table lamp			
Electric radio clock				Tape recorder			
Fan heater				Television set			
Fireplace accessories				Tokens			
Floor rug				Tool kit			
Furniture				Typewriter			
Games				Vacuum cleaner			
Garden furniture				Video cassette recorder			
Garden tools				Washing machine			
Hair drier				Wastepaper bins			
House plants				Watering can			
Lamps				Window blinds			
Lawn-mower				Window box			
Lighting				Wine			
Linen basket				Wood basket			
Luggage				Wood burning stove			
Magazine rack				Writing desk			

12

HEALTH AND BEAUTY

The toast 'your good health' should be taken quite literally at this time – your health is probably the single most important factor determining the amount of enjoyment you get out of life. Good health brings energy and resilience, enabling you to meet with confidence the challenges that are inseparable from getting married.

The following chapter touches on some of the basic considerations affecting your physical well-being and your appearance – good looks depend on good health. A whole philosophy of the body is encapsulated in the idea that your state of health depends as much on what you don't do as on what you do do; there can be positive advantages in negatives – not smoking, for example.

Health

Combating illness over the wedding

If you are especially prone to colds, influenza, sinus trouble, asthma or chest trouble then it would be sensible to avoid getting married during the winter months. January and February seem to be the worst months for all kinds of infections. If the marriage has to take place at these times, see your doctor about having influenza jabs (vaccine) well ahead of the wedding date. A course of antibiotics as a preventative might be recommended.

Other conditions such as various allergies can be seasonal. For example, someone who suffers from hay fever should, ideally, avoid timing the wedding during the high pollen season. If needs must, there is a course of desensitizing injections which can be taken beforehand.

Some stomach upsets like indigestion, colicky pains, and diarrhoea can be due to gastric flu, or food or drink, but can also be affected by tension and nervousness. Be sensible about your diet; although vitamin C may help to combat infection, if you eat too much fresh fruit this in itself can upset your digestion. There is usually no need to take any patent medicines, tonics, or expensive vitamin preparations except on the advice of your doctor.

Other annoying types of infection are cold sores on the lips, caused by a virus, and mouth ulcers, the exact cause of which is still uncertain. Both can be treated and rapid healing promoted.

One of the most distressing ailments is so-called 'honeymoon cystitis', an infection of the bladder. It is frequently associated with sexual intercourse in the inexperienced when some minor bruising or other disturbance occurs that encourages the growth of the organisms responsible for the infection. The complaint has nothing whatever to do with venereal disease.

The symptoms are the frequent and painful passage of urine, some slight fever, and general malaise. It is important that the condition be treated by a doctor but there are methods of self-help; washing carefully between the legs and the infected part, avoidance of nylon tights and nylon briefs unless these are made with a cotton gusset, and if possible taking a shower in place of a bath.

A booster

When one of the members of the wedding is going through a bad time emotionally and psychologically there is a case for enlisting medical assistance in order to help them get through the day. A doctor will be able to prescribe drugs which help in the short term. If the sufferer is the bride, she may have to face the classic dilemma of drawing a distinction between pre-wedding 'nerves' and a more serious development which might have its origin in real doubts about the marriage. If the latter is a probability, the implications should be faced sooner rather than later.

Self-knowledge – the key to coping with pressures
(Contributed by Dr F.E. Kenyon)

In fact, it is good to be under some pressure. A little anxiety can keep you alert and it ensures that you give the best of yourself. People who do not care about anything in particular are neither reliable nor efficient, nor very pleasant.

On the other hand, it is nice to have a few human failings – occasionally to be late, forgetful, angry or unsure of yourself. No one wants to marry a computer. How you cope with extra pressure – like planning your wedding, finding somewhere to live while holding down a full-time job – depends on your personality. Although you can often surprise yourself by tapping reserves of energy within yourself that you hardly knew existed, living on your nerves for too long can burn up quite a lot of energy.

However, it is perfectly normal to have occasional doubts about your own judgement; for example, are you doing the right thing, are you *really* in love?

Certain elements of risk, surprise or adventure can thrill and challenge one person but can leave another feeling anxious and inadequate. Sometimes doubts and fears are barely recognized by your conscious mind but tend to pop up again, often unexpectedly, in moments of panic or in your dreams.

Let us now look at some of the ways in which you may react and what you can do to help yourself deal with them. They are all very common and understandable for the simple reason that we all have in us the potential for becoming overanxious. It's like being in a state of perpetual stage-fright.

No energy

Feelings of listlessness or apathy, although very real, vary from person to person and are difficult to measure. Beware of using tiredness as an excuse to avoid situations or in order to get sympathetic attention. You *may* also be anaemic but this can be easily proved by a blood test. If you are not sleeping properly, you will, of course, feel tired. Learn to share, delegate and leave some things up to others. Sit down and relax as often as you can and eat a sensible diet. Do not rely on tonics, vitamins, any sort of pep pill, too much tea, coffee or iron pills (unless you turn out to be anaemic). The tiredness will right itself when you are no longer under pressure or it can be helped by some of the other measures detailed below.

A state of tension

This means not only feeling tense and strung-up but painful muscular tension as well – literally worried stiff. Tension headaches and backache are examples of this. The headache feels like a tight band round the head or can be mainly at the back of the head going down the neck into the shoulders. Even your scalp can feel tender. Neck and shoulder pain and backache can be made worse by poor posture and unsuitable shoes.

The key to overcoming tension is to learn how to relax. Begin by lying on your back on a firm bed or sofa, in a quiet, warm, semi-darkened room. Empty your bladder beforehand and loosen all tight clothing. You could also play yourself some soothing music. Take the telephone off the hook and shut the outside doors.

Put a low pillow under your head and neck, another under your thighs and a pillow under each arm if that feels the most comfortable. Breathe deeply, slowly and quietly through the nose.

You must now learn to 'tune in' to your muscles, particularly the tense and painful ones, by deliberately tightening them and then relaxing them as fully as possible. Continue sending the original message of 'letting go' to the muscles and take note of the new position of ease.

Repeat this with less tightening in the exercise until only slight tension can be produced in the muscles.

This basic approach can be applied to any part of the body and, indeed, to all parts in succession, from head to toe, to achieve total bodily relaxation. Practice should be both regular and purposeful. If you are very tense try two half-hour sessions daily; if only moderately tense, two fifteen-minute sessions daily. Remember that fifteen minutes of complete relaxation can be as beneficial as an hour's sleep. Avoid the regular use of tranquillizers, pain-killers or other drugs unless under medical supervision.

A crosspatch

When you are very anxious, you tend to get snappy and angry both with yourself and others. You are also oversensitive to criticism and intolerant of noise. A judicious mixture of relaxation and physical activity will help.

Low moments

You often get much more emotional than usual, easily moved to tears by sad news or sentimental plays on television. Occasionally letting go and having a good cry can bring great relief and this is nothing to be ashamed about. Whatever you do, try to preserve your sense of humour.

Forgetfulnes

You may well find yourself getting confused, absent-minded and indecisive, unable to make up your mind. For decisions on minor matters, be firm with yourself, act on the first sensible answer that occurs to you and do not dwell endlessly on the pros and cons. In more important matters, ask the advice of people you trust.

Otherwise try and concentrate only for short stretches at a time. You will usually find certain times of the day better than others for doing this, like the late morning or early afternoon.

Trembling and shaking, particularly in your hands, can be a nuisance and make you rather clumsy. If you drop something, apologize straight away and then forget it – don't worry about it.

Sleep

The usual trouble is not being able to get to sleep; occasionally it can be waking yourself up with a sudden jerk or just fitful sleep.

Do not fly to the sleeping pills; try simple measures first. Go for a stroll in the evening, go to bed later, have a warm drink (but not tea or coffee), read or listen to some music.

Practise relaxation and instead of worrying about the future concentrate on a pleasant situation. Imagine that you are lying on a lovely beach in warm sunshine beside the sea (much better than counting sheep). Invest in a reliable alarm clock so that you need not worry about waking up at a particular time.

Eating and drinking

You may well temporarily go off your food. Appetite is usually worst in the mornings but do not try to force yourself to eat. However, do sit down at breakfast time and have something to drink and a small piece of toast. Small, frequent, easily digested meals may be better than conventional meals at conventional times.

Sometimes you eat too much so you end up putting on weight. Food and sometimes drink is then being abused and used like a tranquillizer.

When you are nervous, you often want to pass water more frequently. Don't restrict your fluid intake too severely but practise holding your water for as long as you can – until you begin to feel discomfort.

Finally, it is a good idea, two or three months before your wedding, to go to see your doctor for a medical check-up. This will give you the chance to ask your doctor about any health problems you may have or have had, and it is also a good time to get contraceptive advice, especially if you are thinking about going on the Pill or coming off it to start a family.

Contraception

Few couples come to marriage without some knowledge of birth control, whether or not they have had direct personal experience of sexual intercourse.

Contraception is a sensitive word in many parts of the world, and any act which controls the future generation is likely to have a profound effect on society as a whole. The facts call into question many moral, emotional and religious issues. To a woman, contraception amounts to the right to control her body and her own future.

Personal decisions on which method to adopt are worth considering seriously and should be shared between the two of you, not in spite of, but perhaps because of, the independence that the Pill gives a woman.

There are several different methods of contraception and which one you choose will depend on several factors: the health risk to the woman; how important it is to you to avoid pregnancy; and how your body responds to a particular drug or device. Science has not yet produced a reversible, fail-safe, convenient and cheap contraceptive, and the advantages and disadvantages of the various methods should be considered carefully.

The Pill and the IUD have the best records for preventing pregnancy, but may have unwelcome side effects, and both methods can also carry some long-term health risk to the woman. The barrier methods have no side effects and do not endanger health, but on the other hand the risk of pregnancy is greater with these methods.

The Pill

The Pill is the most effective and usually the most convenient method of contraception available. However, you should be aware of the doubts that are expressed by medical opinion on the unknown long-term effects of the Pill, which distorts the body's natural hormonal balance over a long period of time.

There are two types of Pill, both of which work on the same principle. The combined Pill, which is available in medium and low doses, contains two hormones, oestrogen and progestogen, similar to hormones that occur naturally in the body. These prevent the monthly release of the egg cell from the ovary, and so inhibit pregnancy. The combined Pill is taken for twenty-one days, followed by seven Pill-free days, making up the twenty-eight-day monthly cycle. The second type of Pill, sometimes called the mini-pill, contains progestogen only and is taken every day. This is considered to be less effective than the combined Pill but is associated with fewer reported side effects.

The considerable advantages of the Pill are that it is convenient, almost one hundred per cent effective and readily available – a prescription can be obtained before or after marriage from any Family Planning clinic or from a GP. The disadvantages are the side effects, which are felt in varying degrees according to the individual, and the possible more serious and long-term effects. The so-called minor risks, which may be temporary, include weight gain, pains in the breasts, legs and ankles, bleeding or vaginal dryness, loss of sex drive, nausea, acne and slight depression. The more serious risks include blood clotting or thrombosis (more common in those who take the Pill over a number of years), pulmonary embolism, depression and migraine.

For these and other reasons the Pill is not suitable for everyone and should not be taken at all by women over forty years – thirty-five if they smoke, are overweight or have already been taking the Pill for five years.

To be set against the lesser side effects are the sense of freedom and sexual confidence which stem from the Pill's high rate of effectiveness as a contraceptive.

The IUD or coil

The intra-uterine device, known as the IUD, is a plastic or copper device placed in the uterus by a doctor. When it is safely in place the IUD prevents conception.

It is not a method that would be recommended for use by a virgin, however.

It is important for the woman to be correctly fitted with the type of IUD which is most suitable for her. It can stay in place for several years with an annual check-up by a doctor.

The greatest advantage of the IUD is that it provides long-term protection, is inexpensive and does not require any effort of memory or will on the part of the user. Nevertheless the disadvantages and side effects cause a substantial proportion of women who are fitted with an IUD to have it removed during the first year. Side effects include pain and heavy bleeding during the menstrual period; there is a risk that the uterus may be perforated when the device is being inserted; sometimes the device becomes dislodged and an unwanted pregnancy may then occur.

Barrier methods

There are three so-called barrier methods – the cap, the condom and chemical barriers such as creams, gels, pessaries and foams.

The cap

This is also known as the Dutch cap or diaphragm. It is a dome-shaped cap of rubber with a springy, flexible rim. It is placed in the vagina so that it covers the neck of the womb, so preventing the male sperm from reaching the female egg cell. For maximum effectiveness it is necessary to use a spermicidal cream or gel as well.

The advantages are that it is safe and inexpensive, and, correctly used, a reliable method of contraception. The disadvantages are that it has to be fitted correctly and its use explained by a doctor, gynaecologist or trained nurse; it may present problems to those who are shy about manipulating their own bodies. Its effectiveness depends on the motivation of the couple and anyone who is likely to be vague or irresponsible about putting the diaphragm in place as a matter of routine should use some other method. (The diaphragm should be placed in position about an hour before sexual intercourse.)

The condom

This is a protective used by the man; it is also known as the sheath or French letter. A condom is rolled on to the erect penis before intercourse. Afterwards care has to be taken that no semen escapes when the condom is removed.

The advantages are many: condoms are available from chemists, barbers and Family Planning clinics. They are inexpensive and effective. The disadvantages are the woman's dependence on the man's sense of responsibility and control, and the psychological objections to the need to interrupt love-making in order to put the condom on before intercourse and to withdraw immediately afterwards. Some couples also consider the method to be unaesthetic.

Chemical barriers

Creams, gels, pessaries, foaming tablets, pastes and aerosol foams are not reliable means of contraception on their own, but they add to the efficacy of other methods.

Natural family planning

The growing doubts about methods dependent on drugs or the insertion of objects into the body has led to renewed interest in the rhythm method; couples using this method have sexual intercourse only during the infertile period of the woman's menstrual cycle. Its efficacy depends on charting the periods of fertility and infertility, and there are various methods of doing this, some more reliable than others, but none infallible.

The advantages are that it is free and the responsibility is shared. The disadvantages can have the most serious consequences – the Family Planning Association reports a high degree of failure. The method requires considerable motivation and can put some strain on the relationship, as the couple must refrain from vaginal love-making during the woman's fertile phase.

Withdrawal and the douche are most unreliable – the douche may even increase the chances of becoming pregnant – and should not be used as methods of contraception.

If you do not want children

If you are both certain that you do not want to have children sterilization (female) or vasectomy (male sterilization) might be considered, but doctors are reluctant to sterilize anyone who is under thirty or who has not had at least one child, as the operation is usually irreversible.

A medical check-up

If you are unaccustomed to using contraceptives, are considering changing your existing method or would simply like to know about some of the choices, the best source of information is your doctor or the local Family Planning clinic. Virgins and the sexually inexperienced should have no anxieties about talking to a doctor or trained counsellor about contraception – they have heard it all before. They will explain the biological facts and put the medical choices before you.

If you hope to start a family right away you might like a medical check-up. It is important to discuss coming off the Pill – you should use some other method of contraception for two or three months before trying to conceive – or stopping any artificial method of contraception you may have practised.

Unwanted pregnancy

This is a most miserable dilemma for everyone involved but delay in deciding what to do narrows the range of options for the pregnant woman. Only those concerned, bearing in mind all the conflicting rights and priorities involved, can decide whether they want to terminate a pregnancy. If termination is decided upon, the sooner that decision is reached the better – both from the medical and the psychological viewpoint. There is no easy advice to give except to listen to the arguments and to consult your heart of hearts.

The woman should consult her GP, who may recommend a termination on the NHS. If he is not helpful, go to one of the non-profit-making agencies – the British Pregnancy Advisory Service or the Pregnancy Advisory Service.

Menstruation

The general ignorance that surrounds a woman's sexuality means that some men and women find menstruation an embarrassing subject. In marriage, they may come face to face with that fact for the first time.

Unpleasant euphemisms for menstruation, a history of association with uncleanliness, and awkwardness between the sexes in talking about bodily functions have all helped to contribute to the creation of a taboo.

This is some of the background to what may or may not be an issue for a couple who are sexually inexperienced. Unfamiliarity may make it difficult for men and women to behave naturally towards each other when the woman has her menstrual period. Men sometimes admit to an almost biblical dislike of some of the physical manifestations and may be put off by a stain or an odour. Some women are unsure about how men feel in relation to a bodily excretion which is to a woman a natural expression of her sex. She may wonder whether to tell him about her menstrual cramps or pre-menstrual tension or whether to keep them to herself.

It is always best in these matters to speak out, so long as you don't expect too much in the way of sympathy. If you say nothing, your partner may misinterpret what seems to him to be your odd behaviour and may reach some unfortunate conclusions.

Unless a couple are on intimate sexual terms with each other, it is sound practise to try to get the dates right for the honeymoon. The timing of the holiday should if possible avoid the days during the month when the honeymooner is due for her period. However, it is by no means unusual for all the excitement of the wedding to bring forward the onset of menstruation, and it is as well to travel and to pack with this in mind. Periods can be suppressed through prescribed drugs and, in certain cases, this might be considered.

On the question of sex during menstruation, personal attitudes vary widely. Some men and some women, perhaps because of some of the reasons touched on earlier, feel obliged to impose limits on love-making. Others take little notice of the inconvenience and follow their inclinations.

The point should be made here that in sexual relations, shared responses are the ideal and love-making is rarely rewarding when one partner, for some reason, holds an act to be distasteful.

Beauty

On looking yourself

Guidelines on clothes, make-up and hair-styles are notoriously difficult to apply. On a wedding day, however, it is no bad thing to look like yourself. Curiously, this may not be as easy as you think. A wedding is an occasion when the rituals and regalia, formality and finery can take over, and the individual may lose her own identity.

Part of the problem is that the understandable desire to dress up and do justice to the great occasion can lead to excesses and generally overdoing the effects. It is easily done – the combination of a special dress, head-dress and veil can turn into a virtual disguise without anyone wishing this to happen.

Fortunately, there are no rules that maintain that a bride has to lose her own identity. The criterion for choice is always the same – does the fashion, hair-style, flower or jewel contribute to the wearer's feelings of confidence and enjoyment? If not, leave it off.

Sometimes a radical change of appearance is planned – either a transformation through a new hair-style or innovatory make-up idea. One word of caution here – make some allowance for masculine suspicion of change in the appearance of women. Fairy-tales and legends testify that men secretly dread the moment of meeting their bride at the altar for fear that she has turned into some stranger. The modern equivalent is the man with anxieties that his partner will prove unrecognizable in her bridal extravaganza.

A guiding principle is that it is you that your partner wishes to marry and, presumably, wishes to be seen marrying. However, the line between a change that shocks and one that comes as a pleasant surprise may be fine. If in doubt and some smart departure from your usual style or approach is planned, it might be wise to tip off your partner about the likely outcome. There are, of course, exceptions to the foregoing: where the bride is known to be particularly adroit in changing her image or, perhaps, where her partner has had a hand in creating a fresh approach.

Make-up

Make-up for the wedding day should be whatever you know you look good in, applied with extra care, bearing in mind the shade of your dress.

One of the very few general rules in a subject which is almost wholly a matter of personal preference and how you see yourself, is that fair-skinned complexions look best in soft, subtle shades that enhance natural tones. Vivid contrasts sometimes sit uneasily on fresh complexions. But not on all, and those whose looks are a daily work of exotic art should keep on with the good work, especially on their wedding day.

Wearing white

Soft white, cream and ivory are flattering to most complexions, but some dresses in nylon polyester can cast a somewhat hard light on the face. A little more compensatory make-up colour on the cheeks, eyelids and lips is the answer and a brightening up of all the effects. But avoid branching out into a theatrical level of make-up, as this could become garish.

All changes and experiments should be tried out in advance using the actual brand of cosmetics intended for the wedding day. Then if you are using any new products which cause problems, allergies or are just plain ineffective, there is time to make adjustments. If possible try out the whole effect with the dress, head-dress and make-up to see if your face treatment fits.

Colours for your colouring

Choosing the best colours for your complexion depends on the colouring of your skin, eyes and hair, the way you wish to be, and the shade of your dress and effects. Those who need a lead here can find a starting point in the basic skin-tone chart overleaf. The sheer diversity and individuality of faces defies simple pigeon-holing, but the broad categories given in the chart apply in most cases.

Choosing a foundation

A foundation adds a colour tone to your natural complexion colour and should impart a smooth finish to the face. The general principle is to select the tone that is closest to your natural skin shade. If hesitating between a darker and a lighter preparation, choose the paler one. Dark or sallow skin tones gain from the maximum translucency. People with a high colour and those who tend to flush should select a foundation with a minimum of pink in the colour.

Choosing a blusher

A blusher adds colour and definition to a face. Those with good natural colour in their cheeks can use a blusher to shape the face and to heighten an impression of rosy health. When applying two separate shades, brush the paler over the upper cheek bone and the brighter one on the cushion of the cheek.

All eyes

Using a new eye make-up is one of the easiest ways of transforming your appearance. The whole of the eye setting can be treated as a canvas for colour, the lid, the eye line, the lid line, the lashes, the under eye, the under brow. If in doubt as to how far you can go with a special effect, the best check is to start with the works in full colour and to take it down shade by shade until you reach the point that satisfies. If you work the other way about, and build up from a low-key start, you may never reach the peak performance.

The best free beauty treatment for eyes – whitening the whites, brightening the pupils, taking away the stretched taut feeling in the skin surrounding the eye which stems from tiredness – is a good night's sleep. Rest and sleep can virtually rescue some eyes from skulking in shadowy hollows.

As marriage is in many ways a new beginning, make sure that you can see the picture. If you need a new prescription for glasses or contact lenses, or wish to treat yourself to some shaded lenses on prescription, the wedding makes a good excuse for the indulgence.

Face Treatment

If you intend to have a facial make the appointment for at least a week before the day. Treatments may bring any impurities in the skin to the surface and these should be given time to clear up. If eyebrow shaping and plucking and moustache waxing have to be done, allow a day or so for any smart caused to the complexion to subside.

Everyone will have their own make-up routine but one principle applies to all methods. Your skin is a living organism and its pores must be allowed to breathe properly. Heavy applications of foundation and face powder may function momentarily as camouflage or cover-up but it will prevent the skin from functioning effectively. Antidotes to a shiny nose or dull complexion are an effective cleansing routine, a sound diet and a light touch on the base make-up. Two fine dustings of face powder will last longer and create a smoother effect than a single heavy coating.

If you enjoy a face pack try one of the fresh kitchen-product recipes using whisked egg white or sliced cucumber or oatmeal. Gentle steam opens the

Skin-tone chart

	COLOURING	FOUNDATION	BLUSHER	EYESHADOW	LIPSTICK
FAIR SKIN	*Light eyes, light hair*	ivory beige	golden pink	pastel shades	pink/red
	Light eyes, dark hair	ivory beige	pinky rose	grey/mauve/ blue/green	pink/red/ mauve
	Dark eyes, light hair	golden beige	golden amber	grey/mauve/ blue/green	amber/red/ coral
	Dark eyes, dark hair	peachy	amber/copper	grey/magenta/ navy/green	deep pink/ red/mauve
FAIR-TO-MEDIUM SKIN	*Dark eyes, dark hair*	pinky beige	russet/amber	green/brown/ russet	amber/rose
	Dark eyes, light hair	golden beige	tawny	green/brown	coral/rose
	Light eyes, dark hair	beige	deep rose	grey/mauve/ blue/green	rose/red/ mauve
	Light eyes, light hair	beige	golden pink	pastel shades	rose/pink/ red
DARK SKIN	*Dark eyes, dark hair*	medium beige	russet	green/brown	russet/ amber/coral
	Light eyes, dark hair	medium beige	dark pink	mauve/grey/ blue/green	pink/red/ crimson
	Dark eyes, light hair	pinky brown	golden	green/brown	rose/coral/ amber
	Light eyes, light hair	dark beige	golden/honey	pink/grey/ gold	pink/gold/ amber

pores, and after cool water is splashed on, the face will feel refreshed. On a hot day, cleanse the face of make-up and apply, for a few minutes only, an ice pack wrapped in a towel; this is wonderfully refreshing.

Hand Care

Long-term treatment is required to allow fingernails to grow into shape and rough skin to become smooth. Hands respond well to a few days' cossetting with hand cream and protective care. If nails are irreparably short or damaged you might consider fake nails which look remarkably genuine and take enamel well. When hands are in a depressingly unkempt state and there is no time, an expedient is to wear gloves or mittens – in cotton, lace or kid – at the wedding.

Time is of the essence for an effective manicure: an hour is not over much if the fingernails are to be varnished. Use a base coat and a top coat for a longer-lasting effect. Two thin applications of colour in which the first is permitted to dry before the second is applied will produce a prettier effect than one heavy coat of colour. If you are doing your own nails remember that the colour does take some time to dry completely. Don't do something else; just sit there until the enamel is completely set.

People who object to brightly enamelled fingernails can bring out the shine by buffing with a special powder. If they are not averse to a cosmetic touch, a clear varnish or a pale pearly shade of varnish adds a groomed finish.

Feet First

Toenails can be glamorized in no time at all with enamel and the colour dries out unscathed as you trip around in bare feet.

You will spend much of the wedding day on your feet so take good care of them. A pedicure is rarely wasted, nor is a first visit to the chiropodist. Young corns, uncomfortable swellings, ingrowing toenails, verrucas, callouses or hard skin can all be treated. Even a healthy foot feels fresher, cooler and springier after treatment. If you prefer to look after your own feet, one remedy for hard skin is to apply the pumice stone regularly when you take a bath.

Problems

Spots

If a spot surfaces on your face close to the wedding, or on the day, leave well alone. The temptation to touch, squeeze, medicate and generally treat the offending impurity should be resisted. Rely on simple cosmetic cover-ups and camouflage. Take consolation from the undoubted truth that the spotty person is much more aware of the imperfection than anyone else.

Preventive measures would not come amiss if you are prone to spots. If eating chocolate, or having a fit of the weeps, or an excess of make-up regularly brings you out in spots, you know what to do about it. If your skin tends to erupt into spots during the pre-menstrual stage, and you worry about it, bear this factor in mind when deciding on the date of the wedding.

High colour

A high complexion colour may be basically nervous in origin, but in many cases is an inherited characteristic. As part of your natural appearance it is best

Opposite: Mirella Ricciardi, 1980
Overleaf left and right: Dick Ballarian, 1979

accepted as it is. However, if a cover-up is important to you, cosmetics can sometimes take down the colour by a shade or two. Green-based foundation and face powder may help to neutralize the red tones.

Unwanted hair

Depending on the heaviness of the natural growth of bodily hair, you may wish to have a finer line to the eyebrow, unhairy underarms, smooth legs, or a trimmer pubic hair line. Unwanted hair can be controlled by several methods which can be carried out at home, or by a professional beautician.

The most effective treatment is waxing, best done by a trained beautician. Heated wax is spread over the appropriate body area, allowed to cool in order to seal the hair into the wax, and rapidly stripped off, taking the hairs from their roots. It sounds painful, but in practised hands is a momentary discomfort only. Eyebrows, legs, arms, bikini line are suitable areas for treatment.

Eyebrows can be plucked with tweezers into shape. If you are doing the job yourself, remember to take the hair from under the top line of the brow only. The natural line of the top of the brow should be left in peace.

Legs and underarms can be treated at home with a commercial depilatory but test a small amount of the preparation on your skin first.

Self-consciousness about body hair is a typically British reaction, due perhaps to our many surviving inhibitions about bodily functions and sex. Women tend to worry about it, on account of what men may think, but these anxieties may well be groundless, as few men object to such a basic manifestation of femininity. The main problem is likely to be the woman's self-consciousness about her physical hairiness. If this applies, consider the cosmetic remedies that are available; these are likely to be effective if treatment is maintained. For more serious problems, electrolysis can be recommended which, though not fail-safe, has a fair rate of success.

Hair-style

There is a good case against the idea of wearing a special hair-style for the wedding day, whatever the length of your hair. If you prefer to be free of concern on the matter, one way of feeling relaxed is to wear your everyday style looking its absolute best.

Short hair depends for its effectiveness on a good cut as the line is the thing. If possible arrange to have a hair-cut before choosing your head-dress or hat, as it may affect the selection of styles that will suit you. Short hair needs to be considered in relation to whatever is to be placed on top of it – think of the effect of head-dress and hair as one design.

Opposite: Mirella Ricciardi, 1979

If you need to get your hair in good condition start to work on it some time before the wedding day. Dandruff, split ends and limp locks respond to intelligent care, the right shampoo and conditioner, and a balanced diet.

Staying Cool

There is no need to become frantically over-hygienized – you are not a product but a person. Do what seems best, and having taken all reasonable precautions to ensure your cool and fresh appearance, relax and let go.

Don't believe manufacturers' claims that cosmetics possess singular staying-powers on the face. If make-up is to retain its freshness, renewed applications are required. For this purpose it makes sense to take along a make-up repair kit to the wedding or arrange for someone to bring one for you.

A few beauty tips may help. Mascara will last longer on the eyelashes if several applications are made, allowing each one to dry completely before the next one is applied. Finally, brush gently in order to soften and separate each eyelash. If a lasting colour change is required, eyelashes and eyebrows can be dyed. Foundation spread thinly and evenly over the eyelids and lips forms an efficient base for holding cosmetic colour placed on top. Lips can be outlined in colour with a brush or applicator and then filled in with the lipstick – this guards against smudging. It is worth noting that some of the new cosmetic applicators really do allow a greater degree of control, so giving a more precise effect, less subject to smudging and wear and tear.

Those troubled by excess perspiration should take steps to come to terms with it; it is a natural function, essential for the control of body temperature. Avoid choosing a fabric which darkens on contact with moisture; keep sleeve-lines and armholes loose and free and easy; use an effective deodorant frequently; see if there are any new preparations on the market that might help; if feeling hot and tacky try running cool – not cold – water over the wrists. Finally, take consolation in the saying that inspiration is 90 per cent perspiration – and be generous with your perfume on your person.

Diet and Slimming

Less of you

Most women like to lose a few pounds in weight before the wedding, encouraged by the prospect of a trio of rewards – the day, the dress and the photographs. Oddly enough, many women tend to lose weight before the wedding in the natural course of events, but it would be tempting providence to count on it.

If you wish to be slimmer by resolve, it is far smarter to adopt a gentle course of bodily self-improvement than to follow a crash diet. The problem about crash diets is that they are liable to cause unpleasant side effects. These are especially unwelcome at a pressurized time when you need to retain your natural good humour and the energy to bounce back after reverses. Unsupervised fasting can produce nausea, stomach pains and dizziness and, unless counteracted, will almost certainly cause constipation, bad breath and fractiousness. The condition of your skin and hair may also suffer ill effects. So gently does it.

What you eat and drink, the hours set aside for sleep and relaxation, regular exercise, good posture, cutting down or cutting out smoking, are all factors that affect your state of health and your figure. Your partner might also use the event of the wedding as an opportunity to improve his person. If so, you could go through the rigours of dieting and saying 'no' to a choc ice together. This is not the place in which to recommend programmed diets as so much depends on the weight-loss objectives, the dieter's health and the time factor.

Some guidelines are:

- The watchword is a balanced diet for keeping up strength and energy.
- All foods supply energy which is measured in calories or joules, but some foods provide energy and very little else, whereas other foods provide a combination of energy and nutrients.
- It is important to choose foods intelligently so that the body receives all the nutrients it needs while still losing weight.
- Food intake should be distributed through the day so you take in fresh supplies of food energy while expending physical energy.
- Eating breakfast is an important aspect of a balanced diet.
- Nourishment should be digested during your active hours so it is converted mainly into physical energy.
- If possible try to avoid eating a large meal before going to sleep at night.
- Ingredients that supply what dieticians call 'empty calories', such as alcohol or sugar, should have no place in a serious slimming regime.

It is impractical for anyone who is doing a fulltime job and, in addition, planning a wedding, to take on a diet involving special cooking. It is best to observe the general diet principles of your selected regime which will provide guidelines when eating in a canteen, or pub or restaurant.

Do's and don'ts

General disciplines are: always carry an artificial sweetener if you normally take sugar, and use skimmed milk powder instead of milk whenever possible; when eating out, don't mull nostalgically over prohibited luxuries on the menu, quickly decide on a grilled or salad dish; move the basket of bread rolls to the other side of the table; resist importunate demands by well-meaning friends and relations to break your diet; remember to thank anyone who is supportive, especially when this causes them inconvenience.

Your doctor can supply a medically approved diet. Women's magazines are often prepared to supply their current diet or diets if you write giving details and enclosing a SAE. Diets by wellknown nutritionists can also be found in books on the subject.

More of you

Whereas no woman wishes for a fatter stomach, many desire a bigger bosom or rounder curves. The problems of the thin receive scant attention and are rarely recognized by plumper people. Certain exercises will develop pectoral muscles, but short of cosmetic surgery there is no known way of changing a person's physical type, nor of putting on selective curves. If you are concerned about being underweight, see your doctor and discuss your diet, eating habits and general health record with him. Marriage may make a difference – sometimes feeling happier and contented has the effect of rounding you off.

Order of Dressing

On the morning of the wedding, take conventional advice and eat a little something. Do not force yourself, however, or allow yourself to be persuaded to eat against your better judgement. A piece of toast and a cup of something is better than nothing if you can manage it.

Allow plenty of time for all the preparations involved in getting dressed but don't be ready too far ahead of schedule. Standing around waiting in a dress which has to be maintained in a perfect state is a bit of a strain, and accidents to it can easily occur.

The timing depends on what has to be done and such variables as whether you are going to a professional hairdresser, or a stylist is coming to the house, or you are doing your own hair at home – a comfortable allowance is about three hours for a manicure, hairdressing at home, a bath, and getting dressed.

One order of dressing is as follows:

- Take a warm scented bath.
- Have a manicure.
- Put on your base make-up – moisturizer, foundation if you usually wear one, face powder – reserving the colour cosmetics until a later stage. The point of this move is to remove the risk of disarranging your hair-style, which might happen if you put on your basic make-up after hairdressing.
- Do your hair or have it arranged by a hairdresser.

- Complete any make-up effects. Now is the moment to add mascara, eyeshadow, blusher and lipstick or whatever you like to wear. Place a tissue over lipsticked lips (if the wedding dress is to be slipped over the head).
- Put on the wedding dress.
- Arrange the head-dress and veil, or hat or hair decorations.

Have to hand a spare pair of tights in the right shade and size, and a sewing kit for emergency repairs. Check that the zips and slides or fastenings on the dress are in good order before dressing. Should difficulties arise, the bride will not be the first to be sewn into her dress.

The jitters

Be prepared for possible feelings of panic at the last moment. It is by no means unusual for someone who is about to go through the ceremony of marriage to feel jittery on departure. Experience suggests this is unlikely to be indicative of fundamental doubts and fears but is a momentary departure of self-confidence which will soon pass.

Revivers include: for drinkers, a small one poured by a friendly hand; music played to taste. A calming exercise is to hold up the hands, fingers apart and to shake them gently. This is a great improvement on waiting around with clenched hands. In the car travelling to the place of worship, the bride should breathe slowly and deeply. One bride was remarkably self-possessed until, on the point of entering the church, she paused and felt a wave of panic. Her father, who was giving her away, breathed into her ear, 'I shall say "one, two, three", and on the third beat in we go.' And in she went.

IRIBE 1920

13

THE HONEYMOON

The honeymoon is above all a holiday in which tastes, interests, likes and dislikes are of paramount importance. It is a well-worn cliché that the bulk of holiday complaints come from people who have chosen, or have been sold, the wrong holiday for them, and it is specially important to choose your honeymoon wisely.

It is also important to choose a holiday that you will *both* enjoy. This will probably involve a certain amount of compromise. Most men, for instance, find lying on beaches tedious, whereas most women will at the very least pretend to like it, if only for the sake of acquiring that all-important tan. If one person's idea of perfect holiday bliss is to sit in the shade with a good book and the other's is to rush off sightseeing at every available moment, it is unlikely that a hot barren island in the middle of the Mediterranean would be an intelligent choice. Pick a honeymoon destination which has enough variety to ensure that, for at least part of the time, each of you will be able to do what you want.

The Holiday of a Lifetime – or a Brief Break?

Another essential consideration in deciding on a honeymoon is whether you want to go for a 'holiday of a lifetime', or whether you would rather save your cash for curtains and your free time for more practical purposes. The case for a really special, glamorous honeymoon is a strong one. After all, whenever else would you be able to justify the expense? The original definition of the word honeymoon was the month after marriage, referring to the moon's monthly cycle. Few couples, however, can afford to take four weeks' holiday these days, but many do choose to spend two or three weeks on honeymoon, often in romantic – and expensive – places. They feel, quite naturally, that the occasion of marriage calls for something rather more exciting and romantic than an immediate return to domesticity.

On the other hand, the arguments in favour of 'just a few days away', or even just one night, are also persuasive. A short break after the wedding has a great deal to recommend it as a honeymoon idea. It is ideal for couples who have neither the time nor the money for a full-scale honeymoon but who want to celebrate the beginning of their married life in some way. Two or three days away, not too far from home, can be the perfect solution. It is long enough to sample all that unfamiliar territory right on your doorstep, do a little sightseeing and recover from the excitement of the wedding before diving back into daily life. One variation of this idea is to spend one night in a romantic hotel, and defer the honeymoon proper until less traumatic times. The advantages of the one-night honeymoon are many. The travelling time is minimal and the doubts, delays and frustrations, now sadly so often associated with international air travel, can be avoided. What's more, some of the money saved on actually getting to your destination can be spent on a really special first-class hotel. After the expense of the wedding, resources may be very limited and the couple may feel that any available cash would be better invested in putting a deposit on a house or saving for the future. In addition, there is the emotional aspect. Getting married can be just as draining emotionally as it is physically. It may often be wiser to take a brief break in calm, peaceful surroundings in order to draw breath and wind down, rather than set off on some exhausting trip half-way across the world.

Some couples even dispense with the formal honeymoon altogether, preferring to get on with settling down together in their new home.

Whichever option is chosen, however, the decision as to what kind of honeymoon – if any – to take, is probably as much influenced by the relationship between the bride and groom, by how long – and intimately – they have known each other, as by anything else. Many couples marrying have known each other for many years. Some may have been living together and have taken several holidays together before the wedding, in which case the honeymoon is less important than for the whirlwind-romance couple, for whom the honeymoon may often be the first chance they have had to spend some time together.

How to Travel

There are, however, certain practicalities and guidelines that will probably apply to every kind of holiday. Once you have decided where to go, for instance (and there are literally thousands of possibilities – beach holidays, city holidays, touring holidays, self-catering holidays, boating and caravanning holidays – to name but a few), you will also have to consider both how to get there, and whether you are going to organize the holiday yourself or rely on a travel agent to do it for you.

By air

It has been said that air travel is what this irreligious age has devised to take the place of purgatory. When things go wrong, as they do with alarming frequency, air travel can be quite simply the most unpleasant way of (trying) to get from A to B. On the other hand, when everything works smoothly (and it does sometimes), flying is the most efficient and quickest way of travelling.

All scheduled fares are settled by the governments of the countries of the various airlines, but unfortunately this is very little help to the traveller seeking some sort of consistency among the thicket of fare prices. The cheapest tickets come from the so-called 'bucket shops', which can be found in the advertisements of magazines and newspapers. If you choose one of these, it is essential to check with the airline that the flight actually exists, and *not* to part with your money until you have got your tickets. On the whole, although many of these organizations are reputable, it is inadvisable to book your flight through the bucket shops, especially when it is your honeymoon that is at stake.

Charter flights are not, as is often thought, any less safety-conscious than scheduled flights. They use the same aeroplanes and are subjected to the same stringent regulations. The only thing you lose on is creature comforts – there is less leg-room, less in-flight service – and the fare is considerably lower. Another cheap way to fly, and one which means you can choose your own timetable, is an APEX flight. This is a seat on a scheduled flight (economy class) on which you can save up to 70 per cent by purchasing your ticket in advance (usually one month before, but it varies with different airlines).

The actual logistics of travelling seem complicated to the inexperienced. The watchword is check everything and allow for plenty of time for accidental hold-ups. Experienced travellers can afford to cut it fine, but airport formalities often take longer than you think, particularly if you are unfamiliar with the procedures. Once on the aeroplane, the first hurdle is over. But flying, particularly on long or charter flights, is not always the most comfortable of experiences. Air travellers generally feel better for cutting down on smoking and drinking. (Alcohol, that is; cabin crews are advised to take a pint of liquid every hour to counteract the dehydration that the pressurized atmosphere of the cabin causes.) For the same reason, the body tends to swell a little in flight, so take off your shoes and loosen clothes. Killing time, except on the shortest flights, is generally the biggest problem, so take reading material or scrabble or a sleeping pill, or chat to your neighbour.

By car

Travelling by car, whether your own or a hired one, gives you freedom, fun and flexibility. But it can be tiring. Try not to push yourself too far when planning your route. Distances look deceptively small on a map, and over-tiredness can cause fatal accidents. Make sure to stop early in the evening if you do not have accommodation arranged in advance. If you are taking your own car, take it in for a full service before you leave and ensure that you have all the appropriate documents. The AA and the RAC provide advice and rescue services as well as insurance to cover accidents or breakdowns.

By boat

Travelling by water, whether as a means to an end or as an end in itself, can be both relaxing and relatively cheap. There are many companies serving the Channel crossing and most have facilities for car drivers. Cruising is rarely cheap, but can provide a pleasant and leisurely sightseeing holiday. Both in Britain and on the Continent, canal cruising is a popular way of seeing the countryside.

By coach

Going by coach is an undoubtedly economical way to travel, but for many people its price advantage does not compensate for the discomfort and tedium it involves. Coach travel gives two distinctly different services – transport from one place to another and touring holidays. The former can be excellent value for money, especially on short trips, but the latter is hardly ideal for a romantic honeymoon, unless you want to share it with fifty other people!

By rail

With traffic hold-ups on the roads and chaos in the air, the railways are staging something of a come-back as a means of transport. Both at home and abroad the railways cover a vast network of routes, and prices are still relatively low. On some trains, the romance of the railways still lives, and there is something really adventurous about hurtling through the night knowing that in the morning you'll wake to strange sights and sounds. On long journeys, however, travelling by train does have a time disadvantage.

The non-traveller

Not everyone is a born traveller. It is quite common to feel apprehensive, if not downright panicky, at the prospect of taking a trip by train or plane. Difficult as this may be for the confident traveller to accept in someone else, the worrier should not be further diminished by having his or her concern derided or ignored. It is best to recognize that few anxieties respond to exhortation, and fewer people feel better for being told that they will forget all about it once they are off and away.

On honeymoon, it might be wiser to choose the destination or the form of transport in the light of whatever will give confidence.

Planning Your Own Timetable?

If you're a bit of an individualist, or mistrust travel agents, you'll probably be tempted to arrange your holiday yourself. There are, of course, all the advantages of planning your own timetable, the fun of poring over maps, Michelin guides and travel books, as well as the knowledge that if things go wrong it will be your own fault, but at least you'll know better next time. There are, however, just as many minus points as there are plus points in do-it-yourself travel. It is fine if you are able to devote considerable time and trouble to making all the arrangements, but you will probably not have much time to spare just before the wedding. Travel agents exist to take that burden off your shoulders. Often the deal they can offer you is cheaper, and certainly for the cautious or first-time traveller, agents will be able to help you find the best holiday to fit your needs, interests and resources.

Make sure, however, if you do decide to consult a travel agent, that the agency is a member of ABTA (the Association of British Travel Agents) and that any tour operator they recommend has a licence from the Civil Aviation Authority (ATOL). This is your best protection against disappointment and, if procedures should go wrong, at least you do have some redress.

Insurance, Documents, Money

Wherever you go, and however you get there, the golden rule about holidays is check, check and check again – everything from whether you remembered your toothbrush to the date on the tickets. When you get married, you are not legally required to change the name in your passport, but remember to check that it is up to date. Remember, too, that some hotels and airline authorities have been known to ask awkward questions because the names on tickets and passports do not tally, so take your marriage certificate along to be on the safe side. If you do decide to have your passport altered to your new married name, make sure to apply to the Passport Office at least six weeks in advance.

You should always insure yourself when you travel, covering loss of luggage, loss of tickets and money, cancellations and illness. Some tour operators offer insurance schemes, but do read the small print carefully in order to make sure that it covers your needs adequately – you are not obliged to accept it. If it is inadequate you can take out your own policy elsewhere or supplement the package with outside insurance. It really is worth paying a little extra to cover yourself adequately – it will cost you more in the end if you are under-insured. It is also possible to insure yourself against strikes, go-slows and air traffic delays, although most of the reputable tour operators have their own schemes to deal with the often appalling consequences of industrial action. Even though money may be small compensation for a delayed, or even cancelled, holiday, especially when that holiday is your honeymoon, it's worth checking on this. If arranging your own insurance, it's a good idea to use a company that you deal with already for, say, car or house insurance. They will probably be more helpful.

Even if you are going on a package holiday with full board (all meals provided), you will need to take some money with you. Most countries have exchange control regulations which you must observe, although you may take out as much money as you want from this country. It is usually better to take travellers' cheques than cash, but never keep them together with your passport, and don't carry your wallet in your hip pocket or in an easily accessible shoulder bag. It's just asking for trouble from pickpockets. Credit cards are also a good idea, much safer than cash, and if you lose them you don't have to foot the thief's bill – the credit company does. But you will need a small amount of ready cash, as well as travellers' cheques and/or a credit card.

Your Health

The subject of health, or ill-health, may seem rather a gloomy consideration when going on honeymoon, but you may well be glad to have taken a few precautionary measures. Find out early if you will need to be inoculated. If you need a jab, have it done in good time. Apart from the inconvenience of not being able to swim for the first few days, there is nothing worse than wasting your precious honeymoon feeling ill if the vaccination flares up. If you wear glasses, take another pair with you. Take a supply of non-prescription medicines. A short list might be: aspirin, antiseptic, plasters, insect repellent, stomach pills (both preventive and curative), indigestion tablets and calamine lotion for sunburn.

Do not make the mistake of thinking you can lie in the sun like a lizard on the first few days and get away with it. Be careful. Sunburn is one of the most common troubles experienced by British travellers and it can ruin your holiday. If you do overdo it, take a day off in the shade, apply masses of calamine lotion and take some aspirin to lower your temperature. Another very common holiday ailment derives from a similar kind of over-indulgence, that of eating different food and drinking more than you are accustomed to. Upset stomach is known by a multitude of strange names – most of them half affectionate as a cover for the embarrassment of it all – but in many cases the fault is as much our own as the cook's. If you are worried, ask your doctor for a prescription for some preventive pills. If afflicted, avoid unpeeled fruit, ice cream, salad, raw foods and water from the tap, and take things easy for a few days to let your body get accustomed to the change. Both too much sun and too much alcohol compound the problem.

Jet lag can be a problem if you're a business man going straight into an important meeting, but if you are on holiday, it should be relatively easy to cope with. At any rate, it won't affect anyone unless you are travelling through a time change of more than six hours. Just make sure that you get plenty of sleep, and don't try to do too much all at once. Let your internal body clock adjust slowly.

Holiday Beauty Routine

Hair can react badly to holiday conditions unless you are careful. Rinse it with fresh water if you can after swimming, use plenty of conditioner to replace lost natural oils, and if your hair is dyed or bleached cover your head with a scarf or hat. This will also help to avoid heat exhaustion. (This can be very unpleasant, with light-headedness, fainting, fatigue and nausea. If you get it, go straight to bed and take plenty of fluid and salt.) Make-up, too, will need holiday adjustments. Too much make-up can appear overdone and out of place on the beach, so keep to the natural look. Sea water can play havoc with mascara – even the waterproof kind – so you might consider having your eyelashes dyed. Lip gloss, as well as looking good, will protect your lips from the drying effects of the sun. Eyes can become sore or inflamed from too much sea-water or sun glare. Sunglasses should be regarded as preventive medicine here, not just fashion accessories, so it's really worth paying for good lenses.

Packing

Experienced travellers have got the business of packing down to a fine art, but most other people get in a fine old muddle, ending up with either too much or too little. The former is probably the lesser evil, but you should remember that, apart from having to pay excess baggage charges if your luggage is too heavy (the usual limit on scheduled flights is 44 lbs (20 kg), sometimes less on charter flights), it is a bore having to lug a heavy suitcase around in hot climates.

It is better for husband and wife not to share a case – it may lead to squabbles. Two small cases are easier to carry than one big one, and you're unlikely to lose both. Statistically, lost luggage is a comparatively rare occurrence, although that can be very little consolation when you land in Athens and your luggage is winging its way to New York. You can lessen the chances of this happening by labelling your luggage assiduously, inside and out, with both your home address and your holiday destination, including the dates between which you will be staying there. Stick-on labels are best. Remember to tear off any old labels. They may look attractively cosmopolitan, but they are very confusing to foreign baggage handlers. If the worst does occur, and your bags do not turn up, report it immediately to the airline or tour representative. They will probably have reserve funds to keep you going until your luggage does turn up – usually not more than a day or two.

In order to minimize the inconvenience of this situation, however, it is advisable to take a sensibly packed cabin bag. It can save a lot of trouble. Make sure it contains all the essentials: washbag, bikini, change of underwear, minimal change of clothes (a T-shirt, for instance, a light skirt and a pair of sandals), contraceptives and, of course, all money and documents.

People's needs differ, and that is why the choice of suitcases is so large. Soft-bellied luggage, either in fabric or plastic, looks good and is very light, but is less resistant to battering than moulded cases, and therefore does not protect your clothes as well. Leather cases last well, but are both expensive and heavy. So if you are buying a new suitcase for your honeymoon, it's worth bearing these points in mind.

A minimum wardrobe

What to take on honeymoon is mostly a matter of common sense. Obviously, you should take clothes that are appropriate to the kind of holiday you have chosen and the country's climate. The tourist boards will be able to advise you on average temperatures. On the other hand, it may be useful to be reminded of useful things to take, especially at a time when your mind is much preoccupied with other things.

Try to take things with a double life in order to minimize packing. A cover-up for lunch in the restaurant or when shoulders get burnt can double as a dressing gown; likewise, beach sandals can also be used as slippers. Some hotels expect guests to change for dinner, so take a cool dress for the evening – men should remember to take a jacket and tie as many hotels insist on it. Remember as well that even in the hottest climates it can get chilly at night, so a shawl or jacket is a must. Another essential is a fold-up macintosh. It rains, at times, everywhere in the world and many famously sunny places have notoriously unpredictable weather (the Caribbean, for example, has short rain showers all the year round) – a plastic mac won't take up much space. If possible, take more than one swimsuit or bikini. If you are going to a seaside resort you will be wearing one all day and every day, and sea water can play havoc with elastic.

Footwear should be comfortable whether you are having a beach holiday, a city holiday or a country holiday. High heels and straps will make your feet ache in no time, and can cut into sunburnt feet. Take clothes in fabrics that will shed travel creases easily.

Holiday check list

If you are bad at packing and usually forget something, it might be useful to make a list under the following headings and tick them off as you pack: washbag and overnight things, unders, overs, outers, accessories, extras. A few optional items you might include are a *travelling iron, hair drier, travelling clock* and *small sewing kit*. Many people would class all four as essentials. Don't forget *sunglasses, camera, reading matter*. If you like picnics, a *bottle/tin opener, sharp knife* and *plastic plates and glasses* are indispensable. If you are taking *electrical appliances*, check with the Tourist Board of the country you will be visiting to find out about the voltage and what plugs you will need. Many large department stores stock international adaptors. An additional *fold-up bag* that can do double duty as shopping bag, beach bag and something in which to bring home presents and duty-frees is invaluable. Take duty-free drinks with you on the way out – foreign bar prices can be astronomical.

Crease-free packing

Efficient packing saves space and helps keep clothes uncreased. Start with the awkward shapes, and spread shoes, books, electrical appliances and bottles (wrapped in plastic bags in case of spillage) over the base. Fill in the gaps with T-shirts and underwear. Build up clothes in even layers, with trousers and skirts on their hangers. If you fold everything lengthways, creases will hang out more easily at the other end. Finish off the packing with a top layer of something big and soft, a cardigan or shawl. Try to fill the suitcase to the top, otherwise everything will slide about inside, but it's better not to have to jump on the lid to get it shut.

Coping with Emergencies

However well-planned your holiday may be, things do sometimes go wrong. The emergencies listed below may be intensely frustrating and worrying at the time, but most, however, are not insoluble problems.

Passports

Remember to make a note of your passport number and its date and place of issue. If it does get lost or stolen, report it at once to the local police and contact the nearest British embassy or consulate, who will be able to issue emergency travel documents.

Money

If you lose all your money and have no local friends who can help you out, you will have to telephone to the UK for more. Having first informed the local police and British consulate, go to a bank; they will telephone, telex or cable your own UK bank and ask them to telegraph money to you. This will probably take two to three days, so if you are really broke ask the British consulate if they will consider making you a small loan.

Tickets

Once a booking has been made for airline tickets, the computer should have a record of it. If you lose your tickets, go immediately to the ticket office and explain the situation. They may be able to check with the computer to make sure the ticket was issued, but this is by no means a general rule.

Luggage

Report lost luggage immediately at the airport to the tour operator's or airline's representative. They will ask you to fill in a form with a full description and will then set about looking for your bags. You can usually claim a small amount of money for necessities. If you lose your luggage report it to the police; you will need a receipt from them to claim your insurance.

Local laws

If you break the law in a foreign country, ignorance is no defence. If you do get arrested, try to contact the British embassy who will put you in touch with a local lawyer.

Flights

If your flight is diverted, it is the airline's responsibility to provide the cost of accommodation and arrange for you to get to your final destination. If your flight is delayed due to industrial action, the airline or tour operator must provide meals and overnight accommodation if necessary. Some tour operators offer compensation for long delays.

Car breakdown

Abroad, go to the nearest garage or in extreme emergency contact local police. In Britain, call the AA or RAC if you are a member, or walk or thumb a lift to the nearest telephone or garage.

Post-wedding Blues

Apocryphal stories abound on the subject of honeymoons that go disastrously wrong, and honeymooning couples are the butt of many a heavy-handed joke. These tall tales and jokes do, however, often have their basis in fact. It unfortunately seems to be the case that many couples set off on honeymoon with unrealistically high expectations and when the reality does not live up to the rosy picture in their mind's eye, they are left feeling somewhat disappointed and disillusioned.

Even couples who have been sleeping together for some time may find that their sex life, for reasons they find hard to analyse, may not be as happy and successful as they had expected it to be. All those jokes about the wedding night – the groom being too drunk, or sitting down to watch 'Match of the Day', or the bride forgetting her contraceptives – play (as most other jokes do) on people's anxieties, fears and expectations. After all the excitement, tension and emotion of the day itself, the wedding night may sometimes be something of a disappointment.

It is important to remember that the first few weeks of married life can be a testing time. Few couples are accustomed to the experience of sharing a sudden rush of unoccupied time together. Days in which the worries, chores and distractions of daily life are conspicuously absent may seem joyful in anticipation, but may, in reality, result in restlessness and boredom. All the weeks of planning and preparation leading up to the wedding itself will probably not only have left you physically exhausted but also mentally and emotionally drained. And the more anxious you are that everything should be perfect, the more selfconscious you will become, leading to undercurrents of tension and tetchiness.

The best advice is probably to try not to expect too much, to allow yourself to wind down slowly and to combat the boredom factor by choosing a destination where there is plenty to do and see; and take along plenty of books, games and other distractions in case your inner resources need refuelling. After all, however much you are in love, sex is a part-time occupation and simply gazing into each other's eyes for days on end can lose its attraction after a while.

A final point to bear in mind is that although you may want to broadcasting your newly married state to the world, this almost always results in winks and nudges from strangers. So if you wish to avoid this, make sure that you get rid of all traces of confetti before you set off on honeymoon. Another way of looking at it is that all the bawdy that surrounds the wedding is a part of getting married, and most people look back on it all with nostalgia. The best thing to do is simply to grin and bear with it.

A long-standing mystery

A tradition which might have been expected to die beneath a weight of practicalities is the secret honeymoon destination. Some men like to keep up the custom of making all the travel arrangements on their own and reserving the news on the precise honeymoon location until after the wedding is over and they are setting off on the journey. Cynics may claim that this is due to the masculine suspicion that this may be the last holiday decision they can take on their own. A more charitable, and probably more truthful, explanation is that the tradition of secrecy is almost as old as the wedding, and a pleasant surprise never goes amiss.

BRISSAUD 1931

EPILOGUE

It is an axiom that in any comprehensive list, the particular thing you are looking for is not on it. I hope that readers will not assume that because a topic is omitted I necessarily regard the point as unimportant. There are all kinds of activities, issues and advice which lie outside the scope of my coverage. Others better qualified than I should be consulted.

Getting married is an experience which calls on so many different aspects that it almost encompasses life itself. The work could go on for ever.

INDEX

HARRIET MESEROLE   1925